Praise for *Keeping Our Cool*

"Colourful and outspoken academic [Andrew Weaver] ... gives a sobering account of climate change and includes colourful commentary on the increasingly wacky weather."—*Edmonton Journal*

"At last, a look at climate that is accessible, fascinating, and ultimately, a call for action. Over the past century, humanity has become so powerful we are altering the chemical makeup of the atmosphere. *Keeping Our Cool* is an insider's story of climate change. Andrew Weaver is a distinguished scientist who has been a major contributor to the Nobel prize–winning work of the IPCC. Beset by naysayers and skeptics, pressures from corporations and laggard politicians, Weaver keeps us focused on the science and the urgent need to act. A gripping narrative, this should be the final alarm that galvanizes us to move onto a different energy path of renewables and efficiency."—David Suzuki, founder, The David Suzuki Foundation

"Weaver is one of Canada's most influential thinkers on global warming, an expert on how oceans shape climate."—*The Globe and Mail*

"*Keeping Our Cool* is a wonderful gift from a premier climate scientist to the rest of us. In the most reader-friendly prose, Andrew Weaver explains clearly and honestly what scientists do—and do not—know about our overheated planet. Andrew Weaver has given the rest of us a great gift—a clear, non-forbidding tour through the current state of climate science. *Keeping Our Cool* acknowledges our deepest fears even as it respects our intelligence."—Ross Gelbspan, author of *The Heat Is On and Boiling Point*

"[*Keeping Our Cool* presents] lucid science explaining the history of our understanding of climate change and the state of the knowledge today ... It's a shocking tale ... [As Weaver] explains successfully in this valuable book, global climate change is real, and it will have dire effects on human civilization ... This book ... holds out a real chance of taking another crucial step to turning things around."—*Canadian Geographic*

"Weaver answers the otherwise confusing questions of climate change with confidence and clarity. As this book demonstrates, Weaver is not just one of the world's foremost climate modellers, he's a great communicator."—James Hoggan, chair, The David Suzuki Foundation and founder of DeSmogBlog

"There are diagrams and tables ... to present graphically what [Weaver] admits is an inherently complicated truth. But this has always been one of Weaver's strengths. Without ever dumbing the issue down, he keeps it as simple and understandable as he can."—*The Vancouver Sun*

"From Canada's top climate scientist, a vastly informative, deeply personal, and truly moving account of the climate crisis racing toward us. Writing with elegance and precision, Weaver takes us on a journey through global warming's complex science to show us how Earth's climate works, what we know (and don't know) about how we're changing it, and why these changes are of urgent concern. Throughout this journey, Weaver remains optimistic that we can still solve this problem, and he offers a host of suggestions for practical policies by governments—and for steps we can all take at home—to protect our children's and grandchildren's future."—Thomas Homer-Dixon, Cigi chair of Global Systems at the Balsillie School of International Affairs, and author of *The Upside Down* and *The Ingenuity Gap*

"Weaver outlines in a comprehensive way what climate change is, why it's real, what causes it, and what obstacles politicians and industrial interests place in the way of countering it."—*Ottawa Citizen*

"It is crucial that Canadians understand the stakes in the climate debate, and Andrew Weaver has both the credentials and the straightforward style to get that job done. This is a necessary book."—Bill McKibben, author of *Deep Economy: The Wealth of Communities and the Durable Future* and *The End of Nature*

PENGUIN CANADA

KEEPING OUR COOL

DR. ANDREW WEAVER is a professor and Canada Research chair in Climate Modelling and Analysis in the School of Earth and Ocean Sciences, University of Victoria. A lead author in the Nobel Peace Prize–winning organization Intergovernmental Panel on Climate Change (IPCC), Weaver recently won a Guggenheim fellowship. He lives in Victoria with his family.

ANDREW WEAVER

KEEPING OUR COOL

CANADA IN A WARMING WORLD

PENGUIN
CANADA

PENGUIN CANADA

Published by the Penguin Group

Penguin Group (Canada), 90 Eglinton Avenue East, Suite 700, Toronto, Ontario, Canada M4P 2Y3
(a division of Pearson Canada Inc.)

Penguin Group (USA) Inc., 375 Hudson Street, New York, New York 10014, U.S.A.
Penguin Books Ltd, 80 Strand, London WC2R 0RL, England
Penguin Ireland, 25 St Stephen's Green, Dublin 2, Ireland (a division of Penguin Books Ltd)
Penguin Group (Australia), 250 Camberwell Road, Camberwell, Victoria 3124, Australia
(a division of Pearson Australia Group Pty Ltd)
Penguin Books India Pvt Ltd, 11 Community Centre, Panchsheel Park, New Delhi – 110 017, India
Penguin Group (NZ), 67 Apollo Drive, Rosedale, North Shore 0632, New Zealand
(a division of Pearson New Zealand Ltd)
Penguin Books (South Africa) (Pty) Ltd, 24 Sturdee Avenue, Rosebank,
Johannesburg 2196, South Africa

Penguin Books Ltd, Registered Offices: 80 Strand, London WC2R 0RL, England

First published in a Viking Canada hardcover by Penguin Group (Canada),
a division of Pearson Canada Inc., 2008
Published in this edition, 2010

1 2 3 4 5 6 7 8 9 10 (WEB)

Manufactured in Canada.

 Recycled
Supporting responsible use
of forest resources
FSC www.fsc.org Cert no. SW-COC-002358
© 1996 Forest Stewardship Council

 **ANCIENT FOREST** ™
FRIENDLY

LIBRARY AND ARCHIVES CANADA CATALOGUING IN PUBLICATION

Weaver, Andrew, 1961–
Keeping our cool : Canada in a warming world / Andrew Weaver.

Includes bibliographical references and index.
ISBN 978-0-14-316825-6

1. Global warming. 2. Climatic changes—Canada.
3. Greenhouse gas mitigation—Canada. 4. Environmental protection—Canada. I. Title.

QC981.8.G56W42 2010   363.738'740971   C2009-906280-1

Visit the Penguin Group (Canada) website at **www.penguin.ca**

Special and corporate bulk purchase rates available; please see
www.penguin.ca/corporatesales or call 1-800-810-3104, ext. 2477 or 2474

To David, Maria, and Helen

Contents

Illustrations

Illustrations

Tables

Introduction

A Change in the Wind

BEFORE HEADING OFF TO FRANCE and Greece for a one-month family holiday, I had a few things to clear up at my office at the University of Victoria. It was one of those relatively uneventful workdays: I dealt with myriad emails, mostly academic spam; found reviewers to assess submissions to the *Journal of Climate*, a scientific journal for which I am the chief editor; responded to a local reporter's questions about the adequacy of current carbon dioxide emission reduction targets; and met with two graduate students who were about to submit their master's theses.

Leaving for home after work felt good. Everything was wrapped up and I eagerly anticipated the July warmth of Greece and southern France. Victoria had come off a horribly wet and dreary winter, recording 48.5 centimetres of precipitation over the previous six months, 11% above normal. In January, we expect more than 2.5 centimetres of rain on only four days in five consecutive years (about four out of 155 days). But in the first seven days of 2007, we already received more than 2.5 centimetres of rain in each of four days. For Victoria, we call these "extreme events."

As on most evenings, I decided to watch the eleven o'clock news while in bed. I was surprised to see Missy Higgins performing live from the Sydney Football Stadium instead of Lloyd Robertson on the *CTV National News* telling me about the kind of day it had been. I had completely forgotten that the Live Earth concert was receiving non-stop coverage on CTV.

All the hoopla surrounding the concert made me question what had caused such a change in public opinion on global warming over the last year. Was it Al Gore's film, *An Inconvenient Truth*? Was it the 2007 scientific assessment report released by the United Nations Intergovernmental Panel on Climate Change? Or the devastation of Hurricane Katrina in August 2005, which brought nature's power into the living rooms of North Americans, or the destruction of Stanley Park in Vancouver by strong winds in December 2006? Was it that the Rideau Canal Skateway didn't open until January 26 in 2007 (the second-latest opening on record) and that Ottawans were playing golf instead of skating in early January for the first time in living memory?

I wasn't sure. In fact, I wasn't sure whether this event indicated a sustained change in public opinion or just a passing fad. The cynic in me agreed with George Marshall, the founder of the U.K.-based Climate Outreach Information Network, who wrote at www.climatedenial.org:

> Live Earth also played strongly to another powerful denial strategy—the adoption of minimal and tokenistic behaviours as proof of our virtue. We are constantly encouraged to believe that we are "making a difference" and "saving the world" with small steps that, in terms of our overall emissions, have little, if any, effect.

I watched the Live Earth concert for a while and reminisced about the year I spent in Australia in 1988 as a post-doctoral fellow at the School of Mathematics in the University of New South Wales, not far from the Sydney Football Stadium. Prior to arriving in Sydney, I had spent three years as a doctoral student at the University of British

Columbia, where I worked under the supervision of Professor Lawrence Mysak, now at McGill University. During my Ph.D. I investigated, among other things, how the mid-latitude atmosphere responded to anomalies in surface heating arising from warm sea surface temperatures. It was my first exposure to the field of climate.

Australia brought back many fond memories. A post-doctoral research position is the most rewarding time in one's research career: no thesis to worry about; no courses to prepare; no grant applications to write; no students or post-doctoral fellows to supervise. As I was studying the physics of the Leeuwin Current off Western Australia, I was unaware that across the globe, in Washington, D.C., James Hansen, the director of the New York–based NASA Goddard Institute for Space Studies, was testifying before the U.S. Senate Committee on Energy and Natural Resources that he was 99% confident that global warming was underway. His now-famous June 23, 1988, testimony has often erroneously been attributed as the beginning of scientific concern about global warming. I was also unaware that in Geneva that month, the 40th Session of the World Meteorological Organization Executive Council, an agency of the United Nations, established the Intergovernmental Panel on Climate Change (IPCC).

Twenty-seven years old and straight out of my Ph.D., I was still early in my career. Little did I know that an apparently uneventful meeting in Geneva in June 1988 would fundamentally affect the rest of my research career.

My attention snapped back to the Live Earth concert when the John Butler Trio took to the stage. It was neither their music nor their performance that struck me, but rather the lead singer's T-shirt, which declared in front of a worldwide audience: "Say No to Nuclear Energy."

I was dumbfounded. Here was an international event drawing attention to global warming and one of the only viable existing solutions was being dismissed as a non-starter. It made me question whether the musicians actually understood the causes of global warming, the severity of the problem, and the level of carbon dioxide emission cuts required to deal with it.

I have given scores of public lectures on global warming across Canada. At the end of my talks, I point out that in order to get to 100% global carbon dioxide emission reductions (see Chapter 6), we need the widespread introduction of non-carbon-based energy sources. Recognizing safety and waste-disposal issues, I nevertheless believe that nuclear power must represent one option in a basket of viable possibilities. (It's worth noting that nuclear energy already produces 78% of France's electricity.) Needless to say, resistance to the N-word on ideological grounds is common.

I asked myself again: Why had it taken so long for the public to believe that global warming was a scientific reality? In March 2007, I was pleasantly surprised by the Angus Reid poll that found that 77% of Canadians believed global warming was real. While there was some provincial variation with Quebec (83%) and British Columbia (80%) reporting significantly higher percentages than Alberta (69%) and Manitoba/Saskatchewan (69%), almost no one was adamant that global warming was not happening (only 2% nationally). However, deeply disturbing to me as a climate scientist was that only 69% of Canadians believed that global warming estimates were based on real science. Nationally, 12% of Canadians, and 21% in Alberta, believed these estimates were founded in junk science.

So what is junk science? It is a term usually attributed to data, models, or theories put forward by advocates with ideological, political, financial, personal, or other motives. It is analyses and claims that avoid the scientific method and the vetting of the work through the broader scientific community. In today's internet age, junk science is only a mouse-click away. Anyone can build a website with a scientific-sounding name and campaign for a particular agenda. Could it really be possible that 21% of Albertans believed that thousands of atmospheric and climate scientists worldwide had conspired with their entire peer group to pull the wool over the eyes of the world? That would be a truly amazing feat—as by our nature, scientists are an argumentative, suspicious, and skeptical bunch.

Perhaps some of the public's suspicion comes from the belief that global warming is just the latest in a long string of crusades by "environmental zealots." You can hear the collective scoff: "Here we go again. The same crowd that protested in front of the nuclear plants are now placarding my coal plants." The difference between global warming and many other environmental issues, including the use of nuclear power, is that some of the loudest voices calling for policy to deal with the issue are coming from the scientific community.

And where are the loudest voices coming from that undermine the science and scientists? Industries and individuals involved directly or indirectly with the production, transportation, and end use of fossil fuels, of course. The scientific community has a very solid understanding of what is causing global warming: It is overwhelmingly because of the combustion of fossil fuels. As such, any solution to the problem will have to involve the near elimination of fossil fuel use in our energy-dependent economies. So I ask: Which group might be accused of promoting junk science? Could it be the global scientific community that publishes its findings in international peer-reviewed journals where all the methods and approaches are open to public scrutiny? Or could it be individuals and organizations linked to industries that could potentially become subject to government regulation, who vet their agenda through the opinion-editorial pages of newspapers, the airwaves of radio phone-in shows, and elaborate websites with scientific-sounding names? I hope the answer is obvious. If not, it will be when you finish reading this book.

• • •

AFTER A WEEK VISITING FAMILY in southern France, we arrived in Athens, Greece, on a late July evening. The next day we planned to check out the Parthenon. We hadn't factored in the weather.

The city was in the middle of another heat wave, and Athenian heat waves are a lot more uncomfortable than Victoria heat waves. Just a few weeks earlier, Victoria broke all-time high temperature records. On July 11, the daytime high was 36.3°C; in the evening, the temperature dropped to only 19.6°C, the warmest night ever recorded. I would have welcomed these temperatures in Athens.

Athens seemed eerily quiet, as many of the locals had escaped to the villages to avoid the searing heat. Just foolhardy tourists roamed the streets. We lasted only a short while walking around the Acropolis before heading for relief in the air-conditioned National Archaeological Museum of Athens.

Back in the cool hotel, I decided to catch up on world events. I was stunned that much of the television news was focused on weather-related disasters. England had received its wettest May to July since the first records were taken in 1766. The rains of July 20 had left vast areas still under water. Stunning images showed boats being paddled through normally dry village streets. In contrast, Romania, Hungary, Austria, and Bulgaria were suffering from extreme heat. I was glad to be on holiday, knowing I had avoided the barrage of calls from reporters asking if these events were because of global warming.

Conveying the significance of global warming to the public is a difficult task for scientists. Extreme-weather events generate a lot of media attention, but the dilemma is that when asked, "Are these events caused by global warming?" we have to respond with a long discussion of weather, climate, and the relationship between the statistics of weather and climate. The media often simply want a yes or no.

Weather is the state of the atmosphere at a particular time and place. For example, as I write this in Victoria, it is partially cloudy, the temperature is 16°C, and the winds are about 5 km/h from the north. Climate, on the other hand, would give the likelihood of occurrence of a particular weather event. Another way of looking at climate is that it is the statistics of weather. Climate is what you expect; weather is what you get.

When scientists make projections of future changes in climate, they are not making long-range weather predictions. Instead, they are making predictions of the change in the statistics of weather. In climate prediction, we examine how the shape of the distribution of a particular aspect of weather, such as temperature or precipitation, changes in the future. We might make predictions of the change in mean temperature or the change in the likelihood of occurrence of a particular extreme precipitation event.

The figure "Temperature Distribution" illustrates what I mean by distribution of a particular aspect of weather. These graphs have a vertical axis labelled "Probability of occurrence" and a horizontal axis showing temperatures ranging from cold to hot. Each of the three graphs shows two curves: a present-day curve ("Previous climate") and a future-climate curve ("New climate"). The present-day curve is centred around the "Average" temperature, with the average temperature also being the most probable temperature you would get in the present-day climate. There is an equal probability in the present-day climate that you could have warmer than average or cooler than average temperatures. That is, the area under the present-day curve is the same to the left and to the right of the average temperature. The tail of the present-day distribution has low values of probability. These are the extreme high and low temperatures.

Part a) in "Temperature Distribution" shows the average (or mean) temperature warming, but the width of the distribution (or the variance, often measured by its square root, known as the standard deviation) does not change in the future climate. Let's suppose this curve represents the daily-averaged temperature (over both day and night) at

Toronto's Pearson airport in July, which we know from Environment
Canada climatological records to be 20.8°C. We also know that this
temperature has a standard deviation of 1.3°C.

Temperature Distribution

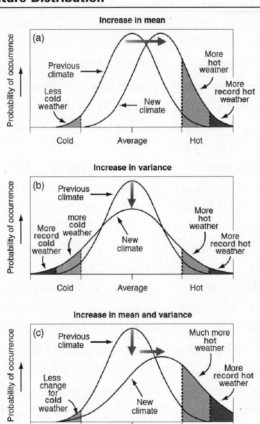

A sample distribution of temperature in the present-day climate and a future climate.
Part a) shows the average (or mean) temperature warming, but the shape of the distribution (or variance) not changing in the future climate. Part b) shows the average
temperature not changing, but the distribution spreading out in the future climate.
Part c) shows both the average temperature and the temperature distribution
changing in the future climate. *Reproduced from Folland et al. (2001) with permission
from the IPCC.*

If we assume that the temperature distribution has the same shape as in part a) of "Temperature Distribution" (a normal, or Gaussian, distribution or shape), we would expect that the most probable daily-averaged July temperature in Toronto would be 20.8°C and that 68% of the time the daily-averaged July temperature would fall between 19.5°C and 22.1°C (within one standard deviation of the average). We would further expect that 95% of the time the temperature would be within two standard deviations of the average (between 18.2°C and 23.4°C), and 99.7% of the time it would be within three standard deviations of the average (between 16.9°C and 24.7°C).

Now let's suppose that by 2050 the daily-averaged July temperature at Pearson airport has warmed by 1.5°C, but the variance (or standard deviation) has not changed (as in part a) of "Temperature Distribution"). We would now expect the most probable temperature to be 22.3°C and that 68% of the time the daily-averaged temperature would fall between 21.0°C and 23.6°C. Similarly, we would expect that 95% of the time the daily-averaged temperature would fall between 19.7°C and 24.9°C, and that 99.7% of the time it would fall between 18.4°C and 26.2°C. The result is that we expect more hot and record-hot weather but less cold and record-cold weather.

Alternatively, let's suppose that by 2050 the average July temperature at Pearson airport has not changed, but the variance measured by its square root (the standard deviation) has increased from 1.3°C to 1.8°C (as in part b) of "Temperature Distribution"). A wider distribution is shown for the future climate, with the most probable temperature remaining the same (20.8°C). We would expect that 68% of the time the daily-averaged temperature would fall between 19.0°C and 22.6°C, 95% of the time it would fall between 17.2°C and 24.4°C, and 99.7% of the time it would fall between 15.4°C and 26.2°C. In this case, we expect both more record-hot and more record-cold temperatures. You would say that the weather has become more variable although the average remained unchanged.

Part c) of "Temperature Distribution" shows an example with both the mean and the variance increasing. If we use the same values for the Pearson airport (a 1.5°C increase in average temperature and a 0.5°C increase in its standard deviation), we would expect that 68% of the time the daily-averaged July temperature would fall between 20.5°C and 24.1°C, with a most probable value of 22.3°C. We would further expect that 95% of the time the daily-averaged temperature would fall between 18.7°C and 25.9°C, and 99.7% of the time it would fall between 16.9°C and 27.7°C. In this case, we have a much greater probability of occurrence of hot weather, with little change in the probability of occurrence of very cold weather.

Scientists will never be able to say that the rainfall on July 20, 2007, in England or the record-breaking temperature on July 11, 2007, in Victoria was because of global warming. Rather, what science can offer is a quantification of the change in the likelihood of such an event (see Chapter 5). It's the projected future changes in the likelihood of occurrence of these extreme events (tail ends of the probability distributions) that pose the greatest problems for societal adaptation to global warming.

It might now be clear why my colleagues in the atmospheric and climate science community were dismayed by the September 27, 2006, interview Prime Minister Stephen Harper gave to the Quebec newspaper *Le Devoir*. In his discussion of climate science, Harper noted, "It's a complicated subject that is evolving." By itself this statement is relatively innocuous, as it could be applied to most areas of the sciences. But, not content with leaving it at that, Harper added, "We have difficulties in predicting the weather in one week or even tomorrow. Imagine in a few decades. "

This statement was such a fundamental misunderstanding of the difference between weather and climate that it made me and my colleagues question who was advising the prime minister. It certainly could not have been the government's own scientists or any of the international meteorological societies. Any one of them would have pointed out the difference between weather and climate. They may have even informed him of the American Meteorological Society's official policy statement on weather forecasting, formally approved by its council January 13, 1991, which included: "It is known from theoretical studies that the limit for which useful forecasts of daily weather can be made is of the order of 10 to 14 days ahead."

Did the prime minister really think we were making weather forecasts twenty years into the future? I felt deeply saddened that the widely touted "Made in Canada" plan to deal with global warming was going to be put forward by a government whose leader did not understand the difference between weather and climate.

• • •

ATHENS WAS TOO HOT FOR US. We decided to head to Kato Vasiliki, a small village on the north shore of the Gulf of Patras. It's the ancestral home of my in-laws and a place far removed from fast-paced city life. I like to refer to it as the town north of somewhere, between here and there. It's midway between the ancient Venetian port of Nafpaktos and the city of Messolonghi, famous as the site where English poet Lord Byron died assisting the Greeks in their war of independence from the Ottoman Empire. Since there would be no internet access in the village, I checked my email before leaving Athens.

As I waded through the mass of emails, two subject lines jumped out at me. The first read: "Vancouver breaks wet record for July." The second read: "England under water: scientists confirm global warming link to increased rain."

I frequently get news stories emailed to me, but something about these two subject lines seemed intriguing. Much of British Columbia had been experiencing record temperatures this summer, and *The Province* (Vancouver, B.C.) piece stated that a new record was broken in both Vancouver and Victoria. Never before had seven straight days of rain been recorded in July. Maybe the heat in Athens wasn't so bad after all?

The Independent piece was disturbing. I knew about the record rainfalls in England from the television news, but the first sentence on the July 23 story stated:

> It's official; the heavier rainfall in Britain is being caused by climate change, a major new scientific study will reveal this week, as the country reels from summer downpours of unprecedented ferocity.

Obviously I was skeptical. How could anyone say that an individual storm or two was a consequence of global warming? The drive to Kato Vasiliki would have to wait until I found that "major new scientific study."

It took only a matter of minutes, as I knew it had to be in the scientific journals *Nature* or *Science*. Sure enough, there was a study published in *Nature* by Environment Canada scientists Xuebin Zhang and Francis Zwiers, with collaborators around the world including Susan Solomon of the United States and Nathan Gillett from the United Kingdom. I knew all these scientists. In fact, Francis Zwiers had an office in the same hallway as I did; Susan Solomon was the co-chair of Working Group I of the United Nations Intergovernmental Panel on Climate Change (IPCC), in which I was heavily involved; and Nathan Gillett spent three years as a post-doctoral fellow working in my laboratory from 2002 to 2004. There is no way they would have claimed that the British rain events were because of global warming.

My suspicions were confirmed. What the authors had done was undertake an elegant and thorough climate change detection and attribution study, to conclude:

We show that anthropogenic forcing has had a detectable influence on observed changes in average precipitation within latitudinal bands, and that these changes cannot be explained by internal climate variability or natural forcing. We estimate that anthropogenic forcing contributed significantly to observed increases in precipitation in the Northern Hemisphere mid-latitudes, drying in the Northern Hemisphere subtropics and tropics....

In somewhat less-scientific jargon, this can be translated as:

We show that increasing human burning of fossil fuels has led to changes in annually- and latitudinally-averaged precipitation that are larger than anything you would expect from natural climate variability, changes in solar radiation, or volcanic eruptions. We provide a best estimate that 50%–85% (19 times out of 20) of the observed increase from 1925 to 1999 in total annually-averaged precipitation over land between 40°N and 70°N, and 20%–40% (19 times out of 20) of the observed reduction in precipitation between the Equator and 30°N, is due to the human combustion of fossil fuels.

Nowhere did they say that the July 20 rainfall in England was caused by global warming. Rather, they provided the first compelling evidence that the lion's share of the observed increase in middle to high latitude northern hemisphere precipitation, and the observed decrease in subtropical and tropical northern hemisphere precipitation, was a consequence of human-induced global warming. In other words, the likelihood of occurrence of increased overall precipitation at the latitudes that include the United Kingdom had gone up.

• • •

HAVING SATISFIED MYSELF that the "major new scientific study" did not actually claim that global warming caused the July 20 rainfall that left "England under water," it was time to leave for Kato Vasiliki. I've driven or taken the bus from Athens to Patras a number of times. It's a beautiful road along the south shore of the Gulf of Corinth lined with flowering shrubs during the summer months. As a family ritual, we stop for a break at a rest area near Kiato, about halfway between Athens and Patras.

Shortly after leaving the rest area, we noticed a few planes flying back and forth between the Gulf of Corinth and what seemed like distant mountains. None of us could figure out what these planes were doing, although it became more obvious the farther we drove. The charred remnants of recent fires were everywhere.

Small roadside fires are not uncommon in Greece during the summer. They are usually started when careless motorists toss smouldering cigarette butts out their window, but are easily controlled. This year was very different. The roadside fires had spread up the hillsides and in many places had jumped the road. To our horror, we noticed flames sweeping across the hillsides close to the highway. A conveyor belt of water bombers dumped seawater on the flames. Fire crews were at the side of the road to ensure flames did not cross over the highway. Another expected sign of global warming, I told myself—but once again, there would be no way to prove that global warming contributed to the uncontrollability of any individual forest fire.

In 2004, Nathan Gillett, Francis Zwiers, Mike Flannigan (of the Canadian Forest Service), and I published the first study to quantitatively link the combustion of fossil fuels to increases in the area burned by forest fires. We showed that the observed increase in area burned over Canada from 1959 to 1999 occurred in association with an observed warming of May to August temperatures. The biggest forest fires typically occurred in the remote north and western regions of our country (see "Forest Fire Area Burnt"). We further showed that increasing carbon dioxide levels in the atmosphere associated with the combustion of fossil fuels had a detectable influence on both the May to August warming and the increase in burned area. Since that time, subsequent studies have found further links between global warming and increasing forest fires.

From an extensive database of forest fires that they compiled for the western United States, scientists at the Scripps Institute of Oceanography in San Diego noted that around the mid-1980s there was a sudden, dramatic increase in the number of large forest fires and the area burned by them. They, too, found that these changes were strongly linked to increasing spring and summer temperatures. They discovered a further link with the timing of spring snow melt, although this in itself is not independent of the spring temperatures (warmer temperatures make snow melt earlier). In particular, since 1986 they found that there had been a 400% increase in the number of forest fires and a 650% increase in the area burned in the western United States, compared to the period 1970 to 1986. In another example, NOAA researchers led by Pavel Groisman in Colorado, in collaboration with Finnish, Russian, Canadian, Swedish, and Norwegian scientists, discovered that warming and precipitation changes over Siberia have led to increases in forest fire danger indices during the latter half of the twentieth century, although they found no change in these indices over northern Europe during the same time. That is, weather conditions were becoming more and more conducive to forest fires in Siberia, but remained unchanged over northern Europe.

Intuitively, one would expect that increasing temperatures would lead to an increasing likelihood of forest fires. For forest fires to start, you need three things: oxygen, ignition, and fuel. Finding oxygen is not a problem, as it makes up 21% of the volume of the atmosphere. The small year-to-year variations in atmospheric oxygen content, which

Forest Fire Area Burnt

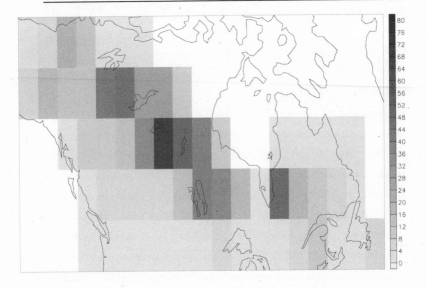

Total area burned in thousands of square kilometres over Canada from 1959 to 1999. The data have been averaged into five-degree by five-degree boxes and come from the large fire database of Stocks et al. (2003). *Reproduced with permission from Gillett et al. (2004).*

affect the fourth decimal of this percentage, aren't significant. Naturally occurring wildfires are usually ignited by lightning. In Canada, only one-third of forest fires, yet more than 85% of the total area burned, is caused by lightning strikes. People's careless practices also ignite forest fires (causing approximately two-thirds of forest fires in Canada), although it is difficult to imagine what would cause humans to be more careless one year over the next. The forest fire ingredient that is most susceptible to interannual fluctuations is the availability of fuel. As every Boy Scout or Girl Guide knows: If the soil and vegetation are moist, it is harder for a forest to burn than if they are dry.

There are strong warming trends over Canada and the United States that can be attributed to the human combustion of fossil fuels.

Snowpacks are melting earlier than they used to so that stream flows are peaking earlier in the year. Combine this with the increased likelihood of summer drought and you have an increased likelihood of ideal fuel conditions for forest fire outbreaks.

We are fooling ourselves if we think we can deal with global warming by planting trees. There are many positive reasons for planting new forests (afforestation), replanting old forests (reforestation), or reducing the destruction of existing forests (deforestation), including the restoration of natural habitat and the prevention of loss of biodiversity. However, trees only store carbon over the course of their lifetime. When these trees die, or if they burn, the carbon is released back to the atmosphere.

Millions of years ago when the atmosphere had much higher concentrations of carbon dioxide, trees, ferns, and other plants were abundant. These plants used the sun's energy, together with carbon dioxide from the atmosphere and water, to create glucose or sugar and release oxygen back to the atmosphere (photosynthesis). As the years went by, plants would grow and die, and some of these dead trees and other vegetation would fall into swampy waters depleted in oxygen. In this environment, the organic matter only partially decayed and so turned into peat, a precursor for coal formation. Over time, shallow seas covered some of the swampy regions, depositing layers of mud or silt. As the pressure started to increase, the peat was transformed, over millions of years, into brown coal, then soft coal, and finally hard coal.

A similar process occurred within shallow seas where ocean plants (phytoplankton) and marine creatures would die and sink to the bottom to be buried in the sediments below. Over millions of years, the sediments hardened to produce sedimentary rocks, and the resulting high pressures and temperatures caused the organic matter to transform slowly into oil or natural gas. The great oil and natural gas reserves of today formed in these ancient sedimentary basins.

Today when we burn a fossil fuel, we are harvesting the sun's energy stored from millions of years ago. In the process, we are also releasing the carbon dioxide that had been drawn out of that ancient atmosphere. So, unless we can actually figure out a way to speed up the millions of years required to convert dead plants into peat and then coal, the idea that we can somehow stop global warming solely by planting a few trees isn't realistic. This is precisely why I was critical of the Liberal government's Climate Change Plan for Canada released November 21, 2002. It offered little in the way of real emissions reductions for the heavy industries producing the lion's share of Canadian carbon emissions. Rather, it exploited credits for existing and future forest management practices and tinkered around the edges of the problem with a host of inconsequential initiatives. The terrestrial biosphere will soon cease its ability to sequester carbon anyway (see Chapter 5). This will leave us with only one natural sink—the ocean. The consequences of this ocean drawdown of carbon dioxide over the next several centuries are not pleasant (see Chapter 3).

A few of the most notorious players in the climate change denial industry are geologists who like to claim that climate has always varied in the past so we shouldn't worry about its variation in the future. They might point to a climate millions of years ago when the Earth was warmer than today; they may even argue that during the Late Ordovician around four hundred and forty million years ago a major glaciation event occurred in association with atmospheric carbon dioxide levels that were many multiples higher than today. I will lay out what we know about paleoclimates and how changes in climate have affected human migration, early civilizations, domestication, and agriculture (see Chapter 3). I will also look at the relationship between past and present climate change, and will tackle head-on the common non sequiturs put forward by the denial industry.

• • •

DURING THE REMAINDER of the drive to Kato Vasiliki, I pondered how one could convey the urgency of dealing with global warming when unable to point at a devastating natural disaster and say, "Global warming caused this." I knew upon my return to Canada I would be asked about the Greek fires. I didn't really want to go into a long monologue about forest fire ingredients; that the heat waves hit Greece all summer; that many regions were experiencing ongoing drought conditions, which were so bad in the Cyclades that the government had to declare a state of emergency when the water ran out. I knew that people would want a short answer to the question "Is it or is it not caused by global warming?" After some thought, I decided I would simply say three things: 1) You would expect an increased likelihood of such forest fire events because of global warming, so 2) Get used to it, since, in the words of Randy Bachman, 3) You ain't seen nothing yet.

• • •

IT'S BEEN EXACTLY FOUR WEEKS since we returned from Greece. Just two days earlier, local media reported that the last of the fires had been extinguished; ironically, these same news stories were reporting that heavy rainstorms were now causing flooding in northern Greece. I was surprised there was little mention of the forest fires during the first two weeks after I returned. A few Canadian media outlets reported August 17 that a forest fire had destroyed dozens of homes in an Athens suburb, but it wasn't until August 25 that the real news coverage got underway. What suddenly caused this media attention? The headline in *The Vancouver Sun* story said it all: "Fires ravage southern Europe; Ten die in 'Biblical catastrophe' in Greece; parts of Italy and Portugal also burn."

It was the fact that, tragically, people had died. As the death toll rose over the next few days and as fires closed in on the UNESCO World Heritage Site of Olympia, birthplace of the Olympic Games, the news coverage grew dramatically.

In Victoria, the weather was on everyone's mind. Despite a wonderful start, Victoria had gone through a dreadful summer, receiving 58% more rain than normal in July and August. As if this wasn't enough, 87% of the rain fell on weekends, with seven out of ten weekends between the end of school and Labour Day being wet. I kept quiet about having just spent a month in southern Europe.

I was also troubled by the fact that four of us had just taken a return trip to Europe and had each released about 2.3 tonnes of carbon dioxide (one metric tonne is equal to one thousand kilograms). Numerous websites that sell carbon offsets made this easy to calculate. While certainly worthy in their goals, these offsets concern me. Today you can buy offsets for your car travel, household emissions, as well as your air travel. You can even offset someone else's emissions by compensating for any number of tonnes of carbon dioxide. My main objection is that buying carbon offsets makes it easy for individuals to believe they no longer have to worry about global warming. They can pay a few dollars and feel good about the fact that global warming is now someone else's problem as they have done their share.

Enhancing carbon sinks (planting trees) is often used to offset emissions. It is not clear how one can assure that these trees will survive in perpetuity. Who would replant the trees if a forest fire occurred? What was there before the tree was planted? If there was a forest, the carbon that used to exist is simply being replaced. In some sense, you are paying for past emissions rather than dealing with current emissions.

Many companies give carbon offsets by investing in alternative energy technologies. I wonder to what extent these investments would have occurred anyway. Others use the money to increase energy-use efficiency in developing nations. My favourite is the purchase and cancellation of so-called Certified Emission Reductions/European Union Allowances. The idea is relatively straightforward. Under the Kyoto Protocol, the European Union developed an emissions trading scheme. As part of the scheme, emission allowances were doled out to large industrial emitters. These were tradable so that a heavy emitter having difficulty reducing emissions could buy allowances from an emitter that had an excess. A carbon offset company could buy an allowance and throw it away, thereby increasing the overall cost of these allowances. In theory, this would cause the cost of non-compliance (or, rather, the cost of not reducing carbon emissions) to go up for heavy industrial emitters.

The widely used argument to justify the carbon offset market is that a molecule of carbon dioxide has the same radiative effect on climate whether it is released in Canada, the United States, China, Antarctica, or Botswana. Replacing incandescent light bulbs with fluorescent light bulbs in Djibouti, which gets 100% of its electricity from fossil fuels, can be used to justify driving a gas-guzzling SUV in downtown Toronto. Dealing with global warming requires fundamental behavioural and technological change on a scale much larger than can be dealt with through carbon offsetting schemes (see Chapter 6).

While I have bought carbon offsets, I have never felt overly comfortable doing so, as I was never sure how the money was being used and how I could verify that carbon reductions were actually achieved. My own approach to air travel has been to reduce significantly the amount I fly. In 2005, I clocked more than 80,000 kilometres; in 2006, I travelled 56,000 kilometres; and in 2007, only 26,500 kilometres. It is very difficult to imagine off-the-shelf solutions to cut airplane emissions. Hopefully, zero-emission air travel will be available one day, but for now I have taken steps to reduce my air travel.

How many of us have wasted up to three days to attend a meeting that could have been held by video or audio conference? Over the past year, I was able to avoid five such trips. On February 2, 2007, the United Nations IPCC released its Fourth Assessment Report on climate change. A press conference was scheduled in Ottawa on the same day so that the seven Canadian lead authors involved in the report could answer media questions. I was dumbfounded at the optics of flying seven scientists, five of whom were based in Victoria, to Ottawa. That's about 4.4 tonnes of carbon dioxide emissions for a one-hour press conference. I agreed to participate in the press conference but insisted it be by telephone. Other meetings involved my February 19 testimony before the Legislative Committee on Bill C-30 (Canada's Clean Air and Climate Change Act) and also my November 22, 2007, and January 30, 2008, testimonies before the Standing Committee on Environment and Sustainable Development. Once more, experts were being flown to Ottawa to testify before these committees, but this time the committees clearly recognized the optics of appearing in person and so made video-conferencing readily available. Choosing video or audio conferencing over flying to Ottawa saved time, money, and carbon emissions.

• • •

RECENTLY I RECEIVED a number of emails asking whether I would be willing to participate in a debate on the science of global warming on a syndicated national radio show. I was told that the host thought the debate would benefit the public. I refused, as I have done several times in the past (for reasons I will expand upon in the next chapter). Briefly, I pointed out that there is no such debate in the atmospheric or climate scientific community, and that making the public believe that such a debate exists is precisely the goal of the denial industry. There is a clear, well-understood reason for global warming: It is largely because of carbon dioxide emissions from the combustion of fossil fuels. In fact, much of the science has been well established for more than a century (see Chapter 2).

Any policy on global warming will obviously have to involve dramatically reducing carbon dioxide emissions from fossil fuel combustion. It's not difficult to imagine that there are lots of vested interests at stake here, many of which might have operations in Alberta, Texas, and the Middle East. A strategy these vested interests might use to block such policy measures would be to convince the public that the science of global warming is still uncertain. Scientific debate over global warming would therefore imply uncertainty; uncertainty would imply that more time was required before we are sure there was a problem; the public would not pressure politicians for action. I have never understood the denial industry's argument that climate scientists are only saying global warming is a problem so we can get big research grants. It would be in our interests to say the problem was still very *un*certain and we needed to do more research.

Nevertheless, I agreed to appear on the show provided I was contacted and asked to do so by the host directly. I received an email invitation, in which he wrote:

> I am very doubtful of the prevailing argument that human-created climate change is the key cause for any global warming. I have done the lay-person's research for several years now. Nevertheless, I am very interested to hear your side of the issue.... My key interest has always been to arrange a debate between proponents of both sides of the issue. That still hasn't happened, unfortunately.

I pointed out in my email response that I was not surprised he could not arrange such a debate, as there was no such debate in the atmospheric and climate scientific community. I mentioned that it was extremely important to discuss and debate what, if anything, we should do about global warming. Should we worry about mitigation (trying to stop global warming) or adaptation (dealing with its consequences) or both? I further pointed out that science was not about opinions, ideology, surveys, or popularity contests. I asked him whether he thought we should have a scientific debate as to whether a rock would fall down or up if thrown off a cliff. Obviously, I suggested, the answer was no. I pointed out that we might want to debate the ethics involved in throwing the rock in the first place; we might want to debate about what could be done to stop the rock from hitting a person on the head in the valley below. My experience over the years is that many members of the general public have extensive experiences with policy-related debates but have very little understanding of science, the scientific method, or the whole concept of scientific uncertainty.

The climate change denial industry has been very perceptive in realizing that the public is generally unable to distinguish between scientific and policy-related debates. For example, extensive public debate occurred during the lead up to the 1994 North American Free Trade Agreement. Extensive public debate also occurred in the months prior to anti-smoking legislation that continues to be implemented across Canada. Such debates are not only important but are essential to the functioning of a democratic society. Was there extensive public debate about whether smoking actually caused cancer? History is quite clear that special interest groups were very involved in trying to create the impression that the scientific link between smoking and cancer was uncertain. History is also clear that these same special interest groups were not basing their opinions on the scientific evidence at hand.

Finally, I gave the host a very specific example illustrating the potential for such a debate to confuse rather than enlighten the public:

Let's suppose Someone A with a Ph.D. and scientific-sounding credentials stood before a camera and said, "Volcanoes produce more carbon dioxide per year than humans produce."

Let's further suppose Someone B, also with a Ph.D. and scientific-sounding credentials, stood before the same camera and said, "That's not true. Each year, humans produce more than 130 times the carbon dioxide that volcanoes produce."

Which one of these people does the viewer or listener believe? Most would probably have no idea who was right or who was wrong, and so would think there was still a debate in the scientific community as to whether humans produce more carbon dioxide than volcanoes produce. I would hope that no one would think that Someone A was referring to the amount of carbon dioxide humans release when they exhale in respiration, the opposite of photosynthesis. The atmospheric science community is certainly not concerned about climate effects of human breathing.

In fact, the U.S. Geological Survey has an easily accessible educational website that points out that globally, volcanoes annually emit between a hundred and thirty and two hundred and thirty million tonnes of carbon dioxide into the atmosphere. It further points out that humans give off about twenty-seven billion tonnes of carbon dioxide a year into the atmosphere. Someone B is right and Someone A is wrong; and that's not debatable. It turns out that in this case, Scientist A is both wrong and misleading.

Volcanic emissions of carbon dioxide are part of an extremely long timescale cycle that takes hundreds of thousands to millions of years to complete. The cycle involves the subduction (or the moving under) of tectonic plates into the Earth's mantle and chemical weathering. Pure rain is actually slightly acidic because carbon dioxide in the atmosphere can dissolve in water to produce carbonic acid. When this slightly acidic rainwater comes in contact with certain minerals (in particular, silicates), a reaction known as weathering can take place. In the weathering process, minerals are broken down and the chemical by-products, including bicarbonate ions that contain carbon, are eventually transported to the ocean through river runoff or groundwater. Certain marine organisms combine calcium and bicarbonate ions in the ocean to produce their shells. These organisms now contain the carbon that originated in the atmosphere and when they die, they can sink and transport this carbon to the sediments of the ocean floor. As the tectonic plates that contain these sediments subduct under other tectonic plates, the carbon is sequestered into the Earth's interior, ready to be released to the atmosphere by volcanoes hundreds of thousands to millions of years in the future. This whole process, which involves volcanic outgassing of carbon dioxide as well as removal of carbon dioxide through chemical weathering, has a timescale much longer than anything relevant to the existence of humans on Earth.

I normally would not have participated in a weekend interview as weekends with my family are precious to me. I don't remember why I made an exception this time. Perhaps it was because I was pestered by a host of emails trying to get me to appear on the same show; this was my way of appeasing everyone. Perhaps it was because the host had informed me that he would be taking calls from listeners on his show; I always enjoy attempting to answer questions from the public about the science of global warming. Perhaps it was because I knew the host was "very doubtful of the prevailing argument that human-created climate change is the key cause for any global warming." I was sure he must have aired these views on his program, so I thought it would be useful to his listeners to have some of his questions addressed. Whatever the reason, I looked forward to participating in the Sunday show.

• • •

WHAT A MISTAKE. I have done many hundreds of interviews over the years; I have participated in numerous talk shows, phone-in shows, and public forums. This was, without question, the most biased and bizarre interview I had ever been part of. After introducing me, the host proceeded to assault me with a multitude of questions from the denial industry's list of nonsensical assertions about climate science. How is it that when carbon dioxide was rising in the 1960s, temperatures were falling? Climate has always varied in the past, are you telling me it has never been warmer than it is today? Scientist A says X: How do you respond? Scientist B says Y: How do you respond? As I would start to answer one question, I would be interrupted with another. At one point

I said to the host, "You are not really interested in the answers to these questions, are you?"

Several times during the forty-minute segment, the host said he would get me back on his show. Yeah right, I was thinking, I am really going to come in on a weekend to take this abuse from you—you must be dreaming. It was not because I minded being challenged. I am a scientist and it is the very nature of science to be skeptical: to challenge and to be challenged. Rather, it was because I had been told that I would be taking listeners' calls. I thought that although I would be asked difficult questions, I would actually be allowed to respond.

• • •

INSTEAD OF DEVOTING an entire chapter to the common assertions of the global warming denial industry, I have included and addressed, throughout this book, many of the questions I have received from the public and the media over the years.

My goal in writing this book is to provide a detailed account of the science of global warming from someone who is an active researcher in the field of climate dynamics. I will not sensationalize the science with outlandish claims of apocalyptic proportions. As the chief editor of the *Journal of Climate* published by the American Meteorological Society, I can provide insights to publishing peer-reviewed science. As a lead author in the 1996, 2001, and 2007 IPCC Assessment Reports, I can also provide an insider's perspective of the IPCC process. And finally, as someone who has conducted hundreds of interviews on the topic of global warming over the years, I can offer some insight into the media and their role in conveying scientific knowledge to the public.

This book follows the outline of the many public lectures I have given on the science and politics of global warming over the years. While I cover global-scale phenomena, there is a very distinct Canadian focus to the expected impacts of and solutions to global warming. I sincerely hope this book assists you in understanding why I believe that global warming is the single biggest issue facing humanity today. As I have said to my friends and colleagues many times before: "People have simply no idea how serious this issue is."

When you have finished this book, I hope you will know what is certain and uncertain about the science of global warming, and you will come to agree with me that the problem is extremely serious and we need to deal with it sooner rather than later. Finally, I hope I will have armed you with a sense of optimism: There *is* much we can do as individuals and as a nation both to slow global warming and to prepare for its climatic consequences, provided that we keep our cool.

1

Global Warming in the News

FOR DECADES, the scientific community's concerns about global warming have largely fallen on deaf ears. In Canada, it seems that we've only recently begun talking about what we can do about global warming. These discussions occur mostly at individual, municipal, and provincial levels, with federal leadership still sorely lacking in the present Conservative (and previous Liberal) government.

Unfortunately, scientists are not always the best communicators of science to the public. For the average person, the scientific jargon emanating from our mouths translates into gobbledygook. Getting a yes or no from scientists is almost impossible. They may offer a yes but will invariably follow it with a list of circumstances under which the yes is valid and invalid. Their answer will be framed in caveats, a discussion of uncertainty and what it means, and perhaps even a sojourn into statistics. Typically, scientists want to be left alone to do what they do best—science. Most major science journals, scientific societies, research institutes, or universities realize this and have science writers either on staff or under contract to provide a buffer between the scientist and the media.

The media are well aware of scientists' natural instinct to engage the public as if they were colleagues. Prior to conducting extended on-air interviews, a reporter will usually call a scientist and ask a number of questions to see whether the answers are given in an intelligible manner. If the pre-screening goes well, the scientist will be put on-air live. If the live interview also goes well, you can bet that an asterisk will be added next to that scientist's name and phone number. One successful interview will lead to many more requests.

I haven't noticed a systematic change in the ability or desire of climate scientists to respond to media requests over the years. So what then explains the apparent dramatic increase in the amount of global warming news coverage? From the ProQuest Canadian Newsstand database, I tallied the number of stories from the *Calgary Herald*, *The Globe and Mail*, and *The Gazette* (Montreal) since 1985 that contained the phrase *global warming*. I chose the *Calgary Herald* because it is widely distributed in the centre of the Canadian oil and gas industry. *The Globe and Mail* represents a national newspaper available in all provinces. *The Gazette* is read in the province containing the greatest percentage of Canadians who believe that global warming is occurring and is founded in real science (see Introduction).

The results are very illuminating (see "Newspaper Articles on Global Warming"). Global warming hardly made the news until 1988. Media interest continued to pick up over the next two years and temporarily peaked in 1990, the year the First Assessment Report of the United Nations Intergovernmental Panel on Climate Change (IPCC) was released. On December 11, 1990, the Conservative government under the leadership of Brian Mulroney published *Canada's Green Plan for a Healthy Environment*. Under Section V of the plan, entitled "Global Environmental Security," the Mulroney government was already pledging a goal "to stabilise national emissions of carbon dioxide and other greenhouse gases at 1990 levels by the year 2000." This is quite remarkable, as there was little public pressure on politicians to deal with global warming at that time. It's no wonder Mulroney was honoured April 20, 2006, as the "greenest" prime minister in Canadian history by *Corporate Knights* magazine.

Newspaper Articles on Global Warming

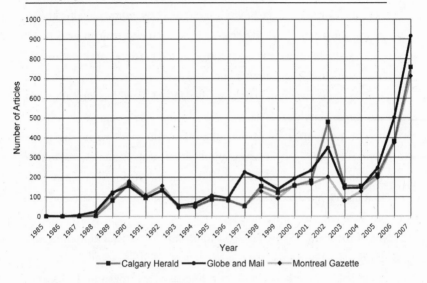

Number of articles between 1985 and 2007 containing the phrase *global warming* in the *Calgary Herald*, *The Globe and Mail*, and *The Gazette* (Montreal). *Data were acquired from ProQuest Canadian Newsstand database.*

Media interest in global warming was consistently lukewarm until 1997, although there was a brief increase in 1992 when the United Nations Framework Convention on Climate Change (UNFCCC) was created. The UNFCCC's ultimate objective was to achieve:

> ... stabilization of greenhouse gas concentrations in the atmosphere at a level that would prevent dangerous anthropogenic interference with the climate system. Such a level should be achieved within a time frame sufficient to allow ecosystems to adapt naturally to climate change, to ensure that food production is not threatened and to enable economic development to proceed in a sustainable manner.

The UNFCCC was open for signature at the now-famous United Nations Conference on Environment and Development (also known as the Rio Earth Summit) held in Rio de Janeiro from June 3 to 14, 1992. Canada signed the Convention at the Earth Summit on June 12 and ratified it December 4. In total, 192 countries (including the United States) are now parties to the UNFCCC, which formally came into force March 21, 1994.

The next surge of media interest was in 1997 when the Kyoto Protocol to the UNFCCC was adopted. No peak occurred in 1996, the year the IPCC released its Second Assessment Report. It's pretty clear that in 1997 media coverage was being driven by policy discussions and not new advances in science.

During 1997, *The Globe and Mail* ran 225 articles containing the phrase *global warming*; the *Calgary Herald*, 52 articles, and *The Gazette*, 57 articles. There were about four times as many stories in the national newspaper than the local papers. This is somewhat surprising, as Canada was committing itself to 6% reductions of greenhouse gas emissions below 1990 levels when averaged over the period 2008 to 2012. Such a commitment would require major new policy initiatives dealing especially with the energy and transportation sectors of the Canadian economy. Perhaps the disconnect between local and national coverage arose from the fact that it was difficult to imagine, at this stage, how international negotiations and national policy would affect the average person in any particular city.

The Globe and Mail coverage died off after the Kyoto Protocol was signed and only peaked again to follow the political discussions leading up to Canada's formal ratification of the protocol December 17, 2002. What is most striking in 2002 is that the *Calgary Herald* had 478 articles dealing with global warming, considerably more than the 348 appearing in *The Globe and Mail* and more than twice the 199 stories appearing in *The Gazette*.

By 2002, Canada's greenhouse gas emissions had grown 20.1% higher than 1990 levels, with the direct or indirect effect of fossil fuel combustion accounting for 81% of these emissions. Meeting the Kyoto target of 6% reduction below 1990 levels was going to be very difficult, and the Alberta oil and gas sector based in Calgary was obviously concerned because any policy to deal with greenhouse emissions would have to involve deep cuts in their sector. The *Calgary Herald* was filled with letters to the editor and opinion articles on Canada's Kyoto position.

As in 1997, the 2002 peak was not related to new scientific findings. The previous year, the IPCC released its Third Assessment Report, announcing: "There is now new and stronger evidence that most of the warming observed over the last 50 years is attributable to human activities." While this third report may have been instrumental in influencing Canada's decision to ratify the Kyoto Protocol, it certainly was not the cause of the 2002 media surge.

Media interest dropped again and didn't pick up until 2005. Hurricane Katrina made landfall on August 29 and battered New Orleans; one month later the Arctic sea ice extent reached a new record minimum. Global mean surface temperatures also set a new all-time high in 2005, although much of the media coverage did not occur until official numbers were reported early in 2006. Another important political event in 2005 was the G8 meeting in Perthshire, Scotland. For the first time, much of the meeting was devoted to climate change.

Media interest continued to soar in 2006 with the May 24 theatre release of Al Gore's documentary, *An Inconvenient Truth*, and its subsequent DVD release on November 21. A public acceptance started to emerge that some of the phenomena being observed around us were perhaps associated with our changing climate. And then came February 2, 2007, and the release of the IPCC's Fourth Assessment Report.

I have been fortunate to be one of a handful of international scientists, and the only Canadian, to have participated as a Working Group I lead author in each of the IPCC's Second, Third, and Fourth Scientific Assessment Reports published in 1996, 2001, and 2007 respectively. In the second report, I was a co-author of the chapter evaluating climate models (which I also helped write in the third report) and the chapter discussing and assessing future climate projections (which I was a co-author of in the fourth report).

There has always been some media interest in the IPCC reports, but 2007 was very different. I had so many calls from reporters around the world that I had to accept assistance from the University of Victoria public relations office. Together with my research assistant, Wanda Lewis, they scheduled essentially non-stop interviews over two days. Some of the last interviews were about the level of media interest in the IPCC report. A telling moment in this whole event was a photographer taking a picture of a photographer taking a picture of a photographer focusing on me during an interview with a reporter. He was preparing a story about journalists doing stories on the amount of media interest in the IPCC report. I was exhausted when it was all over.

People had become very conscious of the strange weather events in recent months: unusual warmth in Eastern Canada; the destruction of Stanley Park by high winds; the worst drought on record in Australia; violent storms in Europe, to name but a few. They were eager to learn about new advances in the science of global warming, and the media were keen to oblige. The scientific community did not disappoint. From an organization known for its cautious, conservative approach to scientific assessment, the Fourth Assessment Report contained some of the strongest language to date. Among other things, the report stated:

> Warming of the climate system is unequivocal, as is now evident from observations of increases in global average air and ocean temperatures, widespread melting of snow and ice, and rising global average sea level.

Also:

> Most of the observed increase in global average temperatures since
> the mid-20th century is *very likely* [>90% probability] due to the
> observed increase in anthropogenic greenhouse gas concentrations.

Scientists rarely use words such as *unequivocal,* but when they do, they
are absolutely certain.

Media interest in global warming continued through 2007. On
April 26, the Canadian government released its much-awaited climate
change action plan, *Turning the Corner: An action plan to reduce greenhouse gases and air pollution.* The Canadian government had finally recognized there was a need to deal with greenhouse emissions. At a news
conference, John Baird, the minister of environment, said:

> It doesn't end today. Global warming, climate change is one of the
> biggest ecological threats the environment has ever faced, and it's
> going to require work every day, every week, every month and
> every year.

Wow, I thought. These guys get it. But then I actually read the
Conservative plan and was dismayed. I think my quote in the April 27,
2007, *Times Colonist* (Victoria, B.C.) aptly captures my opinion: "It's
covered in rhetoric, smoke and mirrors, it's oozing in insincerity and it's
pandering to the Alberta oil industry."

Rather than dealing with emissions reductions, the plan focused on
emissions-intensity reductions, which allowed emissions to increase
but put restrictions on emissions per unit of production. Matthew
Bramley provided a lovely example of what this means in his 2007
Pembina Institute report. From the information provided in the federal
plan, we learn that by 2020 the oil sands sector will be required to
reduce its emissions intensity by 23%. But oil sands production is also

expected to quadruple by 2020. The overall net effect of the federal regulation during this period would be to allow a tripling of greenhouse gas emissions from the oil sands sector. Frankly, no matter how you try to package it, that is not a reduction.

This so-called "Made in Canada" plan looked more like a "Made in the United States" plan, with the proposed 18% emissions-intensity reduction by 2010 being the same as the 18% reduction President George W. Bush proposed for 2012 in his February 14, 2002, *Clear Skies & Global Climate Change Initiatives*. Granted, the Canadian plan proposed measures to enforce its targets, but it also allowed significant opportunities for inaction, including the introduction of a technology fund that works just like carbon offset programs (see Introduction).

Mark Jaccard, a resource and environmental economist at Simon Fraser University and director of the Energy and Materials Research Group, together with his colleague Nic Rivers, analyzed the Canadian climate change action plan. As one would expect, they found that the Conservative government's policies would certainly lead to a reduction in greenhouse gas emissions from levels *that would have existed if nothing were done*. However, greenhouse gas emissions would not drop below 2006 levels. The reason was obvious. Emission-intensity targets do not imply emission reductions. Ottawa bureaucrats were probably squirming in their seats June 12, 2007, when the C.D. Howe Institute released the Jaccard and Rivers report. Just two months earlier, the Conservative government was touting the claim that its *Turning the Corner* would lead to 20% reductions in greenhouse emissions relative to 2006 levels by 2020.

Headline-Worthy Weather

IPCC's Fourth Assessment Report and the discussions leading up to and following the release of Canada's climate change [in]action plan were not the only stories being covered by the media. Unusual weather-related stories around the world continued to make the news, and now, whether rightly or wrongly, there seemed to be a greater willingness by the media to link these events to global warming.

Without a doubt, the most stunning event of 2007 was the shattering of the previous Arctic sea ice extent record. Averaged over the five-day period leading up to September 16, 2007, the total extent of sea ice in the Arctic was reduced to an area of only 4.1 million square kilometres (see "Arctic Sea Ice in 2007"). This may still seem like a lot of ice, but the previous minimum, set in 2005, was 5.3 million square kilometres (also see "Arctic Sea Ice in 2007"). The record-breaking 1.2-million-square-kilometre difference in 2007 represents an area of sea ice greater than the size of Ontario. The median September minimum sea ice extent from 1979 to 2000 was 6.7 million square kilometres. This means that half the time during this period Arctic sea ice retreats to a minimum of more than 6.7 million square kilometres and half the time it retreats to a minimum of less than 6.7 million square kilometres (light grey line in "Arctic Sea Ice in 2007"). Compared to the median, the 2007 record involved melting 2.6 million square kilometres more ice (40% of the median), an area the size of Quebec and Ontario combined.

Another way of looking at the scale of this retreat is to examine what has happened to the average September sea ice extent annually between 1979, when satellite observations began, and 2007 (see "Arctic Sea Ice Trend"). Earlier records would have to rely on mapping from Arctic observations taken directly, which would be highly imprecise as so few observations are available.

Between 1979 and 1988, the average September sea ice extent was 7.4 million square kilometres. While natural fluctuations occur every year, there has been a strong downward trend of about 720,000 square kilometres per decade (about the size of Alberta and Nova Scotia combined each decade). This represents about 10% of the 1979 to 1988 average per decade.

Arctic Sea Ice in 2007

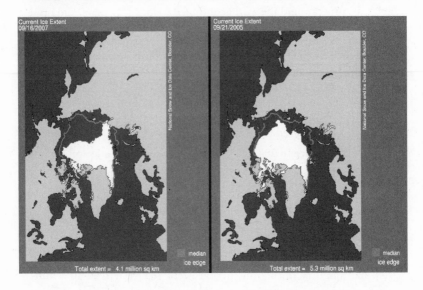

Left: The average Arctic sea ice extent over the five days leading up to and including September 16, 2007. **Right:** A similar figure for the previous record summer minimum set September 20 to 21, 2005. The light grey line shows the median September sea ice extent from 1979 to 2000. *Reprinted with permission from the National Snow and Ice Data Center in Boulder, Colorado.*

In December 2006, Marika Holland at the National Centre for Atmospheric Research in Boulder, Colorado, and several colleagues published a scientific paper showing that the transition to an ice-free summer in the Arctic typically occurred abruptly, rather than slowly. One of their simulations had the Arctic summer becoming ice-free by 2040. In a follow-up study published in May 2007, she and other colleagues analyzed the climate model simulations that were assessed in the IPCC's Fourth Assessment Report released three months earlier. Their main conclusion was quite simple: Most of the models used in the report were underestimating the observed rate of retreat of Arctic

Arctic Sea Ice Trend

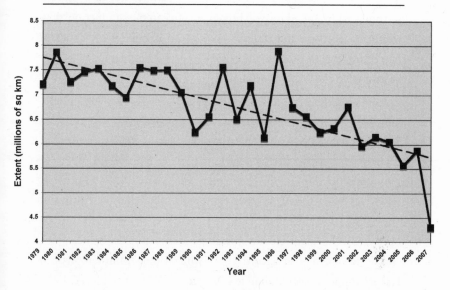

Average September sea ice extent in millions of kilometres from 1979 to 2007. The monthly average sea ice extent in September 2007 was 4.28 million square kilometres. This shattered the previous record minimum of 5.57 million square kilometres set in September 2005. The dashed line represents the linear trend.

sea ice. Holland's research painted a disturbing picture of an Arctic becoming ice-free in the summer sooner than previously thought.

So when along came the 2007 melting of Arctic sea ice, the scientific community was shocked. This event far exceeded the most extreme scenarios predicted by the IPCC report. Even the abrupt scenarios of Holland and her colleagues paled in comparison to the level of melting in 2007. It wasn't only annually produced sea ice that was melting either. Vast areas of multi-year sea ice, ice that had survived previous summers, were now gone. For me as a climate scientist, this was the most striking example I had seen of the early footprint of global warming. Sadly, the Arctic will become ice-free in the summer possibly within my lifetime, and certainly within the lifetime of my children. Any ecosystems that rely on the existence of such summer ice will surely be pushed to the brink of extinction.

Media coverage was extensive, although I still don't believe it adequately conveyed just how much it stunned the scientific community. We had not expected so much melting, and the extent to which it occurred exceeded even the most pessimistic projections. How did political leaders around the globe react? They started squabbling about sovereignty over the Arctic; they appeared thrilled that the Northwest Passage was open to shipping and the Northeast Passage would also be open soon. On August 10, the *Edmonton Journal* ran a story headlined "Arctic ice melting at record pace" while Prime Minister Stephen Harper announced $4 million to construct a military training centre in Resolute Bay, Nunavut, and $100 million to build Canada's first deepwater Arctic port at Nanisivik, on Baffin Island.

Get the Facts Right

In every public lecture I give on the science of global warming, I start by showing a slide of the July 25, 1995, cover of the *Sun* with the headline "OCEANS RISING 150 FT. & flooding coastal areas WILL YOUR CITY SURVIVE?" (see "Will Your City Survive?"). Close inspection of the list of cities included as *danger zones* on the *shocking map inside* reveals both Halifax and Vancouver. I point out that the *Sun* is a tabloid usually available at supermarket checkouts. I mention that the previous week's issue may have had a headline that read something like "Mother gives birth to extraterrestrial," so I recognized that most people would take the *Sun* stories with a grain of salt. In its own words, the *Sun* states: "SUN stories seek to entertain and are about the fantastic, the bizarre

Will Your City Survive?

Cover of the July 25, 1995 (volume 13, #30), issue of the *Sun*, based in Boca Raton, Florida, showing the Statue of Liberty under water. *Used with permission of American Media Inc.*

and paranormal." Nevertheless, I always ask the audience: "Why do you think this headline and front cover would annoy scientists?" Invariably I get the following three answers:

1) It is sensationalistic.
2) It might cause people to dismiss a very serious issue.
3) It represents alarmism and fear mongering.

I have yet to get the correct answer. For scientists, the most upsetting thing about the *Sun* story is of course its accuracy; the cover shows 150 feet (46 metres) of sea level rise reaching up to the chest of the Statue of Liberty. Actually, the Statue of Liberty is 305.5 feet (93 metres) high from the bottom of the foundation of its pedestal (which itself is a few feet above sea level) to the tip of its torch. So a sea level rise of 150 feet would bring the water level up to near the top of the pedestal, but from head to toe, the Statue of Liberty would still stand majestically above the water. The picture actually illustrates a sea level rise closer to 250 feet (76 metres), more than would occur if all the ice on our planet were to melt (if that did happen, the most recent estimate is a rise of about 65 metres).

Joking aside, the *Sun* cover illustrates that the mass media, whether it be radio, television, or print, are usually in the business of selling advertising. In order to sell advertising, they must have an audience; in order to have an audience, they must entice people to their publication or show. How many people would have picked up a tabloid if the headline read: "Oceans rising 50 centimetres this century; low-lying regions have 100 years to adapt." Probably far fewer.

People are usually a little suspicious of articles appearing in the supermarket tabloids, but what about the "Science" section of our local newspapers? The November 22, 1998, *Times Colonist* (Victoria) published a photograph of the Victoria inner harbour with an artist's conception of the effects of a five-metre sea level rise on the causeway. The headline said it all: "Coastal flood feared." I want to emphasize that I am not trying to pick on my local newspaper, but it's the only one delivered to my door and so is the only one readily available to me. What I am trying to illustrate here happens in cities all across the globe.

As I read the article, I realized it was about someone claiming that the Antarctic ice cap is disintegrating, "a nightmare beyond imagination" associated with the collapse of the West Antarctic Ice Sheet that "international scientists have confirmed" is occurring. Within the article, the expert is stated as claiming: "A rise of five metres by Christmas is a very real possibility."

That means that anyone living within five metres of the coast has exactly thirty-three days to move to high ground. The expert obviously believed in his message, as he "spent $2500 buying food in the last two weeks" and left me a long, rambling voicemail telling me to tell everyone I know to get the word out and move to higher ground. Needless to say, the only word I was getting out was that this was utter rubbish. There is simply no way that 2.5 million cubic kilometres of ice could surge off Western Antarctic in the space of thirty-three days. The fastest glacial surge ever recorded was for the Kutiah Glacier in Pakistan when, in 1953, it moved at a rate of 112 metres per day for three months. Let's suppose the impossible, that the West Antarctic Ice Sheet surged from the Transantarctic Mountains northward at 112 metres per day. In order for the whole ice sheet to surge, it would have to travel ten degrees of latitude (about 1110 kilometres). This would take about ten thousand days, which is more than twenty-seven years. A surge rate even ten times slower than that would still be considered extraordinarily fast.

What concerned me most about this article was that it was on a page boldly labelled SCIENCE, with a scientific-looking map at the bottom right of the article. I received calls from several panicked local residents. How were people to know that there was absolutely no scientific foundation to these outlandish claims? Surely the reporter would have sought some secondary fact-checking; surely he or she would have realized that one's ideological belief or opinion is not a scientific theory; surely the reporter would have sought to check whether the expert was indeed recognized as such within the field. In my opinion, this is a major problem with media portrayal of science in general. Often reporters have few, if any, means of assessing who is, or is not, an expert.

· · ·

MOST OF US rely upon local newspapers, radio, or television stations for our news, and many, like me, also keep up-to-date by reading reputable news-related websites. The same is true for science in general and climate science in particular. The public do not keep abreast of scientific advances by reading the latest peer-reviewed academic journals. And why should we? None of us have time to read the monthly, biweekly, or weekly issues of thousands of scientific journals published around the world. Scientific journals are written for a scientific audience and contain specialist language that will be indecipherable to anyone other than experts in the particular field. Here's a sample from an *International Journal of Medical Sciences* article by Anthony Azenabor and colleagues at the University of Wisconsin, Milwaukee:

> Title: *Chlamydia trachomatis* Infection of Human Trophoblast Alters Estrogen and Progesterone Biosynthesis: an insight into role of infection in pregnancy sequelae

> Last two lines of abstract: The implications of these findings are that *C. trachomatis* infection of trophoblast may compromise cellular cholesterol biosynthesis, thus depleting the substrate pool for estrogen and progesterone synthesis. This defect may impair trophoblast functions of implantation and placentation, and consequently affect pregnancy sequelae.

Like most of you, I have absolutely no idea what this means. If this study turned out to be important, I would hope that the *International Journal of Medical Sciences* would have issued a media advisory and that science writers would have picked it up. I would look forward to seeing the importance of this study conveyed to me on the evening news, in the morning newspaper, or on the website of my favourite reputable news organization.

Public reliance on the media for their scientific knowledge puts a heavy burden of responsibility on science reporters. Excellence in science reporting is usually the exception rather than the norm. (Fortunately, there are some excellent science reporters in Canada.) On the other hand, I do not fault the reporters themselves, as many of them will be the first to tell you that they are covering science stories off the side of their desk. They may normally be assigned to the city desk, the provincial desk, or even the national desk. Some may have been political correspondents in an earlier life, but company reorganizations and seniority issues bumped them to the science portfolio.

Media Mood Swings

When the August 17, 2001, *Globe and Mail* reported: "Sun-like star, planets found in Big Dipper" or the June 3, 2007, *Edmonton Journal* reported: "Collision course in physics; Trumping Einstein; Physicists are hoping their massive project to recreate the first trillionth of a second after the big bang will answer a universal question," it probably wouldn't really matter to the average person if a few small errors occurred in the reporting, or if a few quotes were taken out of context. I have no idea whether this was the case with these articles, I chose them because of their headlines. Of course, if there were errors or misquotes, the scientists involved would be going apoplectic and vowing never to talk to the media again.

But what about when one of the "Top Stories" in the January 14, 2001, *Times Colonist* (Victoria) read: "Study deflates global warming." This story was taken off the newswire from the *The Daily Telegraph* (London) and appeared in other Canadian newspapers with equally dismissive headlines. You can imagine sitting around the breakfast table, cappuccino in hand, reading the first sentence:

> Fresh doubt has been cast on evidence for global warming fol-
> lowing the discovery that a key method of measuring temperature
> change has exaggerated the warming rate by 40%.

You can further imagine the average person thinking, I knew it. Finally, a study has proved that this global warming stuff is all non-sense. It's just a left-wing environmentalist conspiracy to transfer wealth to developing nations. It was just a matter of time before someone exposed global warming for what it is. Bunkum.

In this case, I believe it does matter to the average person that a story purporting to report on new scientific advances reads more like an opinion editorial, full of assertions masquerading as facts. The scientific study being discussed was important but hardly worthy of major inter-national news coverage two weeks after it was published. How often do reporters wait two weeks after an event has occurred to write a story? Surely if something is newsworthy, you would want to be the first to get the story out.

In the study, a team of scientists used data from floating buoys in the eastern tropical Pacific to examine the relationship between ocean tem-peratures one metre below the surface and air temperatures three metres above the surface. They found that in the period 1979 to 1999, warming trends were larger for the ocean surface temperatures than for the nighttime air temperatures in the eastern tropical Pacific. When they created a global data set that blended in available nighttime marine air temperatures instead of sea-surface temperatures, they found global warming over the period to be 0.13°C per decade instead of 0.18°C. Their study was well written and included the usual scientific discussions of assumptions, caveats, and uncertainty. Nowhere was justification given for the following statement, or others like it, included in the newspaper article:

> Doom-mongers predicting the dire effects of global warming have seen some of their more cherished notions crumble in recent months as evidence mounts that their predictions have been pessimistic.

The irony of this quote is that evidence suggests that most future-climate projections have been overly optimistic, not pessimistic.

• • •

NINE DAYS AFTER "Study deflates global warming" was splashed across the "Top Stories" page of the *Times Colonist* (Victoria), another article appeared. The headline read: "Global warming severity grows."

You can only imagine what those cappuccino drinkers were saying now. Only nine days earlier, global warming was shown to be bunkum. Now it's worse than ever before. The most likely conclusion they would reach is that scientists are confused and there is still a debate in the community. Certain special interest groups work hard to try to assist the public in reaching this conclusion. Newspaper readers might think that the sheer existence of global warming swings like a pendulum depending on the latest scientific study: one day global warming is on; one day it is off. Worse still, they may dismiss the whole issue entirely.

In this case, the article was reporting on the conclusions from the IPCC's Third Assessment Report. A best estimate of between 1.4°C to 5.8°C global mean warming was projected to occur at 2100 relative to 1990. This range had increased from the range of 1.0°C to 4.5°C given in the Second Assessment Report released in 1996. So why had this range increased, and did it really mean that global warming had become more severe? The reason is very simple and requires only a rudimentary understanding of climate models, the tools we use to make projections of future climate change.

Any simulation into the future using a climate model requires an estimate of future emissions of greenhouse gases, such as carbon dioxide and methane. Similarly, it also requires an estimate of future emissions of so-called anthropogenic (human-made) aerosols. These aerosols are tiny liquid or solid particles suspended in the air and have a net cooling effect. Estimates of future greenhouse gas and aerosol emissions in turn require estimates of population and economic growth, technology advance, land and energy use and efficiency, among others.

In 1992, the IPCC published a special Supplementary Report to its First Assessment Report in which six different greenhouse gas emission scenarios, representing a wide range of socio-economic assumptions, were proposed. None of them included projected changes in aerosol emissions. In the years leading up to the Second Assessment Report, climate modelling groups around the world typically used all or a subset of these six scenarios, as they were the only ones available. The projected global warming range given by the Second Assessment Report (1.0°C to 4.5°C for 2100 relative to 1990) therefore arose from only six emissions scenarios being used. A few studies, however, developed estimates of future changes in aerosol emissions. When an estimate of aerosol emissions was included, the upper bound of the global warming range was decreased to 3.5°C.

In 2000, the IPCC released a 599-page volume dedicated exclusively to providing a wider range of estimates of greenhouse gas, and now also aerosol, emissions. The Special Report on Emissions Scenarios (SRES) contained thirty-five new scenarios engulfing the range spanned by the previous six. The Third Assessment Report's best estimate of 1.4°C to 5.8°C warming at 2100 relative to 1990 was higher than the earlier estimate for two reasons, both of which exclusively involved the emission scenarios being used:

> 1) All SRES scenarios had aerosol emissions eventually dropping off below 1990 levels as the twenty-first century progressed. The IPCC 1996 aerosol emission scenario used to infer the upper bound of only 3.5°C warming by 2100 led to a doubling of aerosols relative to 1990 by the end of the twenty-first century and, remember, these aerosols act to cool the earth.

> 2) The use of a broader range of emissions scenarios led to a broader range of responses.

Global warming had not become more severe as the headline suggested. The scientific community had explored the climate response to a greater range of possible twenty-first-century trajectories of population growth, economic growth, technological advance, change in land and energy use and efficiency, and so forth.

A False Impression

Historically, perhaps the single greatest impediment to accurate science reporting has been the failed application of the ethical obligation of journalists to report *balance*.

Journalistic balance involves seeking out and reporting upon a variety of opinions associated with a news story. Let's suppose that Canada is about to enter into an international trade agreement with China. This agreement would involve policy, and there would be a variety of opinions on that policy depending on your individual perspective. You could imagine an article on this new trade agreement in which an auto industry representative says he or she doesn't like the policy as it might mean job losses in Canada. In the same article, a CEO from an up-and-coming hi-tech firm might say he or she eagerly anticipates new opportunities to sell intellectual property in the world's fastest-growing economy. The journalist would not want the article to appear to be advocating any particular position on the policy that may or may not reflect the reporter's own belief. Ross Gelbspan, an editor and reporter with more than thirty years' experience at *The Bulletin* (Philadelphia), *The Washington Post,* and *The Boston Globe,* summed up this desire for journalistic balance beautifully in his book *The Heat Is On*:

> The professional canon of journalistic fairness requires reporters who write about a controversy to present points of view. When the issue is of a political or social nature, fairness—presenting the most compelling arguments of both sides with equal weight—is a fundamental check on biased reporting. But this canon causes problems when it is applied to the issue of science. It seems to demand that journalists present competing points of view on a scientific question as though they had equal scientific weight, when actually they do not.

In 2004, Maxwell Boykoff and Jules Boykoff set out to test Gelbspan's claims about media balance by examining reports of global warming in *The New York Times, The Washington Post, Los Angeles Times,* and *The Wall Street Journal* for the period 1988 to 2002. They examined a random sample of 636 articles out of 3543 total articles on global warming during this period. Their findings were startling:

> 1) 52.7% of the articles gave approximately equal emphasis to human activity versus natural fluctuations being able to explain global warming.

2) 35.3% focused more on the human causation but still presented a "balanced" view by including the views of those who argued global warming was due to natural climate fluctuations.

3) 6.2% reported only deep suspicions of any human contribution to global warming.

4) only 5.9% expressed the notion that humans were contributing to global warming.

Maxwell Boykoff's follow-up study looked at American television news coverage from 1995 to 2004. He found an equally disturbing result: namely, 70% of the network news stories reported "balanced" coverage. Is there any wonder that the public believed there was a debate raging within the scientific community about what was causing global warming?

In a now-famous study published in the December 2004 *Science*, Naomi Oreskes at the University of California, San Diego, examined the abstracts of 928 articles published in peer-reviewed scientific journals between 1993 and 2003 containing the keywords *global climate change*. Her goal was to see whether legitimate dissenting voices had been left out of the IPCC assessments and other reports. Her conclusions were not unexpected. Not a single study disagreed with the consensus view concerning the role of greenhouse gases in causing global warming.

No published studies existed that refuted a human contribution to global warming. At the same time, balance in the media had left the public with the impression that scientists still couldn't determine if global warming was a result of natural variability. By trying to convey a sense of balance, the journalists have inadvertently fallen into a trap of being biased.

A few years ago, I was asked by a national television morning show to appear live in a debate on the science of global warming. I agreed but emphasized that I would only have such a debate with a climate or atmospheric scientist. I did not want to have a publicly televised scientific debate with, for example, an economist, a politician, or a social scientist for the reasons I outlined in the Introduction. I pointed out the difference between scientific and policy-related debates and argued that they probably wouldn't have me debating Canadian economic policy with the head of the Royal Bank, as I would be way out of my depth. The producers of the show said fine, they would find someone. I chuckled to myself. Sure enough, a few days later they said they could not find a Canadian atmospheric or climate scientist who was prepared to debate the science. Rather than this being the story, they cancelled the show.

Taking on a Skeptic

Of course scientists debate. The advancement of science fundamentally relies on scientists continually challenging one another and arguing about the conclusions of previous studies. Much of this debate takes place at scientific workshops, conferences, lectures, or even casual conversations over coffee. Some of it comes via the anonymous correspondences involved in the peer-review process associated with publishing one's results in scientific journals.

On June 17, 2001, shortly after President George W. Bush pulled the United States out of the Kyoto Protocol, I had a debate with Richard Lindzen of the Massachusetts Institute of Technology that was transcribed by the *Los Angeles Times*. Our subject was "How dangerous is global warming?" Lindzen is one of only a very few atmospheric or climate scientists around the world who is considered a skeptic about global warming—or at least is advertised as such by the global warming denial industry.

In the debate, Lindzen takes exception to alarmism and statements about palm trees in Washington and New York being underwater. He says that "some people argue that man can have no effect on climate, and I think that's nonsense. I agree with you, Andrew, on that. The argument is, will it be enough to worry about?" On many issues, we broadly agree. The discussion ends in conflicting opinions on what policy measures should be taken. Lindzen points out that "policy measure isn't much our domain," a point I agree with.

Both of us have opinions on policy, but the formation of policy requires dealing with ethical issues, various stakeholders, special interests, religious factions, and industry as well as scientists. Science should feed into policy discussions, but in and of itself science cannot and should not dictate what policy directions should be taken. My principal objection is when deliberate attempts are made by special interest groups to misrepresent the science, and its supposed uncertainty, in order to influence public policy in a particular direction.

How Dangerous Is Global Warming?

Los Angeles Times
(reproduced with permission from the *Los Angeles Times* and Richard Lindzen)

Date: June 17, 2001
Section: Opinion; Opinion Desk

Last week, President George W. Bush again denounced the Kyoto global-warming agreement of 1997, insisting it would require unattainable reductions in greenhouse-gas emissions. Moreover, he dismissed a substantial body of science that strongly suggests both that global warming is dangerous and that it is being caused in large measure by fossil-fuel consumption and other human activity. While he called for more research on the issue, he insisted that, at this point, "no one can say with any certainty what constitutes a dangerous level of warming and therefore what level must be avoided."

A vast majority of scientists studying global warming insist that the phenomenon is real, that it is caused by man and that it presents potentially grave dangers. Several scientists, however, take exception. We invited one of them, Richard Lindzen, Alfred P. Sloane professor of meteorology at Massachusetts Institute of Technology, to have a dialogue by phone with *Times* editors and with a scientist more representative of mainstream opinion, Andrew Weaver, who holds the Canada Research Chair in atmospheric science at the University of Victoria in British Columbia.

Question: Professor Lindzen, nine years ago you said, "I can find no substantive basis for the [global] warming scenarios being popularly described." Is that still the case?

Lindzen: That depends. If you're talking about New York being underwater and palm trees in Washington, then the answer is still the same. There's no basis for that. Indeed, even if you accept warming as something that may occur and may be due to man's activities, statements that it will cause increased storminess and more intense hurricanes and so on still have no foundation at all.

Q: Professor Weaver, do you agree with that?

Weaver: Well, I do accept that warming has occurred, and I do accept that it will occur in the future. But to be fair, on both sides there have been alarmist points of views. I have a lovely picture showing the Statue of Liberty under water, which appeared on the front page of a tabloid. That's utter nonsense. On the other hand, you have the ostrichlike mentality of some who would argue that, in fact, nothing bad is going to happen and that maybe global warming is actually good for us.

Q: I'm curious where the points of agreement are. Do you both agree that, whether or not humans are the cause, the planetary temperature is rising in such a way as to slightly raise ocean levels in potentially dangerous ways?

Lindzen: I don't think there's solid agreement on that. You have to understand, the primary cause of sea level at any given location is a change in land level. Superimposed on this might be a small change due to thermal expansion of the ocean. That may very well continue because it has been going on for thousands of years. But it has been happening over millennia, and millennia don't have much to do with man. Sea levels have been rising since the end of the last glaciation. Over the last several hundred years, it seems that it has gone a little bit faster. I don't see much reason to suppose that this will change, and I do think that could have some implications. But what I'm saying is that climate is always changing, and we're always called on to adapt to the change. What I object to is the notion that there is something specifically different about today's change that you think you can identify with man. Normal change has been occurring and will always occur.

Weaver: What you haven't mentioned, Dick, is the rate of change. We know that sea levels have risen since the end of the last ice age by about 120 meters, and of course land rises and falls for natural reasons—because tectonic plates move and collide or because ice sheets melt. But the time scale associated with these changes is very slow. The rise in ocean levels we're seeing now is far too rapid to be solely associated with these natural occurrences. There is a lot of evidence that sea level will continue to rise. The oceans are warming, and warm water expands. It's also likely that glaciers will continue to melt. I do believe that this has implications for regions, like Bangladesh, that are affected by storm surges associated with tropical cyclones and the like. If you put a storm surge on top of increased sea level you have the potential for increased water damage.

Q: In your mind, Professor Weaver, what has caused this change in climate?

Weaver: Two things. First, there's natural variability in the climate system. There is seasonal variability, there is inter-annual variability. There are things like El Nino and La Nina. But there is no known natural climate mechanism to explain the warming over the 20th century. And that is one of the many pieces suggesting that a substantial portion of the warming of the 20th century is associated with greenhouse gases.

Lindzen: Some people argue that man can have no effect on climate, and I think that's nonsense. I agree with you, Andrew, on that. The argument is, will it be enough to worry about?

Q: What is the impact of humans?

Lindzen: Man is contributing to an increase in carbon dioxide in the atmosphere, and carbon dioxide is one of the greenhouse gases, albeit a minor one. The main greenhouse substances in the atmosphere, as the National Academy points out, are water vapor and clouds. In the models, water vapor and clouds act in such a way as to magnify what carbon dioxide alone would do by a factor of three or four. But there are highly uncertain aspects of the model. So we have a circumstance wherein the prediction that causes concern is based on parts of the model that are extremely dubious. Models have varying degrees of failure. They don't produce many phenomena that we know exist. It is a very profound assumption that the models can replace nature.

Weaver: I agree with Dick about the fundamental importance of clouds and water vapor. But these climate models are not as uncertain as he makes out. There has been great success in recent years comparing the paleo-record of climate with modeling results of the same period. We've found that, yes, indeed, the models do a very fine job of capturing global climate changes of the past.

Q: Professor Lindzen, to some degree you're a lone voice in the wilderness here. As we looked for people to represent the two sides on this issue, we didn't find many researchers embracing your point of view. Why do you think that is?

Lindzen: This notion of examining who's voting "yes" and who's voting "no" on climate issues is disguising the fact that there's broad agreement that some areas of the research are quite dubious.

Q: But aren't you standing somewhat alone on the issue of whether humans are a primary cause of global warming?

Lindzen: If you look at the United Nations Intergovernmental Panel on Climate Change report, the actual report points out that we're in no position to make an attribution. Then, in the summary, it says that the group's opinion is that changes may be largely attributable to humans. I don't know what you do about that. You may wish to go ahead and believe that, but you should be aware that it's opinion. When you ask researchers what they really know, they tend to agree that it is not very much.

Weaver: I think we know a lot. I am not aware of a single study that can explain the warming that has occurred over the course of the 20th century without the incorporation of greenhouse gases as a factor. So that's one thing. We have a lot of studies that have detected warming. But I am not aware of a single one that can explain this without using greenhouse gases.

Q: And how does all this relate to policy? Should we be embracing the Kyoto Protocol?

Lindzen: Policy isn't so much our domain, but one thing that is very clear is that the Kyoto agreement would not change anything. It wouldn't change levels of CO_2 in the atmosphere. It wouldn't reduce warming. So the notion that you propose the possibility of a problem and then proceed to take actions that have no relevance to the problem seems a bit weird.

Weaver: On Kyoto, I agree wholeheartedly, as would almost anyone in the scientific community, that it will have zero effect on global warming. However, for countries like Canada, the U.S. and Japan, meeting the standards proposed at Kyoto will be extraordinarily difficult. The only way to meet them is through changing technology. I support Kyoto not because it will have an immediate climatic effect, but because in order to meet it one needs to develop new technologies and change our conception of energy and how we get it.

Q: Kyoto aside for a moment, should we be trying to reduce carbon dioxide emissions? Do our concerns about global warming require action?

Lindzen: Some concerns have legitimacy, but we should prioritize our responses. You can't just say, "No matter what the cost, and no matter how little the benefit, we'll do this." If we truly believe in warming, then we've already decided we're going to adjust. So what's involved in adjusting? We know that the reason we adjust to things far better than Bangladesh is that we're richer. Wouldn't you think it makes sense to make sure we're as robust and wealthy as possible? And that the poor of the world are also as robust and wealthy as possible? Isn't that a better policy? I think what policy wonks like about Kyoto is that even if it does nothing about climate, it starts putting in place global monitoring and enforcement. Well, that's interesting, but how many people would want to sign on to an experiment in international policing of arbitrary regulations that have nothing to do with a specific problem? I think it's bad policy to tie changes and laws and regulations to problems they don't really address. If you say you are fighting global warming, and you adopt a policy that doesn't relate to it, then there's no way for the public to know if it's endorsed anything that works or not.

Weaver: As scientists, we love to observe change and try to understand it. But this is a dangerous experiment. We are moving into a new climate, and we don't know what it's going to be like. We know it will be warmer, and that the sea level will rise. We don't know, however, even if we were to stop all carbon dioxide emissions today, whether we've pushed the climate system past a certain threshold that would take us into an entirely new climate

state, unlike anything in the last 400,000 years. And it's not us—
it's our children—who will have to live with the consequences of
our experiment.

Understanding the Scientific Method

In undertaking original research, scientists will follow the scientific
method. (I have always disliked this term, as it has much broader application than just science and teaches you problem-solving skills.)
Scientists will seek some phenomenon they are trying to understand.
They will observe this phenomenon, collect data, and describe it as best
they can. They will also see how others have described it to ensure as
much information as possible about the phenomenon is available. This
is called the observational stage.

Next, scientists will try to explain the phenomenon with existing
theories (which may include mathematical formulae). Scientists may
find that the existing theories (or mathematical expressions) are inadequate so they have to develop a new theory. This is called the explanation or hypothesis stage. In the third stage, scientists will use their
explanation, or hypothesis, to predict what will happen to this or other
phenomena in alternative situations. This is called the prediction stage.

Finally, experiments will be designed to test the predictions in what
is—quite logically—called the experimental stage. If the predictions are
correct, the hypothesis stands—at least for now. If the predictions fail,
the new observations would have to be recorded, the hypothesis or
explanation would have to be modified, and the whole process would
repeat itself.

Let's suppose I want to understand why I get a stomach ache every
time I eat dinner. I've noticed this for quite some time and I have a
hunch it's because we shouldn't eat desserts after dinner. My theory is
that something about the mixture of savoury and sweet causes this

reaction. My prediction is that I would avoid stomach aches if I stop having dessert after dinner. It's easy to test this prediction by eating dessert on some days and not on other days. Lo and behold, my stomach ache goes away when I don't have dessert; my stomach ache comes back when I do. My hypothesis seems to be valid.

Inspired by the success of my research, I decide to find out if the fact that dinner and dessert don't mix is a general principle that holds throughout the population. Maybe I should tell everyone about my findings. Before I do, I had better test my hypothesis. First, I get a few friends and family to try dinner with and without dessert. Only one other person notices any difference when they stop having dessert. Most never had stomach troubles in the first place. My hypothesis must be incorrect. Nevertheless, I stand by my observation that dinner and dessert do not mix for me.

My friend comes over and says that my hypothesis that desserts are the cause of my stomach problems is crazy. A raging argument breaks out. He challenges my assumptions and I vigorously defend them. "I'll prove it to you," he finally says. "My hypothesis is that it's the ice cream you have every day with your dessert that's causing you the problems." He predicts that if I continue having dessert but stop having ice cream with it, my stomach problems would go away. I grudgingly agree to do a few tests over the next few days. My friend turns out to be right.

This process of observing, creating, and testing the predictions of hypotheses continues until I conclude that I am lactose intolerant. After many more tests both in the laboratory and with other people, the scientific community concludes that those people missing lactase, the enzyme that breaks down lactose, may experience a range of symptoms including stomach upset when milk products containing lactose are consumed.

Scientists disseminate the results of their research in scientific journals, which are typically published by national or international scientific societies or academic publishers. Common to all reputable journals is a process known as peer review. A journal editor, occasionally in consultation with associate editors, will seek experts in the field to determine whether the manuscript contains original research that advances the field of knowledge in the journal's subject area. The reviewers will check the manuscript for errors in logic, inconsistencies, and other potential pitfalls, and provide the editor with comments. The editor then decides what to do with the manuscript. Recommendations rarely include outright acceptance for publication. More frequently the editor will send the original manuscript back to the author(s), along with comments from reviewers, whose anonymity is preserved, and request major or minor revisions prior to further consideration. A manuscript can also be rejected for publication if the reviewers and editors found fatal problems with it.

Of the 558 manuscripts submitted to the *Journal of Climate* in 2007, 50% were sent back to the authors for major revisions, 18% were sent back for minor revisions, 31% were rejected outright or withdrawn, and 1% were accepted outright. In total, only about 63% of all submitted manuscripts ended up being published in 2007, and most, after at least two rounds with the reviewers. That is, revised manuscripts would be sent back to the reviewers for further examination and this process could be iterated several times.

Mistakes sometimes happen, and very occasionally the reviewers and editors miss something that should have caused a paper to be otherwise rejected. It is extraordinarily rare for the opposite to occur. That is, good papers eventually get published; poor papers usually don't, although the occasional one slips through. What is perhaps most remarkable about the peer-review system is that it is entirely voluntary and without compensation. Scientists agree to review other people's research since they know that someone will have to review their research. Most scientists regard reviewing papers as a responsibility and an opportunity to learn something new.

Key to the scientific method is that all existing observations are explainable by the theory whose predictions have been tested extensively. A scientist simply cannot ignore data because it doesn't fit a theory; rather, the scientist will seek either to modify the theory so that the data is explainable or determine if there was some error in the collection of the data.

So in 2007, when the IPCC released its Fourth Assessment Report, including the statement:

> Most of the observed increase in global average temperatures since the mid-20th century is *very likely* due to the observed increase in anthropogenic greenhouse gas concentrations.... Discernible human influences now extend to other aspects of climate, including ocean warming, continental-average temperatures, temperature extremes and wind patterns,

it means that it encompasses all available observations.

The institution of science does not rely on one person's opinion; the creation and dissemination of assertions on elaborate and unmonitored websites is not considered science; finally, someone's ideological belief, while perhaps influential in forming hypotheses, should play no further role in the scientific method.

Understanding Scientific Uncertainty

The concept of scientific uncertainty is also poorly understood by the public in general and the media in particular. Scientific uncertainty has two categories: epistemic (or reducible) uncertainty, which is associated with incomplete understanding of the system; and aleatoric (or irreducible) uncertainty, which is linked to inherent randomness. Let's suppose I am told that there are one thousand coins stacked neatly in several piles on the floor. Suppose I want to know the probability of a polar bear facing up on any given coin (I know that all of the two-dollar coins [toonies] and none of the other coins have polar bears on one side). From afar, it is difficult to see how many toonies there are—this represents epistemic (or reducible) uncertainty. It's easy for me to eliminate this epistemic uncertainty by picking up a pair of binoculars and counting the number of toonies directly. I know that each of these toonies has a 50% chance of having a polar bear face up and a 50% chance of the Queen of England being face up. If I count one hundred toonies, then the probability is that fifty of these would have polar bears facing up. The probability is then that fifty of the one thousand coins in the stacks, or 5% of the total, would likely have polar bears facing up. This probability would never be reducible and represents aleatoric uncertainty.

Uncertainty in climate predictions can further be broken down into two components, each of which has its own epistemic and aleatoric subcomponents: One component involves uncertainty in climate feedbacks; the other involves uncertainty in the emissions scenario used to investigate the future climate. In terms of overall uncertainty, each contributes about half, the latter being dependent on poorly constrained assumptions of future population growth, social behaviour, economic growth, energy use, and technology change. Compounding the problem of uncertainty is the potential existence of "unknown unknowns" or surprises whose importance only becomes apparent once they are discovered.

Scientific uncertainty has often been used as grounds for not dealing with an issue that would cause various special interests some short-term hardship. Take, for example, smoking as a cause of cancer. For years scientific uncertainty was used to generally confuse the public and stall the implementation of regulatory policies. The same thing occurred with respect to chlorofluorocarbons (CFCs) and the destruction of stratospheric ozone. Even though the precautionary principle would put the onus of proof on an individual or group claiming that their activities were not harmful, especially in light of overwhelming scientific evidence to the contrary, uncertainty has been evoked time and time again by the denial industry to limit government action.

The theory of turbulence provides another example. There are many aspects of turbulence that are still not well understood today. Yet over the years, the scientific community has developed a fairly good understanding of the bulk properties of turbulence. We may not be able to predict exactly where turbulent air motions will take a dandelion seed as it sails in the air, but that doesn't prevent us from getting in an airplane. The parallels between weather and climate should be obvious.

Scientific uncertainty is also frequently framed in the context of percentage certainty. Suppose I said that the scientific community was certain that the continued emissions of greenhouse gases would cause further warming and that this warming over the twenty-first century will have a greater than 90% probability of being larger than the warming that occurred over the twentieth century. Suppose I followed this statement with a host of other projected climate and ecosystem responses to this warming, many of which are not very pleasant. Would you focus on the 10% probability I was wrong or the 90% probability I was right? Would you board an airplane if it had a 90% chance of arriving at your destination safely and a 10% chance of crashing? How about if the plane had a 90% chance of crashing and a 10% chance of getting you safely to the next airport?

Who Is Trying to Sway Public Opinion?

One of the most profoundly revealing yet deeply disturbing examples of deliberate attempts to obfuscate the public over the science of global warming is contained in the now-famous memo from influential political strategist and consultant Frank Luntz to the U.S. Republican Party. On page 137 of his November 2002 memo, he states:

Should the public come to believe that the scientific issues are set-
tled, their views about global warming will change accordingly.
Therefore, you need to continue to make the lack of scientific certainty a primary issue in the debate....

On page 138, he spells out a means to the end:

You need to be even more active in recruiting experts who are
sympathetic to your view, and much more active in making them
part of your message. People are willing to trust scientists, engi-
neers, and other leading research professionals, and less willing to
trust politicians. If you wish to challenge the prevailing wisdom
about global warming, it is more effective to have professionals
making the case than politicians.

In reference to the Kyoto Protocol, the memo provides options to
sway public opinion against support for regulations. It suggests
stressing that regulations will "hit the most vulnerable among us,"
including "the elderly, the poor and those on fixed incomes." It further
suggests emphasizing that food and utility costs will rise, the prospect
of job losses, and that "well-intended regulations will make American
life less safe, not more safe."

Does the approach advocated by the report sound familiar?
Absolutely. We have our very own "Made in Canada" propaganda campaign aimed at trying to sow the seeds of doubt with the Canadian
public. Astroturf organizations (manufactured or artificial grassroots
organizations funded directly or indirectly by oil and coal interests)
have sprouted up and issued "news releases." Letters to the editor and
opinion editorials frequent the pages of a select few newspapers where
there are sympathetic editors. Reporters who happen to write an accurate story updating new developments of the science of global warming
without providing artificial balance receive a barrage of email com-

plaints, as do their bosses. All in all, big money can pay for some big public relations, and big public relations can sway public opinion.

The Shift to Accurate Media Coverage

In Canada, and even the United States, the tide has turned. Media reporting of global warming over the last several years has felt less compelled to include an artificial sense of balance. Maxwell Boykoff has quantified this shift in a recent study that appeared in the journal *Area* in December 2007. He showed that while 36.6% of stories in the major newspapers in the United States gave artificially balanced coverage in 2003, this dropped to only 10.4% in 2004, 8.2% in 2005, and 3.3% in 2006.

We will never be able to point to a single reason for the change, but several events—including Al Gore's *An Inconvenient Truth* and the devastating effects of Hurricane Katrina and numerous other weather-related disasters—must have played a role. Journalists also started to realize that they had been duped into reporting a false sense of uncertainty. And hell hath no fury like a journalist scorned. The litany of skeptic claims would end up being discredited; the projections released in the IPCC reports would come true (with Mother Nature responding at the upper extreme of those projections); the climate scientists' message would remain unchanged while the denial industry's message became a moving target. Acting like a desperate legal defence team that knew it had lost its case, the denial industry was tossing all sorts of mutually inconsistent questions out to the public jury—in the hope of creating a reasonable expectation of doubt that would lead to a not-guilty verdict on the human ability to affect climate.

Over the last two years, investigative journalism at its very best has begun to examine some of the individuals in the denial industry, along with their affiliations and supporters. Three pieces available in Canada stand out as being truly exceptional: an August 12, 2006, *Globe and Mail* article by Charles Montgomery; a CBC *fifth estate* documentary entitled *The Denial Machine* that first aired November 15, 2006; and an August 13, 2007, *Newsweek* story by Sharon Begley entitled "The Truth about Denial."

Reading the Montgomery article and watching *The Denial Machine* were liberating experiences. For years the climate scientist community had been frustrated by the actions of a small group of individuals who seemed to command a disproportionate amount of air time. Climate scientists working in government laboratories or universities do not have the time, or the inclination, to travel the country on Probus lecture tours, write scores of letters to the editor or opinion editorials, and speak out on radio talk shows hither and yon. It is simply not feasible. So, when these reports started to investigate the denial industry, many of my colleagues and I breathed a sigh of relief. In fact, I remember the night of November 15, 2006, as if it were yesterday. Andrew Bush of the Department of Earth and Atmospheric Sciences at the University of Alberta, Guido Vettoretti of the Department of Physics at the University of Toronto, and I were sitting in the basement of the University of Toronto faculty club having a beer after a long day of meetings. We asked the bartender if he would mind changing the television station from the sports channel to the CBC, which was broadcasting *The Denial Machine*. We were one of only a few groups of people in the bar. As the documentary unfolded, we became noticeably restless until eventually we couldn't hold back our cheers. Interview after interview exposed the efforts of the big oil and coal industries to undermine the science of global warming. Parallels with the tobacco lobby and their efforts to discredit the science linking smoking to cancer were made throughout.

At the same time as media reporting started to shift away from biased balance, two especially influential web blogs were created. In December 2004, www.realclimate.org was launched by a group of five

well-established and internationally recognized climate scientists who
wanted, in the words of co-founder Gavin Schmidt of the NASA
Goddard Institute for Space Studies in New York, "to provide context
and background on climate science issues that are often missing in popular media coverage." A year later, www.desmogblog.com, founded by
respected Canadian public relations professional Jim Hoggan, the president of James Hoggan & Associates, was launched with the aim to
counter the disinformation created by the well-oiled denial machine. In
the words of the desmogblog.com team:

> Unfortunately, a well-funded and highly organized public relations
> campaign is poisoning the climate change debate. Using tricks and
> stunts that unsavoury PR firms invented for the tobacco lobby,
> energy-industry contrarians are trying to confuse the public, to
> forestall individual and political actions that might cut into exorbi-
> tant coal, oil and gas industry profits. DeSmogBlog is here to cry
> foul—to shine the light on techniques and tactics that reflect badly
> on the PR industry and are, ultimately, bad for the planet.

The influence that these and other such weblogs have had in shaping
the public discourse, particularly the media portrayal of global
warming, should not be overlooked. They provide one-stop shopping
for updates on some of the latest political controversies and misrepre-
sentations of science in the name of public policy. I visit both sites daily.

• • •

FEW JOURNALISTS have scientific training, and so the distinction between
science and science policy often gets blurred. In the past, journalists sub-
scribed to the notion that balanced reporting required them to give equal
attention to those who believed that global warming was caused by natural variability and those who believed it was caused by humans. While

well intended, such balance inadvertently interjected bias in the reporting since it created an artificial sense of scientific uncertainty.

Journalists often work under ridiculously stringent timelines; stories have to be filed by cut-off times; the editor will require last-minute changes. It must be very difficult to check if the person they are interviewing in response to a press release they received is actually a recognized expert. Perhaps the press release came from a PR campaign masking itself as a grassroots organization. Would the journalist know? Would the journalist have time to investigate if the press release were dumped on his or her desk with instructions to write a story about it?

Moreover, reporters don't often write the newspaper headlines for their stories. Usually an editor or headline writer has only a few seconds to scan an article and come up with something catchy. While the headline may entice you to read the article, it may inadvertently misrepresent the science being written about. I even had one reporter email me sheepishly after his article appeared, saying that he took no responsibility for the headline.

I have enormous respect for the work journalists do. Over the years I have been interviewed by scores of reporters. I have only met a small handful who I believe are more interested in using their stories to influence public opinion through the assertion of their own ideological principles than they are in trying to represent the facts accurately. I have noticed a very significant shift in the reporting of global warming science over the past two years, a move away from "he said, she said" toward a more accurate, less sensational approach. The public discourse is no longer about whether global warming is real but rather what we are going to do about it. And of course, anything we do must involve extensive discussion and debate, which is the foundation of good public policy. I remain optimistic that science, rather than the ideological agenda of a small segment of society, will influence governments as they develop the policies that must inevitably be introduced in the years ahead.

2

A Passage Through Time

It probably comes as no surprise that global warming is one of my favourite conversation topics. I have harangued family, friends, students, and fellow Saturday-morning soccer parents on more than one occasion.

What I hear most is that people think global warming is a recent scientific phenomenon. This is perfectly understandable, of course, as the majority of us keep abreast of science through the media. Global warming received almost no media coverage until 1988, which was a notable year for four reasons. First, Dr. James Hansen of NASA's Goddard Institute for Space Studies (often mistakenly credited as being the father of climate change theory) testified before the U.S. Senate Committee on Energy and Natural Resources that he was 99% confident that global warming was underway. Second, the United Nations Intergovernmental Panel on Climate Change (IPCC) was formed. Third, Canada hosted a major international climate-related conference. Fourth, the central and eastern United States were being baked by heat waves and an extended drought. The agricultural sector suffered severe losses. According to U.S. National Oceanic and Atmospheric Administration (NOAA) estimates, between five thousand and ten thousand people died in the United States because of these heat waves.

These four events occurred more than a century after the basic physics of the greenhouse effect was understood and almost a hundred years since carbon dioxide's contribution to this greenhouse effect was calculated.

Following years of research to develop a theory of heat, well-known French mathematician Jean-Baptiste-Joseph Fourier (see "Joseph Fourier and Svante Arrhenius") wrote an essay in 1834 on the temperature of the Earth and planetary spaces. Unlike his earlier work, Fourier's remarks were not bolstered by mathematical analyses but rather they summarized his previous findings framed in a hypothesis for a generalized theory of heat. Buried within his original article were the words (as translated by J.R. Fleming, 1999):

> ... the temperature can be augmented by the interposition of the
> atmosphere, because heat in the state of light finds less resistance
> in penetrating the air, than in repassing into the air when con-
> verted into non-luminous heat.

Fourier recognized that the atmosphere acted to raise the Earth's temperature, as it was essentially transparent to incoming radiation from the sun but was effective in blocking heat radiated from the Earth's surface, a key element of the greenhouse effect.

In 1859, Irish scientist John Tyndall published a brief note in the Proceedings of the Royal Society of London reporting on some of his ongoing experiments. He described an elaborate instrument (see "John Tyndall and His Experimental Apparatus") he had constructed and noted: "Gases vary considerably in their absorptive power." For the first time, he had shown that different gases warmed by different amounts when exposed to radiation similar to that from the Earth's surface. On February 7, 1861, Tyndall provided more extensive details at the prestigious Bakerian Lecture of the Royal Society of London. Here, the scien-

Joseph Fourier and Svante Arrhenius

Left: Jean-Baptiste-Joseph Fourier (1768–1830). **Right:** Svante August Arrhenius (1859–1927). *Used with permission of The Granger Collection, New York.*

tific community learned that ozone, carbon dioxide, water vapour, and nitrous oxide, among others, absorbed radiation from the Earth's surface, and that nitrogen and oxygen, making up 99% of the atmosphere by volume, were transparent to this radiation.

In 1903, Svante August Arrhenius (see "Joseph Fourier and Svante Arrhenius") won the Nobel Prize in chemistry for "the advancement of chemistry by his electrolytic theory of dissociation." Within the climate community, he is celebrated as the first to develop a theoretical model of how atmospheric carbon dioxide affects the Earth's temperature. Long before calculators, Arrhenius performed tedious, painstaking calculations of the projected temperature change that would occur at the Earth's surface under different levels of atmospheric carbon dioxide. When atmospheric carbon dioxide doubled, Arrhenius predicted that the world would warm by about 5°C in the tropics and about 6°C at high latitudes. He provided the first quantitative estimation of *climate*

John Tyndall and His Experimental Apparatus

Left: John Tyndall (1820–1893). *Used with permission of The Granger Collection, New York.* **Right:** Apparatus used by Tyndall to examine the absorptive capacity of various gases. *Used with permission of the Royal Society of London.*

sensitivity, which is defined as the surface warming that occurs in response to a doubling of carbon dioxide.

Perhaps the most remarkable early contribution to the science of global warming was from British steam engineer Guy Stewart Callendar (see "Guy Callendar") in 1938. He analyzed what would happen to the Earth's temperature under the continued combustion of fossil fuels. Callendar compiled estimates of the then-present concentration of carbon dioxide in the atmosphere. He noted that in 1936 there were 289 parts of carbon dioxide per million parts of air (ppmv). Assuming constant 1936 emission rates, he predicted that atmospheric carbon dioxide levels would increase to 314 ppmv by 2000, 346 ppmv by 2100, and 373 ppmv by 2200. Callendar argued that his assumption of constant future emissions was reasonable due to the "ever-increasing efficiency of fuel utilization" that had stabilized emissions "during the last 20 years." Of course, annual carbon dioxide emissions have grown more than sevenfold since his paper was published.

Callendar calculated that by the time the atmospheric carbon dioxide level reached 330 ppmv (sometime in the twenty-first century),

Guy Callendar

Guy Stewart Callendar (1898–1964). *Used with permission of James R. Fleming.*

the world would warm by about 0.39°C. When it reached 360 ppmv (sometime in the twenty-second century), the world would warm by 0.57°C. In fact, the dramatic increase in emissions over the twentieth century led to carbon dioxide levels surpassing 360 ppmv in 1995. The current level of 385 ppmv has been increasing since 2000 by an average of 2.0 ppmv per year, far beyond Callendar's wildest expectations.

What is perhaps most impressive about Callendar's work is the breadth and depth of his analysis. Not only did he perform theoretical calculations, but he also compiled global temperature records, recognized and accounted for the importance of the urban heat island (which tends to make cities warmer than their surrounding areas), and carefully documented his work. He found that the Earth had been warming by about 0.005°C per year since the late nineteenth century and argued for an important human contribution to this warming. He further predicted an average future warming of 0.003°C annually through the combustion of fossil fuels.

Much like Arrhenius forty years earlier, Callendar viewed warming to be a good thing:

> ... it may be said that the combustion of fossil fuel, whether it be peat from the surface or oil from 10,000 feet below, is likely to prove beneficial to mankind in several ways, besides the provision of heat and power. For instance the above mentioned small increases of mean temperature would be important at the northern margin of cultivation, and the growth of favourably situated plants is directly proportional to the carbon dioxide pressure....

Callendar recognized the potential for longer growing seasons at high northern latitudes and the so-called fertilization effect whereby, all else being equal, certain plants might grow faster when exposed to higher levels of carbon dioxide. Of course, Callendar's optimism was ill-founded, as his assumption of constant 1936 carbon emissions was woefully inadequate.

• • •

HEATING OUR HOMES used to be an onerous task. In the early eighteenth century, we cut down trees and scoured the countryside for fallen branches and twigs. Industrialization, however, took a heavy toll on European forests, which gradually disappeared as the need for energy grew. Fortunately, large-scale coal mining took off in the mid-eighteenth century and increased steadily during the nineteenth century, feeding our hunger for fuel.

Using coal as a primary heat source had its drawbacks. Sulphur dioxide, which is converted in the atmosphere to sulphate aerosols and subsequently rains out as (sulphuric) acid rain, is a nasty by-product of coal combustion. Many early respiratory deaths were caused by prolonged exposure to smog (derived from *sm*oke plus f*og*). Hence, Callendar, Arrhenius, and others were thrilled about the prospects of a warming world: Less energy was needed to keep warm and there was better air quality, a longer growing season, lush plants—a veritable Garden of Eden.

When trying to convince people that the climate has changed, I've come up against an interesting obstacle: Many individuals will only accept this fact if the present climate is noticeably different from the climate they remember. We all know that our memory can play tricks on us and certainly gets fuzzier with time. We'll remember yesterday's weather better than last week's, and last summer's climate better than the climate of 1997. How many of us have heard or told stories about the climate when we were young: "When I was a child we used to get great snowfalls," your parents might say. Never mind that your parents have probably doubled in height since the time of those snowfalls and so have an entirely different spatial perception.

To early nineteenth-century Londoners, normal climate conditions would allow for the River Thames to freeze periodically (see "Frost Fair on the Thames"). Today, we would be flabbergasted if the Thames were to ice over. "An ice age approaches" would be splashed across the front pages of newspapers around the world. Separating what one *believes* to be normal as opposed to what *is* normal requires an examination of the data.

Everyone experiences weather, so at times it seems that everyone believes they are an expert on global warming. If you combine this confidence in the comprehension of global warming with a passionately held belief of what constitutes a normal climate, you can see the barriers scientists face when trying to convince the public of the scale of climate change we have already experienced and how it pales in comparison with what lies in store.

Unless otherwise mentioned, throughout this book I use the internationally accepted United Nations World Meteorological

Frost Fair on the Thames

Frost Fair on the Thames River, January 31–February 5, 1814. Reproduced with permission from the UK Secretary of State for Culture, Media and Sport. © Crown copyright: UK Government Art Collection.

Organization (WMO) definition of *normal climate*. Normal climate will refer to conditions averaged between 1971 and 2000. Following WMO recommendations, this definition is revised at the end of every decade to include averages from the previous thirty years. The next redefinition is scheduled for 2011, when normal will represent conditions averaged between 1981 and 2010.

Understanding the Greenhouse Effect

When Arrhenius and Callendar first published their research, it was vigorously challenged by their scientific peers—a natural and fundamental step required for the advancement of scientific knowledge. Scientists questioned the assumptions, tried to reproduce the results, and tested various predictions arising from the theories put forward. Not only did the cornerstones of their analyses stand up to further scrutiny, but they were also expanded upon by numerous subsequent studies.

Over the last two centuries, we have developed a solid understanding of the greenhouse effect. Everything—including the sun, the Earth, you and me—emits energy in the form of electromagnetic waves known as radiation. Electromagnetic radiation travels at the speed of light and, just like waves in the ocean, is characterized by a wavelength (the distance between the crests of two waves) and a frequency (the number of wave crests that pass a given point in a second). Shorter wavelength radiation possesses more energy than longer wavelength radiation; hotter objects emit radiation with shorter wavelengths than cooler objects; hotter objects also radiate more total energy than cooler objects.

Electromagnetic radiation plays an integral part in our everyday lives. When we go to the dentist, we might be exposed to high-energy X-rays; we sometimes heat our food using microwaves; we listen to FM and AM radio waves; we slap on sunscreen to avoid high-energy ultraviolet rays; we use night-vision goggles or motion sensors to see infrared radiation. While the sun emits radiation at all wavelengths, much of it is in the visible band, the component of electromagnetic radiation that our eyes have evolved to see. We call the sun's radiation shortwave radiation. The Earth is much cooler than the sun and so emits radiation with much longer wavelengths. We call this longwave radiation.

The Earth is in a *global radiative equilibrium* (see "The Earth's Energy Balance") if the total amount of energy received from the sun equals the total amount of energy emitted by the Earth to space. When

The Earth's Energy Balance

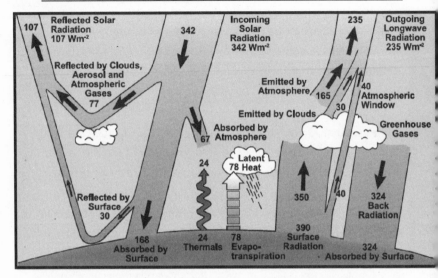

Estimate of the long-term annually and globally averaged energy balance of the Earth, assuming global radiative equilibrium. *Reproduced with permission from FAQ 1.1, Figure 1, of Le Treut (2007).*

this occurs, the annually and globally averaged Earth's temperature does not change. That is, if there is no net heating, the temperature will not rise or fall but will stay constant. It is like having a glass that is half full of water and as you sip through a straw, you pour in water at exactly the same rate—the water level in the glass will not change.

By averaging all over the globe throughout the day and night, we know that the sun heats the top of the atmosphere at a rate of 342 watts per square metre, or W/m² (see "The Earth's Energy Balance"). That's a little less than six 60-watt incandescent light bulbs heating each square metre. Of this incoming solar radiation, about one-third is immediately reflected back to space either by clouds, aerosols, atmospheric gases, or the Earth's surface. We say that the Earth has a *planetary albedo* of 30%, where the albedo is defined as the percentage of incoming shortwave radiation that is reflected back. Only about half of the 342 W/m² of incoming solar radiation reaches the Earth's surface, where it is converted to heat or used to evaporate water. The rest (67 W/m^2, or about 20% of incoming solar radiation) is absorbed in the atmosphere.

Heat is transferred from the Earth's surface to the atmosphere through three processes: thermals, evapotranspiration, and radiation. When an object is heated, its molecules move faster. Solar heating therefore makes the molecules at the Earth's surface move faster. When these molecules bump into air molecules immediately above the surface, the air molecules also start to move faster. By definition, the temperature of an object is a measure of the average energy contained in the motion of that object's molecules. When the molecules speed up, the temperature rises. This mechanism of heat transfer between objects in direct contact with one another is known as *conduction*. When the air immediately above the Earth's surface is heated, it also becomes lighter than the air slightly higher up and so wants to rise through a process known as *convection*. The combined effects of conduction and convection create *thermals*. They account for about one-seventh of all the heat transferred from the Earth's surface to the overlying atmosphere.

Energy can also be used to break the bonds holding liquid water molecules together in a process known as *evaporation*. Plants use this process to keep cool. They draw water through their roots to their leaves, and energy is then used to evaporate that water. In plants, this process is called *transpiration;* in humans, it's called *perspiration*. The physics is exactly the same. When the evaporated water, now in the air in the form of vapour, condenses to form clouds or precipitation, heat is released. The net effect is a transfer of heat from the Earth's surface, where evaporation occurs, to the atmosphere, where condensation occurs. Since 71% of the Earth's surface is covered by oceans, it is not surprising that the combined effect of evaporation and transpiration, known as *evapotranspiration*, is much more effective on the global scale than thermals in transferring heat from the Earth's surface to the atmosphere.

The final mechanism of heat transfer is longwave radiation emitted by the Earth's surface, only 10% of which passes directly through the atmosphere to space via the *atmospheric window* (see "The Earth's Energy Balance"). Naturally occurring greenhouse gases in the atmosphere—most notably water vapour and carbon dioxide, methane, nitrous oxide, and ozone—all absorb radiation (and convert it to heat) differently, depending on the wavelength. The atmospheric window corresponds to those wavelengths for which infrared radiation passes freely through the atmosphere without absorption. The rest of the Earth's longwave radiation is largely absorbed by the atmosphere.

If there were no atmosphere surrounding Earth, the net 235 W/m^2 of incoming shortwave radiation (incoming 342 W/m^2 minus reflected 107 W/m^2, from "The Earth's Energy Balance") would have to be balanced by 235 W/m^2 of outgoing longwave radiation for global radiative equilibrium to exist. A relatively simple calculation reveals that without an atmosphere, the Earth's average surface temperature would be −19.4°C instead of the 14.4°C observed today. The existence of our atmosphere provides a beneficial *natural* greenhouse effect that has made the planet 33.8°C warmer than it would otherwise be. In effect, it acts like a blanket to keep the surface warm.

Like everything else on the Earth, the atmosphere emits radiation in all directions. Clouds and parcels of air emit radiation upwards, downwards, and sideways. Greenhouse gases and clouds throughout the atmosphere continually absorb and re-emit longwave radiation in all directions. The net result is that about 195 W/m^2 end up being re-emitted to space at the top of the atmosphere in global radiative equilibrium.

A *radiative forcing* occurs when something causes a change in the average net (incoming minus outgoing) radiation balance at the top of the atmosphere. A positive radiative forcing acts to warm the Earth's surface, while a negative radiative forcing acts to cool it. A radiative forcing perturbs the balance between incoming and outgoing radiation, and over time the climate system responds to try to re-establish global radiative equilibrium. If you buy a bottle of wine and put it in the fridge, the wine will cool until its temperature is the same as everything else in the fridge. When you take the bottle out of the fridge, the wine warms until it reaches room temperature. The wine is trying to reach equilibrium with its surroundings as a consequence of the laws of thermodynamics.

Adding additional greenhouse gases to the atmosphere is like adding a thicker blanket around the Earth. The extra gases will not affect the amount of incoming solar radiation but will reduce the loss of outgoing longwave radiation. More longwave radiation is absorbed in the atmosphere and re-emitted to the Earth's surface, where it is converted to heat. As a consequence, the Earth's surface must warm until eventually a new global radiative equilibrium is reached. Once more, 235 W/m^2 of longwave radiation will be emitted to space, but now it will be associated with a surface temperature that is warmer than before.

A slight dimming of the sun creates a negative radiative forcing, as there would be less shortwave radiation coming into the top of the atmosphere. In response, the Earth would cool until its outgoing longwave radiation exactly balanced the reduced incoming shortwave radiation. A new global radiative equilibrium will have been reached. Volcanic eruptions also provide a negative radiative forcing, since they usually add aerosols to the stratosphere (the atmospheric layer between about ten and fifty kilometres above the Earth's surface). These aerosols are effective at reflecting solar radiation back to space and so increase the planetary albedo. This effect only lasts a few years since once the aerosols get into the troposphere (the atmospheric layer below about ten kilometres, where all our weather occurs), they are effectively scavenged from the atmosphere when it rains.

The greenhouse effect and global warming are based on elementary principles of physics—principles that were discovered more than a century ago: Warm climates can't be maintained unless there is an excess of greenhouse gases to block outgoing longwave radiation; cold climates can't be maintained unless there is a depletion of greenhouse gases. If the amount of these gases is increased, a positive radiative forcing occurs and the Earth must warm until a new global radiative equilibrium is reached. Because the oceans respond slowly to a radiative forcing, it takes several centuries for the Earth to reach this new warmer equilibrium. We know that even if atmospheric carbon dioxide levels were immediately stabilized at 385 ppmv, the Earth would still warm by about 0.6°C in the years ahead. This is about the same amount as the observed twentieth-century warming. If, on the other hand, we immediately stabilize global emissions at 2006 levels, then, relative to pre-industrial times, global warming of about 1.8°C will occur by 2050 and 2.7°C will occur by 2100. Under this scenario, global warming continues unbounded for centuries with consequences that would not bode well for humanity.

Definitely Not Another Ice Age

Thousands of studies have been published in peer-reviewed scientific journals examining the science of global warming. Obviously it is impossible for scientists to read every article from every journal that relates to their field. In the past, a researcher might have taken a weekly or bi-weekly trip to the library and scanned the titles or read the abstracts of recent articles published in their favourite journals. Nowadays, these journals' tables of contents are emailed to scientists around the world the day they are published. The latest research is only one further click away.

One of the best ways to review research from a particular field is to consult the Thomson Scientific Institute for Scientific Information (ISI) Web of Science, a searchable bibliographic database that currently contains information from 6166 scientific journals. You can track what articles have been published on any topic and by whom. You can find out what's hot in the field by checking for the most referenced articles. A quick search reveals that between 1965 and 2007 there were 30,219 published studies on global warming or climate change. That's a lot of science, and you can bet that if there were an Achilles heel to the theory of global warming, it would have been discovered long ago. The scientific community understands global warming and the greenhouse effect extremely well. Frankly, we have understood it extremely well for decades.

In 1957, Roger Revelle and Hans Suess at the Scripps Institute of Oceanography, University of California in San Diego, published a seminal study explaining that the oceans could not absorb the human emissions of carbon dioxide as fast as they were being produced. They estimated that on average, a carbon dioxide molecule would remain in the atmosphere for ten years before being dissolved in the ocean, noting:

> Human beings are now carrying out a large-scale geophysical experiment of a kind that could not have happened in the past nor be reproduced in the future

since

> we are returning to the atmosphere and oceans the concentrated organic carbon stored in the sedimentary rocks over hundreds of millions of years.

In October 2007, Alvaro Montenegro and Michael Eby (researchers in my group at the University of Victoria), Viktor Brovkin at the Potsdam Institute for Climate Impact Research in Germany, David Archer at the University of Chicago, and I published a new estimate of how long human-produced carbon dioxide stays in the atmosphere.

Using one of the most sophisticated representations of the carbon cycle available, we asked what would happen if emissions followed one of the IPCC emissions scenarios (A2) out to 2100 and then decreased linearly to zero at and beyond the year 2300 (see "IPCC Emissions Scenario A2"). We did not like what we found: 75% of all human carbon dioxide emissions stayed in the atmosphere for an average eighteen hundred years; 25% had a lifetime longer than five thousand years. This was much longer than anyone had ever estimated before. The reason was clear. The terrestrial biosphere eventually changes from being a sink of carbon to a source of carbon (we can only grow so many plants and it takes an incredibly long time for peat and coal to form). The ocean's

IPCC Emissions Scenario A2

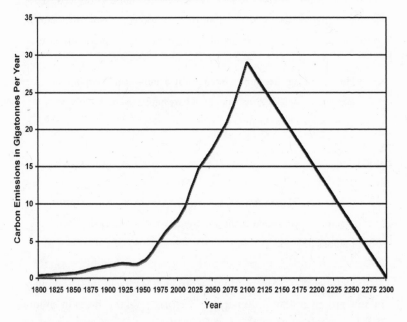

Scenario of carbon dioxide emissions in billions of tonnes (gigatonnes) of carbon per year. The observed emissions are used until 2000; the IPCC scenario A2 is used from 2000 to 2100; after 2100, the emissions linearly decay to zero at 2300.

efficiency of carbon dioxide uptake also slows with time and, unfortunately, it becomes more acidic.

Even the area of climate modelling has its roots in research conducted more than a half-century ago. While the development and use of computer models to forecast weather got underway in the 1950s, the first sophisticated atmospheric modelling studies aimed at investigating the climatic consequences of increasing atmospheric carbon dioxide didn't start until the 1970s. Prior to that, much more idealized representations of the climate system were used to make climate projections.

In 1975, Suki Manabe and Richard Wetherald at the NOAA Geophysical Fluid Dynamics Laboratory, now in Princeton, New Jersey, used a complicated general circulation model of the atmosphere to predict that a doubling of carbon dioxide would lead to 2.9°C global warming. This value of climate sensitivity was about half that predicted by Arrhenius eighty years earlier. What's remarkable about Manabe and Wetherald's result is that the best estimate of warming issued in the IPCC's Fourth Assessment Report thirty years later was the same. Based on numerous experiments from various groups around the world, the IPCC found that the equilibrium response of the climate system to a doubling of atmospheric carbon dioxide was likely in the range 2.0°C to 4.5°C, with a most likely value of 3.0°C.

During the 1960s and 1970s, the radiative effects of aerosols came under scrutiny. These tiny liquid or solid particles are the pesky agents that caused the debilitating smogs of London back in the nineteenth and twentieth centuries. Aerosols can be produced from natural sources (dust, pollen, volcanic eruptions) or as a result of human activity (sulphates). In 1967, Robert McCormick and John Ludwig from the U.S. National Center for Air Pollution Control in Cincinnati, Ohio, wrote a short note to *Science*, suggesting:

> ... that the effects of man's pollution of his environment are monotonically increasing along with the world population. The emission of long-lived aerosol, keeping pace with the accelerated worldwide production of CO_2 may well be leading to the decrease in worldwide air temperature in spite of the apparent buildup of CO_2.

Researchers tried to understand the cause of the apparent drop in world temperatures since the 1940s in spite of increasing greenhouse gases. Some argued that human aerosol production was increasing and overwhelming the CO_2-related greenhouse effect; others pointed out that volcanic activity had increased, especially in the 1960s, causing a cooling effect. Some pointed to small changes in the sun's intensity; and others argued a role for natural climate variability. It turned out that they were all right: The cooling trend cannot solely be explained by natural radiative forcing (volcanic and solar); it cannot solely be explained by human-caused increases in radiative forcing (aerosols dominating over greenhouse gases). It can be explained, within the range spanned by natural variability, when both natural and human-caused forcing are combined.

I have heard it claimed that in the 1970s scientists were apparently predicting an ice age was imminent. This has always bothered me because in my twenty years as an active climate researcher, I have never come across a peer-reviewed scientific study that made this claim. Fortunately, today we have the Thomson Scientific ISI Web of Science, so getting to the bottom of this is easy.

I could not find one original peer-reviewed scientific study that argued the Earth was heading into an ice age. The only paper that came close was published in 1971 by S. Ichtiaque Rasool and Stephen Schneider, then at NASA's Goddard Institute for Space Studies, which noted:

An increase by only a factor of 4 in global aerosol background concentration may be sufficient to reduce the surface temperature by as much as 3.5°K. If sustained over a period of several years, such a temperature decrease over the whole globe is believed to be sufficient to trigger an ice age.

Of course this statement is riddled with weasel words, assumptions, and the hypothetical. Nevertheless, its scientific shelf life was only a few months before the assumptions underpinning the study were shown to be questionable.

However, a number of articles in newspapers and popular magazines alluded to the possibility of an impending ice age if the cooling trend that started in the 1940s continued. *The Globe and Mail* ran a story December 10, 1974, headlined "Does man trigger trouble in the world's climate cycle?" in which it was suggested that an ice age was one possible outcome of continued cooling. *Time* magazine was also a proponent of the theory in its June 24, 1974, article "Another Ice Age?" These stories mostly occurred several years after the Rasool and Schneider article was published.

Obviously there were a couple scientists who believed that the increase in human-produced aerosols was of sufficient concern. The opinions of an outspoken few would have been received eagerly by a popular press looking for attention-grabbing stories. Nevertheless, these opinions did not count as valid scientific arguments and so did not make it into the scientific literature. What I find most fascinating about this early fixation on an imminent ice age is that it continues today. How many of you have heard that global warming may cause an ice age? Wouldn't that be ironic. If it sounds odd, it should: It's utter nonsense.

In 1975, Wally Broecker, an eminent scholar from the Lamont Doherty Earth Observatory, wrote an important and perceptive article in *Science*, noting that:

> ... the natural climatic cooling which, since 1940, has more than compensated for the carbon dioxide effect, will soon bottom out. Once this happens, the exponential rise in the atmospheric carbon dioxide content will tend to become a significant factor and by early in the next century will have driven the mean planetary temperature beyond the limits experienced during the last 1000 years.

Broecker was right.

Knowing Your Greenhouse Gases

We have a solid understanding of the radiative forcing associated with human activities. Taken as a whole, human activities have caused a positive radiative forcing of between 0.6 and 2.4 W/m^2, with a best estimate of 1.6 W/m^2, since pre-industrial times (year 1750). This may not seem like a lot of heating, but there are 511,000,000,000,000 (511 trillion) square metres surrounding the Earth's surface ten kilometres up. Human activities are heating the Earth at a rate of about 818 trillion watts. To put this number in perspective, the massive nuclear generating station in Darlington, Ontario, has four CANadian Deuterium Uranium (CANDU) reactors that supply 20% of Ontario's electricity needs. Each reactor provides 881 megawatts of power, for a total of 3524 megawatts. A 1.6 W/m^2 radiative forcing is equivalent to using the electricity production from 232,000 Darlington nuclear plants, an amount four times greater than the total electricity production on the planet, to generate heat.

The total radiative forcing can be broken down into positive and negative components (see "Radiative Forcing of the Climate System"). Carbon dioxide, produced largely through the combustion of fossil fuels, makes up the single biggest contributor to global warming. Human activity also produces carbon dioxide when limestone is broken down in the creation of cement. In 2004, fossil fuel combustion released 7910 million metric tons of carbon to the atmosphere, while cement production gave off 298 million metric tons. Using wood to produce energy prior to industrialization and converting forests to pasture today has also released carbon dioxide. Deforestation since 1750 accounts for

Radiative Forcing of the Climate System

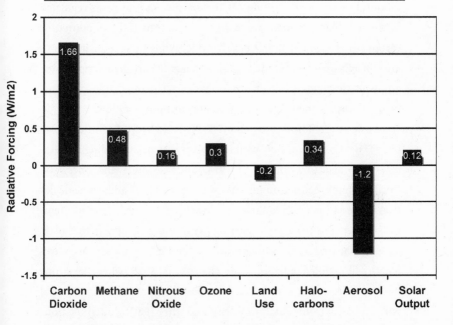

Radiative forcing of the climate system in 2005 relative to pre-industrial times in W/m². Changes in solar intensity are a natural radiative forcing. The rest are related to human activity. The best estimate of the total human-caused radiative forcing relative to the year 1750 is 1.6 W/m².

about one-third of the total radiative forcing arising from carbon dioxide emissions. The remainder is almost entirely due to the burning of fossil fuels.

Methane is the second most important greenhouse gas arising from human activity, most notably from accidental loss in the exploration, drilling, transportation, and delivery of natural gas, from agriculture, and from decomposition in landfills. Natural removal mechanisms in the atmosphere break methane down into carbon dioxide on the timescale of about a dozen years. Nitrous oxide—largely produced from the heavy use of fertilizers in agricultural activities and, to a lesser extent, from the combustion of fossil fuels—is also an important greenhouse gas with a relatively long average lifetime in the atmosphere (about 114 years). Rounding off the six greenhouse gases regulated under the Kyoto Protocol are hydrofluorocarbons (HFCs), perfluorocarbons (PFCs), and sulphur hexafluoride. While these industrial gases are typically extremely effective at absorbing the Earth's radiation in the atmospheric window and many of them have extremely long atmospheric lifetimes, their concentrations are currently very low.

At one time chlorofluorocarbons (CFCs) and hydrochlorofluorocarbons (HCFCs) were widely used in coolant systems, including refrigerators and air conditioners. In 1974, Mario Molina and Sherwood Rowland published a groundbreaking study on CFCs and ozone depletion that eventually led to their winning the 1995 Nobel Prize in chemistry. Ozone is a naturally occurring gas in the stratosphere that plays an essential role in absorbing much of the high-energy (short wavelength) ultraviolet radiation from the sun. In 1985, when the ozone hole in the Antarctic was detected, the world became mobilized to deal with this environmental problem and the 1987 United Nations Montreal Protocol on Substances that Deplete the Ozone Layer was agreed to. The Montreal Protocol came into force January 1, 1989, although it was subsequently adjusted and amended. It provides a wonderful example of how people around the world joined forces, through the United Nations, to solve a global environmental problem. And in doing so, no one suffered repressive economic hardship despite the protestations of certain business interests and the repeated pronouncements of scientific uncertainty trumpeted by a CFC denial industry, many of whom are now associated with today's global warming denial industry.

PFCs and HFCs are typically used as CFC or HCFC substitutes. While not ozone-depleting, they are powerful greenhouse gases. The PFCs, HFCs, CFCs, and HCFCs are all known as halocarbons and arise exclusively from human activities. First introduced in the twentieth century, the halocarbons now cause a 0.34 W/m^2 radiative forcing.

Ozone is a powerful greenhouse gas not regulated by either the Montreal or Kyoto protocols. The destruction of naturally occurring stratospheric ozone by CFCs and HCFCs in the upper atmosphere has actually had a small cooling effect, since less stratospheric ozone allows more of the Earth's longwave radiation to escape to space. The net energy loss is much larger than the small energy gain associated with enhanced ultraviolet solar radiation passing through the Earth's atmosphere. Low-level tropospheric ozone, on the other hand, is a pollutant that would otherwise be almost absent were it not for human activity. It is a component of smog and is produced when the exhaust from automobiles and industrial smokestacks is bombarded with the sun's rays. Ozone was not regulated under the Kyoto Protocol, as its lifetime is relatively short (a matter of weeks at most) and it is not emitted directly but rather arises as a by-product of chemical reactions involving other pollutants.

Aerosols, and in particular sulphates, contribute to cooling both through direct scattering of solar radiation as well as through their effect on clouds. In a cloud, aerosols promote the formation of more and smaller cloud droplets, which increase the albedo of clouds, making them more reflective. Land cover changes also give a small negative radiative forcing. When forests are cut and replaced with pasture, the surface of the Earth becomes lighter (trees are darker than grass). This is especially true in the spring and winter, as snow will blanket a pasture more completely than a forest. The lighter surface reflects more solar radiation, as it has a higher albedo. The best estimate of radiative forcing arising from slight changes in the intensity of the sun since pre-industrial times is 0.12 W/m^2, more than ten times smaller than the human contribution.

So how does Canada stack up as a player on the international emissions stage? Not well at all, I'm afraid. In 2004, Canada produced 2.2% of all global emissions of carbon dioxide, despite having less than 0.5% of the global population (see "Top Twenty CO_2-Emitting Countries"). We were the tenth worst for emissions per capita, behind the United States and a few small countries (such as Qatar, Kuwait, and the United Arab Emirates) with tiny populations and massive industries involved in the extraction and transportation of fossil fuels. Each Canadian produces twice as much carbon dioxide as a German, 3.3 times as much carbon dioxide as a person from France, and more than five times as much as a person from China. Well, you might argue, we are a northern country and require a lot more heating. Maybe so, but how does that explain Canadians producing 2.6 times as much carbon dioxide as Icelanders, twice as much as Greenlanders, and a whopping 3.4 times as much as people from Sweden?

In Canada, carbon dioxide makes up 78% of our greenhouse gas emissions, with methane adding a further 15% and nitrous oxide only 6%. The remaining 1% or so comes from PFCs, HFCs, and sulphur hexafluoride. Alberta, the home of Canada's oil and gas industry, contributes a whopping 31.4% of total Canadian emissions despite having only 10% of Canada's population (see "Canada's 2004 Greenhouse Gas Emissions by Province"). On the other hand, British Columbia, Manitoba, and Quebec produce only 8.9%, 2.0%, and 12.3% of the total emissions, even though they represent 13%, 3.7%, and 24% of

Top Twenty CO$_2$-Emitting Countries

1	Qatar	21.63		1	United States of America	1650020
2	Kuwait	10.13		2	China	1366554
3	United Arab Emirates	9.32		3	Russian Federation	415951
4	Aruba	8.25		4	India	366301
5	Luxembourg	6.81		5	Japan	343117
6	Trinidad and Tobago	6.80		6	Germany	220596
7	Brunei| (Darussalam)	6.56		**7**	**Canada**	**174401**
8	Bahrain	6.53		8	United Kingdom	160179
9	United States of America	5.61		9	Republic of Korea	127007
10	**Canada**	**5.46**		10	Italy	122726
11	Norway	5.22		11	Mexico	119473
12	Netherland Antilles	5.12		12	South Africa	119203
13	Australia	4.41		13	Iran	118259
14	Falkland Islands	4.13		14	Indonesia	103170
15	Faeroe Islands	3.86		15	France	101927
16	Estonia	3.82		16	Brazil	90499
17	Oman	3.72		17	Spain	90145
18	Saudi Arabia	3.71		18	Ukraine	90020
19	Gibraltar	3.65		19	Australia	89125
20	Kazakhstan	3.64		20	Saudi Arabia	84116

Left: Top twenty countries in 2004 ranked by per capita annual emissions of carbon in metric tonnes (one metric tonne is one thousand kilograms). **Right:** Top twenty countries in 2004 ranked by total annual carbon emissions in millions of metric tonnes. *Source: Marland et al. 2007.*

Canada's population respectively. These three provinces make extensive use of hydro power in order to meet their electricity demands.

As a signatory to the United Nations Framework Convention on Climate Change, Canada submits annually to the United Nations its national inventory of greenhouse gas emissions. "Canada's 2004 Greenhouse Gas Emissions by Sector" summarizes the readily available

Canada's 2004 Greenhouse Gas Emissions by Province

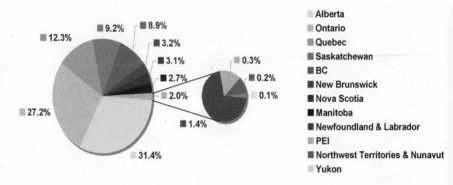

Breakdown of Canada's total 2004 emissions of the six greenhouse gases regulated under the Kyoto Protocol (carbon dioxide, methane, nitrous oxide, HFCs, PFCs, and sulphur hexafluoride) by province. *Data source: Environment Canada.*

data on a sector-by-sector basis. The fossil fuel industry—including crude oil, coal, coke, and oil sands production, petroleum refining as well as natural gas exploration, transportation, and distribution—produces 20% of all Canadian greenhouse gas emissions. Since much of the petroleum industry is based in Alberta, it is no wonder that it's the province with the greatest emissions. Electricity and heat generation emit another 17%, while mining and manufacturing industries provide a further 18% of total emissions. Lumping the three together, heavy industrial emitters produce a total of 55% of all Canada's greenhouse emissions, with the remainder being distributed across the transportation (22%), agricultural (7%), waste management (4%), and residential, commercial, and institutional (11%) sectors. Emissions in the residential, commercial, and institutional sector largely arise from the use of fossil fuel combustion to provide heat for buildings.

Any policy aimed at reducing Canada's greenhouse gas emissions would have to tackle the 55% emanating from large industrial emitters, many of which are based in Alberta and southern Ontario. Policies exclusively targeting residential heating, which account for only 5.7% of

Canada's 2004 Greenhouse Gas Emissions by Sector

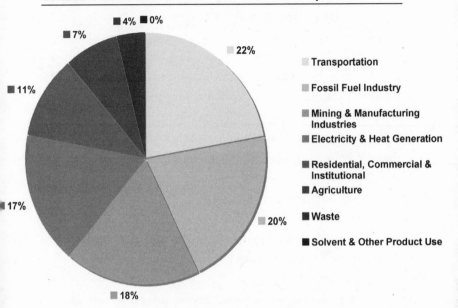

Breakdown of Canada's total 2004 emissions of the six greenhouse gases regulated under the Kyoto Protocol (carbon dioxide, methane, nitrous oxide, HFCs, PFCs, and sulphur hexafluoride) by sector. *Data source: Environment Canada.*

Canada's emissions, or the transportation sector, will simply not be enough. Even if emissions in these sectors were eliminated entirely, we would still need drastic reductions in the large emitter sectors in order to reach the global emissions reductions I believe we need to achieve by the latter half of this century.

Turning Science Into Policy

The greenhouse effect and global warming are based on elementary principles of physics discovered more than a century ago. They are not recent phenomena dreamt up as part of a worldwide conspiracy of self-indulgent climate scientists but rather are fundamental concepts well understood within the scientific community. As early as 1965, global warming began to move from the scientific to the policy arena. Roger Revelle, a distinguished scientist from the Scripps Institute for Oceanography, led a team of researchers to write a section of the U.S. President's Science Advisory Committee's report *Restoring the Quality of Our Environment*. This was the first authoritative assessment to point to rising carbon dioxide as a looming global environmental problem. At the time, however, recommendations were largely for more research to study the issue.

In 1969, Charles Keeling, also from the Scripps Institute for Oceanography, was profoundly concerned about the rising levels of greenhouse gases in the atmosphere. In his April 25, 1969, talk to the American Philosophical Society, he concluded:

> If the human race survives into the twenty-first century with the vast population increase that now seems inevitable, the people living then, along with their other troubles, may also face the threat of climate change brought about by an uncontrolled increase in atmospheric CO_2 from fossil fuels.

It wasn't until 1979 that the U.S. National Academy of Sciences was asked by the director of the Office of Science and Technology Policy to produce a report to "assess the scientific basis for projection of possible future climate changes resulting from man-made releases of carbon dioxide into the atmosphere." The academy struck an ad hoc study group under the auspices of its Climate Research Board, whose task was:

> 1) To identify the principal premises on which our current under-standing of the question is based,

> 2) To assess quantitatively the adequacy and uncertainty of our knowledge of these factors and processes,

3) To summarize in concise and objective terms our best present understanding of the carbon dioxide/climate issue for the benefit of policymakers.

The report—known as the Charney Report after the renowned atmospheric scientist Jule Charney from the Massachusetts Institute of Technology who chaired the ad hoc committee—was 22 pages long and written by only 9 scientists. This is a far cry from the IPCC Working Group I's 996-page Fourth Assessment Report, which had 152 coordinating and lead authors and a further 467 contributing authors.

The Charney Report provided an estimate of climate sensitivity of between 1.5°C and 4.5°C, with a best estimate of 3.0°C, for a doubling of atmospheric carbon dioxide. What's remarkable about this estimate is that it stood unchanged through the IPCC's First, Second, and Third Assessment Reports. Only thirty years later was it slightly narrowed to between 2.0°C and 4.5°C, with a most likely value of 3.0°C, in the Fourth Assessment Report. While the Charney Report stayed away from policy statements, it did emphasize that the oceans had the ability to absorb heat and mix it vertically. This, it argued, would mean a delay of several decades before the climate system would approach thermal equilibrium with atmospheric greenhouse gas levels. It noted that as a consequence "perceptible temperature changes may not become apparent nearly so soon as has been anticipated," so that "we may not be given a warning until the CO_2 loading is such that an appreciable climate change is inevitable." In the foreword to the report, the chair of the Climate Research Board of the National Research Council, Verner Suomi, to whom the ad hoc committee reported, picked up on this summary statement and added: "A wait-and-see policy may mean waiting until it is too late."

The First World Climate Conference—sponsored by the World Meteorological Organization (WMO) in Geneva in 1979—spawned the United Nations World Climate Programme (WCP), whose goals are "to improve understanding of the climate system and to apply that understanding for the benefit of societies coping with climate variability and change," and later in 1980 the World Climate Research Programme, whose objectives are "to determine the predictability of climate and to determine the effect of human activities on climate."

Two further U.S. assessments were published within three days of each other in the early 1980s. The first was again written by a committee of experts under the auspices of the National Academy of Sciences, and the second was a report from the U.S. Environmental Protection Agency. While the academy scientists were "deeply concerned about environmental changes of this magnitude" and noted "we may get in trouble in ways we have barely imagined," they argued that more research and monitoring was needed to assess the regional and socio-economic impacts of global warming. The EPA report was far less tempered, arguing that "agricultural conditions will be significantly altered, environmental and economic systems potentially disrupted, and political institutions stressed." The study further concluded that "changes by the end of the 21st century could be catastrophic taken in the context of today's world. A soberness and a sense of urgency underlie our response to a greenhouse warming."

In the mid-1980s, a series of conferences and reports organized by the United Nations Environment Programme (UNEP), International Council of Scientific Unions (ICSU), and the WMO brought global warming science to the policy arena. Chaired by Canadian James Bruce, the Second Joint UNEP/ICSU/WMO International Assessment of the Role of Carbon Dioxide and Other Greenhouse Gases in Climate Variations and Associated Impact (in Villach, Austria, in 1985) was particularly important. At the end of this influential conference, a consensus statement on the state of the science was issued. Three broad conclusions were conveyed:

1) Many important economic and social decisions are being made today on long-term projects—major water resource management activities such as irrigation and hydro-power, drought relief, agricultural land use, structural designs and coastal engineering projects, and energy planning—all based on the assumption that past climatic data, without modification, are a reliable guide to the future. This is no longer a good assumption since the increasing concentrations of greenhouse gases are expected to cause a significant warming of the global climate in the next century. It is a matter of urgency to refine estimates of future climate conditions to improve these decisions.

2) Climate change and sea level rises due to greenhouse gases are closely linked with other major environmental issues, such as acid deposition and threats to the Earth's ozone shield, mostly due to changes in the composition of the atmosphere by man's activities. Reduction of coal and oil use and energy conservation undertaken to reduce acid deposition will also reduce emissions of greenhouse gases, a reduction in the release of chloro-fluorocarbons (CFCs) will help protect the ozone layer and will also slow the rate of climate change.

3) While some warming of climate now appears inevitable due to past actions, the rate and degree of future warming could be profoundly affected by governmental policies on energy conservation, use of fossil fuels, and the emission of some greenhouse gases.

Canada played an important role in the international policy scene in 1988 by hosting a major world conference in Toronto entitled The Changing Atmosphere: Implications for Global Security. The conference brought together 341 delegates from 46 countries, including

73 physical scientists, 30 social scientists, 50 representatives from industry, 50 representatives from non-government environmental organizations, 20 politicians, and a hoard of 118 policy/legal advisers and senior government officials. Prime Minister Brian Mulroney gave the opening address, concluding: "The government of Canada, and indeed governments around the world, eagerly await your recommendations."

The delegates did not disappoint. Their thirteen-page statement included numerous detailed and specific recommendations, including:

> Set energy policies to reduce the emissions of CO_2 and other trace gases in order to reduce the risks of future global warming. Stabilizing the atmospheric concentration of CO_2 is an imperative goal. It is currently established to require reductions of more than 50% from present emission levels.

And:

> Reduce CO_2 emissions by approximately 20% of 1988 levels by the year 2005 as an initial global goal.

How have political leaders and society as a whole responded to the repeated concerns from the scientific community since the days of Arrhenius through to the Charney and other reports? Take a look at "Global CO_2 Emissions from Human Activities, 1800 to 2004" and you be the judge. Emissions have continued to rise year after year, with the exception of a few short interludes for global economic recessions or U.S oil crises (as with the oil embargo of 1973 when the Organization of Arab Petroleum Exporting Countries announced they would no longer ship oil to countries supporting Israel, and the fall of the Shah of Iran in 1979). In 2004, emissions increased by 5.4% over 2003 levels. Initial estimates have 2005 levels increasing by a further 3.3% over

Global CO$_2$ Emissions from Human Activities, 1800 to 2004

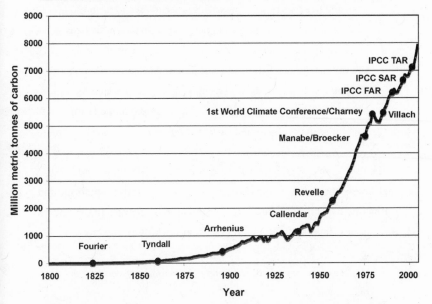

1800 to 2004 global emissions of carbon dioxide from human activities (excluding land use change) in millions of metric tonnes of carbon. The year that several key scientific findings or reports were published has been noted. Refer to the text for a discussion of the significance of these labels.

2004 levels and 2006 levels increasing another 2.6%. And, in 2006, China overtook the United States as the number-one carbon dioxide emitter on the planet as a consequence of its rapid economic growth and surge in coal consumption. What will it take to reverse the trend?

Inside the IPCC

In 1988, the WMO and the UNEP established the IPCC as a means to assess global climate change. The IPCC is governed by United Nations regulations with a mandate (reaffirmed in 2006 at its twenty-fifth session):

The role of the IPCC is to assess on a comprehensive, objective, open and transparent basis the scientific, technical and socio-economic information relevant to understanding the scientific basis of risk of human-induced climate change, its potential impacts and options for adaptation and mitigation. IPCC reports should be neutral with respect to policy, although they may need to deal objectively with scientific, technical and socio-economic factors relevant to the application of particular policies.

The IPCC oversees three Working Groups (WGI, WGII, and WGIII) that assess the science, socio-economic impacts and adaptation, and mitigation aspects of global warming and climate change. In the Fourth Assessment Report, the mandates of these working groups were:

WG I: assesses the scientific aspects of the climate system and climate change;

WG II: assesses the scientific, technical, environmental, economic and social aspects of the vulnerability (sensitivity and adaptability) to climate change of, and the negative and positive consequences (impacts) for, ecological systems, socio-economic sectors and human health, with an emphasis on regional, sectoral and cross-sectoral issues;

WG III: assesses the scientific, technical, environmental, economic and social aspects of the mitigation of climate change.

Another way to think of these groups is: WGI describes the problem of global warming; WGII details its consequences; WGIII assesses what we can do about it.

A common public misconception is that the IPCC working groups undertake their own independent research, collect their own data, or monitor the climate system. This is not the case—they exclusively provide an assessment of the peer-reviewed scientific literature, although they may make passing reference to published technical reports. Websites and newspaper opinion pieces/editorials are not used in the assessment, as they have not passed the standards set by the peer-review system.

The IPCC has published four comprehensive assessments of climate change and a number of special reports on a variety of topics. The First Assessment Report (1990) was influential in the formation of the United Nations Framework Convention on Climate Change (UNFCCC), which currently has 192 member states, including Canada. The Second Assessment Report (1996) had great impact on the negotiations leading up to the adoption of the Kyoto Protocol to the UNFCCC at the Third Conference of Parties in 1997. The Kyoto Protocol, ratified by 175 parties to the UNFCCC, required Canadian greenhouse gas emissions to be 6% below 1990 levels in the period 2008 to 2012. The Third Assessment Report was completed in 2001, and the Fourth Assessment Report in 2007.

The IPCC does not make policy recommendations to governments but rather assesses our current understanding of the scientific, socioeconomic, technological, and environmental aspects of climate change. The reports provide input into the national and international negotiations supposedly aimed at developing policy to deal with global warming. I say *supposedly,* as in Canada our only policy appears to be one of rhetoric, broken promises, and failed leadership on the climate portfolio.

I still have vivid memories of my first IPCC meeting in Brighton, England, in 1995. As a member of an international subcommittee of the World Climate Research Programme, known as the Steering Group on Global Climate Modelling, I was asked to serve as a lead author on the chapters dealing with climate model evaluations and projections. The meeting brought together seventy-eight climate scientists from twenty countries; we met as a whole, as individual chapter groups, and as sub-groups from dawn until dusk. We argued; we challenged one another; and at night and during breaks, we modified our sections. Our combined efforts were to prepare a version for international peer review.

The amount of science condensed and incorporated into the IPCC assessments has grown dramatically. I don't think the public appreciates the work that has gone into the reports and the rigorous nature of the peer review. Here's a brief summary of the process leading to the Working Group I (WGI) contribution to the Fourth Assessment Report, released February 2007. Remember that this is only one of three contributions that make up the whole assessment.

In 2003, climate scientists from around the world attended several scoping meetings, designed to solicit expert feedback about how the report should be laid out. The WGI's Technical Service Unit (TSU) then compiled a formal table of contents for approval by the IPCC at its twenty-first session in November.

During 2004, the TSU put together author teams from lists submitted by governments and international scientific organizations. (Individuals were also added if their expertise was needed to fill gaps in a particular area.) At the first lead authors meeting in September, individual writing tasks were assigned and the chapter contents were fleshed out. Fourteen of us started writing "Chapter 10: Global Climate Projections" on assessing future climate projections from global climate models. Our challenge was to produce a zeroth order draft by January 14, 2005, for the first informal peer review. We asked colleagues from around the world to submit contributions. Those who provided text or figures were formally recognized as contributing authors (of which there were seventy-eight). On April 29, we received our set of peer reviews: 23 pages containing 133 comments. Our revised chapter was due two weeks later for discussion at the second lead authors meeting. The deadline for the formal first draft was August 12.

We got a slight reprieve of three months while the first draft was undergoing peer review. But on my birthday I received what can only be described as the gift from hell: an incredible 172 pages outlining 1331 reviewer comments, concerns, and criticisms. And this was only for the 99-page Chapter 10. The other ten chapters received a similar onslaught of comments. Rookie authors were shell-shocked; veterans were dumbfounded. As lead authors, we had to respond to each comment and indicate how we modified the text to account for the issues raised. The third lead authors meeting was in December. We spent long sessions in plenary, as chapters, and as subgroups discussing, debating, and arguing about the science in our chapter. The goal was to hash out an outline for the second draft, which was due for peer review in March 2006.

The second peer review included not only experts but also an expanded group selected by governments around the world (often scientists who were not involved in the first review). The second set of comments arrived June 16: another 1331 splashed across 173 pages just on our chapter alone. Our fourth meeting was ten days later. More meetings, discussions, arguments, late nights, and writing led to the final draft submitted September 15, 2006.

Throughout the process, a subset of lead authors collated contributions from various chapters to compile the "Technical Summary" and the "Summary for Policymakers." The final draft of the "Summary for Policymakers" was available October 27 to governments for one last set of reviews, due December 8. Since the 18-page summary of the 996-page report is pretty much all that is read by political leaders, you can bet that at this stage government leaders were finally waking up and starting to position their responses for the WGI plenary session (January 29 to February 1, 2007). In Canada, embattled Rona Ambrose was removed from the Environment portfolio and replaced by political heavyweight John Baird. Only a few months earlier, Prime Minister

Stephen Harper couldn't differentiate between weather and climate and now, suddenly, it seemed he was jostling for green-looking photo ops.

Harper's new-found environmental awakening oozed with insincerity. Around this time, the Liberal opposition leaked to the press a 2002 fundraising letter written by Harper revealing his true beliefs, namely:

1) Kyoto is essentially a socialist scheme to suck money out of wealth-producing nations;
2) carbon dioxide is "essential to life";
3) the science of global warming was "tentative and contradictory."

Is it any wonder the scientific community was cynical that he would take this issue seriously?

The WGI plenary session was a *Gong Show*. While the main body of the "Technical Summary" and main report are approved as a package, the "Summary for Policymakers" must be approved unanimously by all parties to the UNFCCC line by line and, hence, word by word. Like previous final plenaries, special interests came to the forefront. Fortunately, the overarching governing rule is that the "Summary for Policymakers" must be based on the science contained in the main report (which virtually none of the political delegates would have read). This placed an extremely strong constraint on any changes that might be proposed. Predictably, the "Summary for Policymakers" was approved by the delegates at the very last minute with only a few minor changes (largely addition of clarifying information from the main body of the report).

The writing of the IPCC assessment reports is without doubt the most intensive and rigorous scientific process in which I have been involved. It is written by leading scientists from around the world and reviewed extensively by a diverse range of individuals. Even members of the denial industry have participated in this review process. In fact, pretty much anyone can. All you need to do is fill out a form and send in your comments. There was no political interference in any aspect of the writing. It is only at the last phase, where the "Summary for Policymakers" must be unanimously approved, that politics rears its ugly head. However, even here it is constrained by what is contained within the report itself. Ultimately, the "Summary for Policymakers" is slightly weaker coming out of the final plenary than it was going into it.

I always recommend that people read the "Technical Summary" and not the "Summary for Policymakers." Both contain minimal amounts of jargon. However, nothing has been filtered out of the "Technical Summary." You will get the straight goods directly from the scientists. The technical summaries, as well as the entire report, are all available at no cost from the IPCC website (www.ipcc.ch). They are well worth downloading.

Receiving the Nobel Peace Prize

My IPCC colleagues and I enjoyed a truly special day October 12, 2007. I had just sat down to write when a barrage of emails and phone calls hit, asking for interviews about the announcement that the IPCC was a co-recipient of the 2007 Nobel Peace Prize. I was stunned. Sure enough, minutes later I received emails from Susan Solomon, chair of Working Group I, and Rajendra Pachauri, the chair of the IPCC, congratulating us all. It was a most wonderful end to a process that had taken up enormous amounts of my time over the last two decades.

In an October 12 press release, the Norwegian Nobel Committee praised the IPCC and noted:

> Through the scientific reports it has issued over the past two decades, the IPCC has created an ever-broader informed consensus

about the connection between human activities and global warming.

The science of global warming is well established from first principles rooted in the early work of Fourier, Tyndall, Arrhenius, Callendar, and a host of other scientists over the last two centuries. It's only been in the last two decades that this research has been synthesized in the IPCC Assessment Reports; it's only in the last few years that the public has begun to appreciate that something needs to be done about global warming. Unfortunately, we have done essentially nothing.

Al Gore was the other co-recipient of the Nobel Peace Prize. Together with the IPCC, he was recognized for his

> efforts to build up and disseminate greater knowledge about man-made climate change, and to lay the foundations for the measures that are needed to counteract such change.

I had been most fortunate to attend a presentation by Al Gore during a visit to Victoria September 29, 2007, less than two weeks before he received the Nobel Prize. Gore delivered a powerful talk to a packed audience on the urgency of dealing with global warming. It was passionate, inspirational, and empowering. Gore finished his address by stating that we are at a crossroads. He believed that our children would ask one of two possible questions when they looked back at the beginning of this century. The first might be: "What in the world were they doing and how could they let this happen?" The second might be: "How did they find the moral courage to rise and solve this problem that so many said they couldn't?"

As a born optimist, I am convinced it will be the second question my children will ask me if I am still alive in forty years. But it will take political leadership coupled with behavioural and technological change on a scale that the world has not seen before.

3

The Nature of Things

CLIMATE HAS ALWAYS VARIED, and it will continue to vary, no matter what we do. This truism sounds innocent enough, but it's a rallying cry for the denial industry looking to delay emissions reduction policy.

Since its formation 4.6 billion years ago, the Earth has experienced climates much warmer and much colder than today. Early Earth was inhospitable, with an atmosphere largely made of water vapour and carbon dioxide. It wasn't until volcanic activity subsided about 4.2 billion years ago that the planet cooled enough to allow condensation to occur—hence the formation of clouds, rain, then rivers, lakes, and oceans. Venus, whose atmosphere is 96% carbon dioxide, has a climate too hot for life (its average surface temperature is 477°C). Mars has such a thin atmosphere that its climate is too cold for life (its average surface temperature is −50°C, with the difference between daytime highs and nighttime lows being as much as 100°C). Earth, however, has a climate with just the right average surface temperature to allow life to flourish.

Primitive forms of life evolved on Earth around 3.8 billion years ago, and the first to use photosynthesis showed up sometime before 2.8 billion years ago (perhaps as early as 3.5 billion years ago). For several billion years, photosynthesis drew down carbon dioxide from the atmosphere and released oxygen. Whereas the early atmosphere may have contained 10% (100,000 ppm) carbon dioxide and negligible amounts of oxygen, today the atmosphere contains 385 ppm carbon dioxide and 21% (210,000 ppm) oxygen. For every million molecules in the air, 385 are carbon dioxide and 210,000 are oxygen. Simply put: Photosynthesis provides the air we breathe.

For hundreds of millions of years, the Earth and its climate evolved. Global glaciations (Snowball Earths) may have occurred around 2.2 billion, 710 million, and 640 million years ago. Less extensive glaciations took place during other intervals. By and large, though, early Earth was much warmer than it is today. Geologists like to classify the world around them, including the time-history of the Earth. They use the term *Phanerozoic* to describe the eon in which multicellular organisms first appeared in the fossil record. This corresponds to the last half-billion or so years of Earth's history. The Phanerozoic comprises three eras, each of which is classified by its own prevailing forms of life: The Paleozoic (Age of Ancient Life) covers 542 to 251 million years ago; the Mesozoic (Age of Reptiles) covers 251 to 65 million years ago; and the Cenozoic (Age of Mammals) covers the time since the extinction of the dinosaurs 65 million years ago.

Reptiles, with few exceptions, are cold-blooded, which means they don't internally regulate their body temperature. Mammals are almost exclusively warm-blooded, which means they are able to regulate their body temperature. To warm themselves, mammals eat food and convert it to heat; to cool themselves, they perspire and use heat to evaporate water. Mammals have an easier time adapting to both warm and cold temperatures, so they are found all over the planet. Reptiles have difficulty adapting to cold climates, so are more common in warmer climates.

Geochemists estimate the carbon dioxide levels in ancient atmospheres using a number of techniques, unfortunately all with large uncertainty (see "Four Hundred Million Years of Atmospheric CO_2 Levels"). These include using plant fossils and our current knowledge of how plants react to different atmospheric carbon dioxide levels, as well as looking at isotope ratios.

Four Hundred Million Years of Atmospheric CO$_2$ Levels

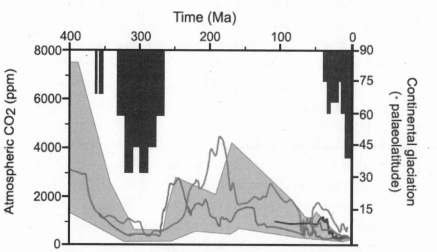

Atmospheric carbon dioxide levels (in parts per million or ppm) over the last four hundred million years (Ma) of Earth's history obtained using four different reconstruction techniques involving boron and carbon isotope ratios or an empirical relationship between atmospheric carbon dioxide and plants. In addition, a shaded range is included from a carbon cycle model. The vertical bars starting from the top of the graph give estimates of timing and equatorward extent of glaciations that are inferred from the proxy record. *Redrawn from the top panel of Figure 6.1 in Jansen et al. (2007).*

Everything is constructed from atoms. Atoms have a nucleus of positively charged protons and neutrally charged neutrons (which keep the protons from repelling one another). Surrounding the nucleus is the same number of negatively charged electrons as protons, making that atom neutrally charged. When individual atoms start to bond together by sharing electrons, they form molecules. Different elements are determined by the number of protons in the atom's nucleus: Hydrogen has one proton, boron has five protons, carbon has six protons, oxygen has eight protons, and gold has seventy-nine protons. The number of neutrons in an atom can also vary, leading to different *isotopes* of the element.

Most isotopes are unstable, meaning that the nucleus eventually transforms itself through radioactive decay (perhaps by ejecting a neutron or a proton) into a stable element. However, some isotopes are stable and do not break down. For example, boron has two naturally occurring stable isotopes: boron-11 (^{11}B) and boron-10 (^{10}B). Boron-11, with five protons and six neutrons, constitutes 80.1% of all boron and boron-10, with only five neutrons, makes up 19.9%. Carbon also has two naturally occurring stable isotopes. The most common is carbon-12 (^{12}C), making up 98.89% of all carbon, and the other is carbon-13 (^{13}C), forming only 1.11%. Oxygen, on the other hand, has three stable isotopes: The most common, making up 99.8% of the total, is oxygen-16 (^{16}O), containing 8 protons and 8 neutrons. Oxygen can also have 9 neutrons or 10 neutrons and still remain stable. These are known as oxygen-17 (^{17}O) and oxygen-18 (^{18}O) respectively.

Because different isotopes of an element have different numbers of neutrons, while the number of protons and electrons remain fixed, they have different masses. This mass difference means that chemical, biological, or physical processes can occur differently for each isotope. This process is known as *fractionation*.

Water made of hydrogen and oxygen-18 ($H_2^{18}O$) is heavier than water made of hydrogen and oxygen-16 ($H_2^{16}O$). It takes less energy to evaporate $H_2^{16}O$ than $H_2^{18}O$; conversely, $H_2^{18}O$ condenses more readily than $H_2^{16}O$. Knowing the temperature dependence of the evaporation and condensation of these two isotopes, which can be determined from laboratory experiments, is an extremely useful tool in developing *proxy records* of temperatures in past climates.

By collecting a sediment core from the deep ocean and measuring the ratio of oxygen-18 to oxygen-16 in the shells of tiny ancient plants and animals in that core, scientists can also obtain a very good estimate of global ice volume. Because $H_2^{16}O$ is easier to evaporate than $H_2^{18}O$, when ice builds up on land, it contains vast quantities of $H_2^{16}O$, leaving the ocean enriched in $H_2^{18}O$. When marine organisms grow their shells of calcium carbonate, they incorporate the oxygen isotopes in proportion to their relative abundance in the seawater.

A similar fractionation process occurs during photosynthesis. Plants (in the ocean and on land) find it easier to use carbon dioxide containing carbon-12 instead of carbon-13, as it requires less energy to do so. This fractionation makes plants depleted in carbon-13 relative to the atmosphere (or water) surrounding them.

The scientific community has a solid grasp of the broad features of the atmospheric history of carbon dioxide over the last four hundred million years, if not the exact magnitude (see "Four Hundred Million Years of Atmospheric CO_2 Levels"). It is relatively clear that the Mesozoic era (Age of Reptiles, between 251 and 65 million years ago) was characterized by high levels of atmospheric carbon dioxide, low levels of land-based ice, warm temperatures, and a preponderance of cold-blooded species accustomed to living in warmer environments. Conversely, the Cenozoic era (Age of Mammals, between 65 million years ago and the present) was characterized by gradually decreasing carbon dioxide levels, cooler temperatures, and a gradually increasing likelihood and extent of glaciation.

As expected from the early work of Fourier, Tyndall, Arrhenius, Callendar, and others, the warm intervals were associated with high levels of carbon dioxide and the cool intervals with low levels of carbon dioxide. Over the timescale of millions of years, changes in the concentration of atmospheric carbon dioxide occurred because of variations in the rates of chemical weathering, volcanic outgassing, and the drawing down of carbon into the great coal, oil, and natural gas reserves prevalent today. Decreasing carbon dioxide levels led to a negative radiative forcing, and the Earth system responded by cooling. The opposite would occur when carbon dioxide levels increased. And life on the planet responded accordingly.

The Six Great Extinction Events

As the climate varied, new species evolved and others became extinct. Since the beginning of the Paleozoic (Age of Ancient Life, 542 million years ago), there have been six great extinctions. The first occurred around 440 million years ago, when most of the Earth's land mass, then a supercontinent known as Gondwana, was located at high southern latitudes that included the south pole. About 80% to 85% of known marine species were wiped out. The second occurred about 360 million years ago and was associated with another massive extinction of marine species, especially coral reef creatures. Once more, 80% to 85% of known marine species were obliterated. The third, known as the Permian-Triassic extinction event, took place at the boundary of the Paleozoic and Mesozoic eras 251 million years ago. This was the largest of the extinction events, eradicating 70% of all land species and 96% of all marine species. It sparked the end of ancient life and the beginning of the reign of the dinosaurs.

The fourth major extinction marks the boundary between the Jurassic and Triassic periods, some 200 to 210 million years ago. About 80% of marine species and many of the land vertebrates perished, including most large amphibians. Approximately 65 million years ago, around the same time as the so-called Cretaceous-Tertiary (K-T) extinction event, an asteroid crashed into the Earth on the northern coast of Mexico's Yucatan Peninsula. The remnants of the impact exist today underneath the Earth's surface as the 180-kilometre diameter Chicxulub Crater. While not as dramatic as earlier events, about 75% of the world's species, including the dinosaurs, were wiped out in this fifth major extinction.

The sixth and perhaps greatest extinction event is occurring as I write. This Holocene extinction event is a direct consequence of human activity.

The accepted causes of the earlier extinction events are not without controversy. Several main theories have been put forward, involving asteroid impacts, sea level drops, and the eruption of flood basalts. In all three cases, it is not the event that causes the extinction but the resulting change in environmental conditions, including climate.

Asteroid impacts have been mentioned as a possible cause for the extinctions of 360, 251, 200 to 210, and 65 million years ago, but direct evidence exists for only the K-T extinction. The asteroid that produced the Chicxulub Crater is thought to have a diameter of at least ten kilometres. It landed in a bed of calcium sulphate (gypsum), so the resulting global dust cloud would have contained vast amounts of sulphate aerosols, those same cooling agents that arise from the combustion of coal. The dust cloud would have made it into the stratosphere and hung around for a few years, cooling the Earth significantly and affecting photosynthesis. When the sulphates rained to the earth, they would have bathed the surface in acid rain.

Reductions in sea level also provide an explanation for mass extinctions, although sea level drop is almost certainly a response to other phenomena such as global cooling and the growth of glaciers on land (as in the case of the extinction event 440 million years ago). The argument is that if sea level falls, the area of continental shelves declines. Since these are the most productive regions of the oceans, a mass extinction may result. Shallow-water species would have the most difficult time surviving.

Perhaps the most appealing explanation for the major extinctions of 251, 200 to 210, and 65 million years ago involves the eruption of flood basalts. We have all watched stunning visuals on television of lava gushing forth from a volcano. You may have also heard stories about the year 1816, known as the "year without a summer," which was caused by global cooling after the eruption of Mount Tambora in 1815. More recently, in June 1991, the eruption of Mount Pinatubo in the

Philippines caused the Earth to divert temporarily from its warming trend. In the past, however, there have been some incredibly large surges of molten rock that burst through the Earth's surface to flood the surrounding area. These typically occurred over geologically short periods (less than a million years) through a sequence of major eruptions, each lasting a decade or more and releasing from one thousand to ten thousand cubic kilometres of magma. That's enough to cover New Brunswick with more than one hundred metres of solid lava.

Twelve flood-basalt events have occurred over the last 250 million years, with three of the largest corresponding to three major extinction events. Some 250 million years ago, about three million cubic kilometres of lava spewed out of the Earth and covered two million square kilometres of Siberia, an area almost twice the size of Ontario. Enormous quantities of sulphur dioxide were also released. Researchers have estimated that each of the individual eruptions that made up a flood-basalt event could release ten billion metric tonnes of sulphur dioxide into the atmosphere. Compare this to the twenty million metric tonnes of sulphur dioxide released by Mount Pinatubo in 1991, which caused the Earth to cool briefly by about 0.5°C. Each eruption in the flood-basalt event would be like five hundred Pinatubos. The climatic consequences would have been profound.

As with coal combustion, sulphur dioxide is converted in the atmosphere to sulphate aerosols and eventually precipitates as (sulphuric) acid rain. Unlike the case of an asteroid impact, however, the individual eruptions making up the flood-basalt event lasted a decade or more. This would mean much longer periods of cooling under the influence of sulphate aerosols and the reduction of light for photosynthesis. In addition, far greater quantities of sulphuric acid would have fallen onto the land and into the oceans. These flood-basalt eruptions would certainly have stressed life on Earth to the limit.

Upsetting the pH Balance

Pure rainfall is slightly acidic, as it contains dissolved carbon dioxide that forms carbonic acid. The term *acid rain* is used to describe precipitation in which sulphates or nitrous oxides, released from industrial activities, are dissolved in the water to form sulphuric or nitric acid. During the flood-basalt eruptions or when the asteroid landed in the calcium sulphate bed off the Yucatan Peninsula sixty-five million years ago, large amounts of sulphuric acid would have ended up in the surface waters of the ocean.

Corals, certain types of phytoplankton (coccolithophores) and zooplankton (foraminifera), molluscs (pteropods or mussels), and other sea creatures form their calcium carbonate $(CaCO_3)$ shells using dissolved calcium ions (Ca^{2+}) and bicarbonate ions (HCO_3^-) prevalent in the surface layers of the ocean. The ocean's surface layers are also presently supersaturated in carbonate ions (CO_3^{2-}), meaning that calcium carbonate does not want to readily dissolve in seawater. Sulphuric acid is rich in hydrogen ions (H^+), and when those rained down into the oceans at the end of the Cretaceous, the hydrogen ions reacted with the carbonate ions. Bicarbonate ions were formed at the expense of their carbonate counterparts. This spelled bad news for the creatures whose shells were made of calcium carbonate, since surface waters were no longer saturated in carbonate ions. Despite the abundant availability of bicarbonate ions, the initial formation of shells would be difficult since there would be a tendency for these shells to dissolve as soon as they formed. At high-enough hydrogen ion concentrations, calcium carbonate shells in living sea organisms, especially coral, would start to dissolve. (To watch this first-hand, drop a piece of chalk [calcium carbonate] into a glass of carbonated water [carbonic acid]. The chalk breaks down rapidly. In doing the same experiment with tap water, which is less acidic, nothing happens.)

At the end of the Cretaceous, not only was there widespread extinction of dinosaurs on land but also of calcium carbonate–shelled mussels, corals, and phytoplankton in the ocean. It took at least two million years before corals started to reappear and about ten million years for their genetic diversity to become re-established.

So what has all this got to do with global warming? Today, the only really big natural sink for the carbon dioxide we are putting into the atmosphere is the ocean. As carbon dioxide is absorbed by the ocean, at a rate far slower than we are putting it into the atmosphere, the ocean becomes more acidic. The number of carbonate ions in the surface ocean goes down and the number of bicarbonate ions goes up. Slowly but surely, creatures whose shells are made of calcium carbonate start to suffer. Some will end up having softer shells; some will eventually go extinct unless they can adapt.

The measured concentration of hydrogen ions, or acidity, in the ocean is represented by a parameter called pH. The lower the pH, the more acidic the solution (there are more hydrogen ions); the higher the pH, the more basic the solution (there are fewer hydrogen ions). On the pH scale of 0 to 14, a 7 implies the solution is neither acidic nor basic; it's neutral. (A one-unit change in pH means a tenfold change in acidity; a change of 0.1 is a 25% increase or decrease in acidity.)

The alkalinity of water is a measure of its ability to neutralize acids— something carbonates are very effective at doing. When we talk about increasing the acidity in the ocean, we are really talking about an increase in the number of hydrogen ions because of a decrease in alkalinity. The time required to replenish the ocean with carbonate ions is very long when atmospheric concentrations of carbon dioxide remain high. It's first associated with the dissolution of carbonates in sediments at the bottom of the ocean, a process that takes thousands of years. On longer timescales, chemical weathering of rocks on the continents is required, which takes many hundreds of thousands to millions of years.

Acidity of Surface Waters

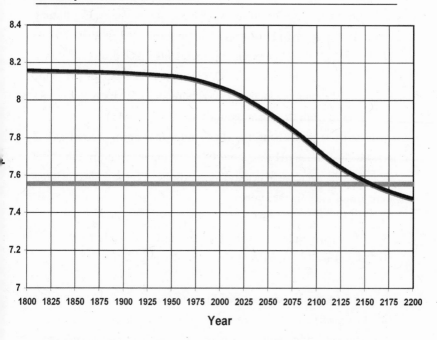

Acidity of the surface waters of the global ocean for the carbon dioxide emissions scenario portrayed in "IPCC Emissions Scenario A2" in Chapter 2. The observed emissions are used until 2000; the IPCC emissions scenario A2 is used from 2000 to 2100; after 2100, the emissions linearly decay to zero at 2300. The horizontal grey line indicates 0.6 pH units below pre-industrial levels (a 300% increase in the concentration of hydrogen ions (H+), or acidity), a level below which there is no evidence the acidity has fallen during the past three hundred million years.

When my colleagues and I examined how long human-produced carbon dioxide remained in the atmosphere (see Chapter 2), we also examined what happened to the acidity of the surface waters in the ocean (see "Acidity of Surface Waters").

Since pre-industrial times, the observed surface pH of the global ocean is known to have dropped by about 0.1 pH units. Consistent with these observations, the University of Victoria (UVic) Earth System

Climate Model predicts a drop from pH=8.16 in 1800 to pH=8.06 in 2007, precisely 0.1 pH units, or a 25% increase in acidity. Continuing forward in time, the pH drops to 8.02 in 2020, 7.93 in 2050, 7.74 in 2100, and 7.48 in 2200. Overall, this represents a 0.68 drop in pH from 1800 to 2200; in other words, a 380% increase in acidity. The pH in the UVic model eventually increases over thousands of years as carbonates are dissolved from the ocean sediments.

In its latest assessment, the IPCC notes that during recent glacial periods the surface pH was about 0.1 units higher than pre-industrial times (a 25% decrease in acidity) as atmospheric carbon dioxide levels were lower. They further noted:

> There is no evidence of pH values more than 0.6 units below the pre-industrial pH during the past 300 million years.

Now find the horizontal grey line in "Acidity of Surface Waters." Unless we start to deal with our emissions, we are on target to take ocean surface acidity into a realm for which we have no known historical analogues. Even the Cretaceous acidity levels would have been short-lived, as the sulphates deposited in the surface waters would have eventually been mixed throughout the ocean and finally precipitated out into the sediments below.

As Stanford University professor Ken Caldeira said in his Roger Revelle Commemorative Lecture at the Smithsonian National Museum of Natural History in Washington, D.C., March 5, 2007:

> It is likely that a continuation of current trends in carbon dioxide emission will lead to the extinction of corals, which have been around for millions of years, and may lead to the extinction of other marine species.

In June 2005, the prestigious Royal Society in the United Kingdom issued a sixty-page scientific report assessing "ocean acidification due to increasing atmospheric carbon dioxide." This conservative group of esteemed scientists conveyed a sense of urgency in their summary:

> Ocean acidification is a powerful reason, in addition to that of climate change, for reducing global CO_2 emissions. Action needs to be taken now to reduce global emissions of CO_2 to the atmosphere to avoid the risk of irreversible damage to the oceans. We recommend that all possible approaches be considered to prevent CO_2 reaching the atmosphere. No option that can make a significant contribution should be dismissed.

This is indeed a powerful call for action from an otherwise staid organization.

Humans are short-circuiting the long-term natural carbon cycle that involves chemical weathering, the transport of bicarbonates to the ocean, their use by marine organisms to create calcium carbonate shells, the deposition in sea-floor sediments of the carbon stored in sea creatures and contained in their waste products, the subduction of these sediments into the mantle, and the eventual release of carbon dioxide in volcanic emissions millions of years later. Every year, we emit more than one hundred times the natural emissions of carbon dioxide from volcanic activity. We are front-loading the natural carbon cycle, and the natural carbon dioxide removal systems, including the ocean and the world's ecosystems, are unable to keep up. The result spells trouble for those ecosystems. Even though there is still a great deal of scientific uncertainty as to how individual ecosystems will respond, one thing we do know is that they must either adapt or become extinct.

It could be argued that we should mine limestone and dissolve it in the ocean to offset the acidification arising from our activities. You might even be able to store vast quantities of carbon dioxide essentially forever in this process. This geo-engineering fix was one of many examined by the IPCC in a 2005 special report assessing the possibility of capturing and storing carbon dioxide. While certainly not advocating this approach, the authors pointed out that 3.5 kilograms of calcium carbonate (limestone) would have to be artificially dissolved in the ocean to sequester 1 kilogram of carbon dioxide without the negative effects associated with acidification. However, they noted that global production of limestone from mining is only about three billion tonnes per year. Even if we dissolved this entire amount in the ocean every year, it would only be able to sequester about 3% of the world's annual carbon dioxide emissions, assuming they remained at 2004 levels. A thirty-three-fold increase in limestone mining to sequester our emissions would have enormous energy requirements (with their concomitant emissions), not to mention the potential environmental impacts of such expanded mining activities. We would also have to stop producing cement, which uses this limestone, throughout the world. Somehow, I just don't see hacking down the white cliffs of Dover and sprinkling them about the ocean as a viable fix to the problem of global warming.

Ice Core Time Capsule

We live in a period of Earth's history known as the Quaternary. Over the last 2.6 million years that define the Quaternary, the Earth's continental geometry has not changed much and our climate has oscillated between ice ages and the periods between them, known as interglacials. The Quaternary is also the time in which hominin (human) evolution occurred.

One of the ways scientists infer what environmental conditions were like during the Quaternary is by analyzing cores taken from land, ocean sediments, lake bottoms, and the great ice sheets covering Greenland and Antarctica. Perhaps the most remarkable Quaternary climate records have come from the European Project for Ice Coring in Antarctica (EPICA) on the Antarctic Plateau.

In 1996, a summer camp was constructed by French scientists at a site known as Dome Concordia (Dome C). By 2005, the camp operated year-round. Dome C is one of the coldest spots on Earth, with an average annual temperature of −51°C and a positively balmy average summer temperature of −30°C. Average winter temperatures of −60°C with lows down to −85°C make the −27°C normal January temperatures of Tuktoyaktuk in Canada's Arctic seem like a tropical paradise. While the science-fiction movie *The Day After Tomorrow* creatively violates every known law of thermodynamics, it accurately portrays the dedication of scientists involved in ice core drilling. At the beginning of the movie, Jack Hall (Dennis Quaid) risks his life by jumping across an expanding crevice in the ice to save the cores he has spent so long collecting. While many of the Antarctic research scientists may not be as good-looking as Quaid (I am sure a number will email me to disagree on that point), they certainly are an amazingly committed and dedicated lot. You would not catch me overwintering on a plateau in Antarctica thirty-two hundred metres above sea level and eleven hundred kilometres from the coast!

Every year it snows at Dome C, and every year some of that snow is buried by subsequent snowfalls. Today only between two and ten centimetres fall there each year, although this amount has varied through time. As snow accumulates, the deeper layers turn to ice under the weight. As the ice grows thicker, the ice sheet begins to creep toward the coast. Trapped within the ice are tiny air bubbles formed when the snow originally fell. These bubbles are a treasure trove of information, as they contain the chemical makeup of the ancient atmosphere. Tens to hundreds of thousands of years after the original snowfall, the EPICA team pitched its camp and drilled through the ice to within five metres of bedrock. Their efforts yielded a Quaternary climate record now dating back some eight hundred thousand years.

Through extraordinarily precise measurements obtained from ice core sections, the EPICA team has been able to determine the concentrations of carbon dioxide and methane in air dating back six hundred and fifty thousand years (see "Antarctic Ice Core Record"). Throughout the last six glacial/interglacial cycles captured in this record, atmospheric carbon dioxide levels have never gone above about 300 ppm or below 180 ppm. Similarly, methane has been sandwiched between about 340 parts per billion (ppb) and 770 ppb. Today, carbon dioxide and methane levels are sitting at around 385 ppm and 1750 ppb respectively. That's almost 30% higher than at any time over the last six hundred and fifty thousand years for carbon dioxide and more than double any observed methane concentration during the same period.

Geochemists frequently use stable isotopes and their known fractionation properties to get a picture of past climates. One such isotope is deuterium, also known as hydrogen-2 (^2H or just D). Deuterium is a hydrogen atom that contains a neutron. It is relatively uncommon, making up only about 0.015% of naturally occurring hydrogen. Water containing deuterium (^2H_2O) is heavier than ordinary water (H_2O), so it does not evaporate as easily. During warm climates, Antarctic ice is enriched in deuterium; during cold climates, it is depleted in deuterium. By measuring the amount of deuterium in the water contained in the Dome C ice core, the EPICA scientists have been able to reconstruct the local temperature conditions over the last eight hundred thousand years, the last six hundred and fifty thousand of which are shown in "Antarctic Ice Core Record."

This graph also includes a proxy record of global ice volume obtained from oxygen isotope records in the shells of *benthic foraminifera*. These minute creatures are similar to the zooplankton found in the surface waters but instead live at the sea floor, or *benthic*

Antarctic Ice Core Record

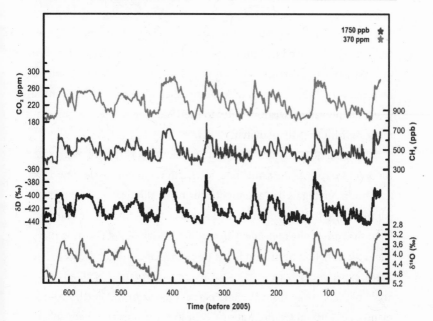

Antarctic ice core record of carbon dioxide (top curve), methane (second curve from top), and deuterium (third curve from top), for the last six hundred and fifty thousand years. Deuterium (δD) is a stable isotope of hydrogen (hydrogen-2), with one proton and one neutron. It provides a proxy record for local air temperature; colder temperatures are indicated by increasingly negative δD. The scale for carbon dioxide (parts per million) is on the left, and the scale for methane (parts per billion) is on the right. Two stars in the top right corner of the figure give the carbon dioxide and methane levels in 2000 using the same scale as for the previous six hundred and fifty thousand years. An oxygen isotope record from ocean sediments, providing a proxy for ice on land, is given in the bottom curve. As δ¹⁸O gets larger (the curve goes down), more ice is present on land. High temperatures and low ice volume are associated with high levels of carbon dioxide and methane. Low temperatures and high ice volume are associated with low levels of carbon dioxide and methane. *Reproduced from Figure 6.3 of Jansen et al. (2007).*

zone. Once more, warm climates are associated with high levels of greenhouse gases and low levels of global ice volume, whereas cold climates are associated with low levels of greenhouse gases and high levels of global ice volume.

What Triggers an Ice Age?

The reasons for the slow undulation of the glacial and interglacial cycles so elegantly displayed in "Antarctic Ice Core Record" are relatively well understood, even though research is still ongoing to explain some of their nuances. While many have explored the causes of ice ages over the years, the prevailing wisdom dates to the 1920 work of Serbian mathematician Milutin Milankovitch.

The Earth goes round the sun in an elliptical orbit once every year (or 365.24 days). At the same time, the Earth rotates once every twenty-four hours, giving us day and night. During its elliptical orbit, the Earth passes closest to the sun on a date known as the *perihelion*. It's farthest from the sun on the *aphelion*. Currently the perihelion falls on January 3 and the aphelion occurs on July 4 (see "Orbital Configurations"). The Earth experiences seasons because its axis of rotation is tilted at an angle of 23.5° away from the line perpendicular to the Earth's orbital plane (see "Orbital Configurations"). In July, the northern hemisphere is tilted toward the sun and the southern hemisphere is tilted away from the sun; the opposite occurs in January. As a consequence, in the northern hemisphere summer, which includes the month of July, we experience longer days and shorter nights and we therefore receive more energy from the sun than we do in the winter.

While we may take this *orbital configuration* for granted, it has not always been constant. The tilt of the Earth varies between 22.05° and 24.5° over a forty-one-thousand-year period (see part b) of "Orbital Configurations"). Also, the Earth's elliptical orbit varies from being more oblong to more circular over the timescale of one hundred thousand years. Finally, the date of the aphelion, and hence perihelion, is continually changing on nineteen-thousand- and twenty-three-thousand-year timescales. So when the Earth's tilt is greater, the differences between the seasons are amplified: winters are colder and summers are warmer. When the tilt is less, winters are warmer and summers are

Orbital Configurations

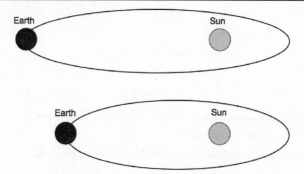

a) Eccentricity of elliptical orbit ~ 100,000 year timescale

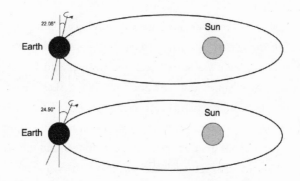

b) Changes in the axial tilt ~ 41,000 year timescale

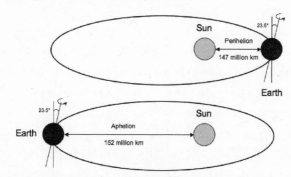

c) Changes in position of solstices ~ 19,000 and 23,000 year timescale

Part a) shows exaggerated changes in the eccentricity of the Earth's elliptical orbit (how oblong it is); part b) shows changes in the tilt of the Earth's axis of rotation; and part c) shows the location of the Earth at its aphelion (July 4) and perihelion (January 3).

cooler. On July 4, the Earth is farthest from the sun at its aphelion, but this is also when the northern hemisphere is tilted toward the sun. Now imagine that the aphelion occurred on December 20 when the northern hemisphere was tilted away from the sun. The northern hemisphere winter would be colder and its summer would be warmer.

As the properties of the Earth's orbit around the sun change (on millennial timescales), the amount of radiation the Earth receives in summer versus winter changes. The total amount of radiation reaching the top of our atmosphere does not change much, but the energy is redistributed slightly throughout the year. Orbital configurations leading to warmer winters and cooler summers in the northern hemisphere are those that lead to glaciation.

Let's turn back the clock one hundred and sixteen thousand years to the start of the last ice age. The orbital configuration is such that the northern hemisphere winter is becoming warmer and its summer is becoming cooler. Since summers are now colder, year after year the snow takes a little longer to melt, especially at higher elevations and latitudes. As the snow sticks around, the surface becomes whiter, especially in the spring and summer when the days are longer and the nights are shorter. This increases the albedo of the Earth's surface, thereby reflecting more of the incoming solar radiation and amplifying the surface cooling.

Cooler temperatures in the high northern latitudes spell bad news for the vegetation there. Forest is slowly replaced by tundra, increasing the albedo of the surface and amplifying the cooling still further. With the soils beginning to freeze a little at high latitudes, a source of carbon dioxide and methane starts to shut down. Organic matter no longer decomposes but rather is locked in frozen soils and eventually permafrost. Atmospheric levels of carbon dioxide and methane start to fall.

As ice accumulates on land, sea level drops and areas of continental shelves start to become exposed, allowing for the growth of vegetation and the drawing down of more carbon dioxide. The Earth continues to cool. The oceans are now capable of absorbing more carbon dioxide, since its solubility increases with decreasing temperature. In addition, a reduction in overall precipitation is ongoing, since all else being equal, there is less water vapour in cooler air than warmer air. This has three effects: 1) there are likely fewer wetlands and hence fewer methane sources; 2) more cooling occurs, as water vapour is a powerful greenhouse gas; and 3) dust can travel greater distances before raining out. But this dust is rich in iron so vital to the growth of phytoplankton in distant parts of the ocean, especially the Southern Ocean and the North Pacific. More dust means more iron, which in turn means more phytoplankton growth in these areas and a further draw down of carbon dioxide. These feedbacks continue until such time as a quasi-equilibrium is reached. Ice sheets can grow no further as precipitation levels no longer overwhelm the combined processes of *sublimation* (whereby ice and snow go directly to the vapour phase), melting at the surface and edges of the ice sheet, and calving of icebergs into the ocean.

If we turn back the clock twenty-one thousand years to the last glacial maximum, after which deglaciation started to set in, the above sequence of events would simply occur in reverse. A very small change in the amount of radiation being absorbed by the Earth in winter versus summer is amplified by many feedbacks operating within the climate system. Land surface, greenhouse gas, albedo, and biogeochemical feedbacks all conspire to enhance the small changes in seasonality associated with changing orbital configuration.

Understanding Abrupt Climate Events

Today we live in a period of relatively stable climate known as the Holocene, which started approximately 11,600 years ago. But this climate stability is certainly not the norm; humans have not always been so lucky. It is generally acknowledged that the first anatomically modern humans evolved in Africa about 195,000 years ago, putting them near the end of the second-to-last interglacial period known as the Hoxnian (see the bottom curve in "Antarctic Ice Core Record"). This is the recently recalculated date for the oldest known modern human fossils found by Richard Leakey in Ethiopia in 1967. It is thought that early modern humans started to expand their geographical range throughout Africa around 125,000 years ago. This period corresponded with the last interglacial, known as the Eemian, from 130,000 to 116,000 years ago. The Eemian was characterized by greenhouse gas levels similar to pre-industrial levels. Summers were warmer and winters were colder because of the orbital configuration. The warmer summers led to melting of a substantial amount of the Greenland ice sheet (with perhaps a small contribution from Antarctica), leading to a sea level about four to six metres higher than today. Hippos were known to roam England and parts of Europe during this time.

Outside of Africa, the oldest fossil remains of modern humans likely come from the Middle East and date to between 119,000 and 85,000 years ago. In China, the oldest modern human fossils date to about 67,000 years ago, although some may date to more than 111,000 years ago. Modern humans did not reach Australia or Europe until much later. In Australia, the oldest fossils date to between 50,000 and 42,000 years ago, while in Europe, they date to about 35,000 years ago. The Americas were the last to be populated, with our early ancestors arriving some 13,400 years ago. While precise dating of early human fossils remains problematic, most scientists conclude that anatomically modern humans evolved in Africa around 195,000 years ago and subsequently began migrating to diverse parts of the world in several waves, the first of which began between 110,000 and 90,000 years ago.

There have been many hypotheses put forward to explain why humans migrated where and when they did. Climate variability almost certainly was a big player in any motivating factor because changes in climate would have led to changes in temperature, vegetation, and the availability of food. We know from various proxy records, including the "Last Glacial Cycle in the Vostok Ice Core Record," that the glacial climate was characterized by an overall cooling trend from the beginning of the Eemian interglacial (130,000 years ago) to the last glacial maximum (21,000 years ago). As the climate system cooled, ice sheets grew on land, especially the Laurentide ice sheet in Canada and the Fennoscandian ice sheet in northern Europe. Our cold-adapted cousins, the Neanderthals, would have needed to migrate southward in Europe in response to the growing Fennoscandian ice sheet. There they would have encountered our ancient human ancestors and competed for dwindling resources. It looks like humans won out in the end and the Neanderthals went extinct 24,000 to 28,000 years ago.

Last Glacial Cycle in the Vostok Ice Core Record

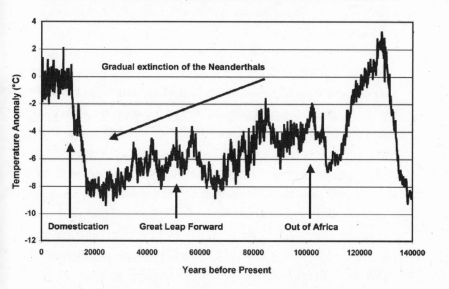

Atmospheric temperature reconstruction over Antarctica expressed as an anomaly relative to present-day values. The data, described in Petit et al. (1999), are derived from stable isotope analysis of the Vostok ice core. Several key events in the evolution of modern humans have also been indicated.

Superimposed on this overall cooling were numerous large-amplitude, millennial timescale fluctuations known as Dansgaard-Oeschger oscillations (D-O oscillations).

In the late 1960s and early 1970s, Willi Dansgaard, a Danish geochemist based at the University of Copenhagen, and his colleagues documented a series of abrupt climate events they discovered through analysis of an ice core from a remote northwest Greenland location known as Camp Century. More than a decade later, Dansgaard and his Swiss colleague Hans Oeschger found additional supporting evidence of these abrupt events in a south Greenland ice core collected at a site known as Dye 3. Other ice cores, sediment records, and a slew of additional proxy records have since revealed that D-O oscillations have a global signature, are pervasive throughout glacial climates, particularly in their coldest phases, and have strong signatures in the North Atlantic. The last D-O oscillation (the Younger Dryas Event) occurred between 12,800 and 11,600 years ago, the end of which marked the start of the Holocene.

D-O oscillations are characterized by an abrupt warming of between about 5°C and 8°C in Greenland temperatures, with a much weaker warming elsewhere in the northern hemisphere and a concomitant cooling in the Southern Ocean. The abrupt transition takes place in only a few decades, and the new warmer North Atlantic climate lasts from several hundred to several thousand years. After a period of slow cooling, this warm phase of a D-O oscillation terminates with an abrupt cooling and the whole process begins anew. In 2002, Andreas Schmittner, Masakazu Yoshimori, and I developed a mechanism to explain this observed D-O variability. We used the UVic Earth System Climate Model to show that changes in the strength of the ocean's ability to transport heat from the tropics to the poles in the North Atlantic played an important role in explaining the variability.

In today's climate, the Gulf Stream brings warm water from the tropics northward. The Gulf Stream leaves the North American coast near Cape Hatteras, and some of the warm water crosses the Atlantic in the North Atlantic Drift Current, eventually ending up in the Greenland, Irminger, and Norwegian seas (GIN Seas). The remainder recirculates around the subtropical Atlantic Ocean. As warm water travels to higher latitudes, it loses heat to the overlying colder air. But this heat loss makes the surface waters colder, and cold water is heavier than warm water. As a consequence, surface waters tend to sink. This is precisely what happens in the GIN Seas where surface waters are converted to deep waters through convection. The now cold, deep water returns to the South Atlantic via a southward-flowing current situated underneath the northward-flowing Gulf Stream. The northward-flowing waters, their conversion to deep water, and their subsequent return flow at depth are part of what is known as the *Atlantic meridional overturning circulation*. It was precisely this circulation that stopped operating in the movie *The Day After Tomorrow*.

In the North Atlantic, the ocean therefore acts as a large-scale conveyor that transports heat from low to high latitudes (see "Great Ocean Conveyor Belt"). In the present climate, high-latitude cooling acts like the accelerator pedal in an automobile and drives the conveyor forward. We know that fresh water is lighter than salt water. As a consequence, if we add a lot of fresh water to the North Atlantic we might be able to make the surface waters so light they no longer tend to sink. This is like the brake pedal in our automobile analogy. In the present climate, high-latitude cooling dominates over high-latitude precipitation, runoff, and ice melt in driving the ocean conveyor. In fact, the Atlantic meridional overturning circulation has several gears and can operate with different speeds.

During the cold glacial climate, the conveyor had a weak mode and a strong mode of operation. When the ocean was in the strong mode, more heat would be transported to high latitudes. This warmed the overlying atmosphere so that more moisture was available to fall as snow on the ice sheets surrounding the North Atlantic; the ice sheets

Great Ocean Conveyor Belt

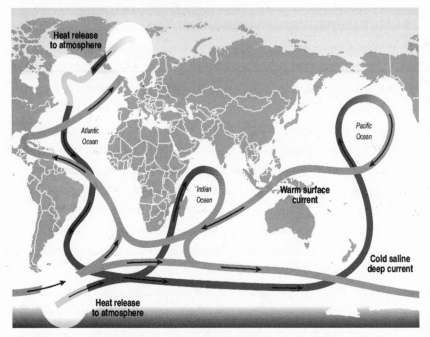

Schematic diagram of the ocean conveyor belt. *Reproduced with permission from Figure 4-2 of IPCC (2001).*

grew accordingly. As the ice sheets grew, they would start to creep toward the coast; several hundred years later, increasing calving of icebergs would follow. But these icebergs consist of fresh water and so a brake is applied to the conveyor. Less warm water would be transported northward, which would in turn lead to less precipitation and eventually less iceberg calving. The whole process would begin again.

While examining the marine sediments in three North Atlantic cores, German scientist Hartmut Heinrich noted several anomalous concentrations of stones and pebbles. There was only one way these stones could have been transported to the middle of the North Atlantic: a vast armada of icebergs. Heinrich published his results in 1988. Several years later, Doug MacAyeal from the University of Chicago proposed an explanation for these iceberg surges, now known as Heinrich Events. As ice sheets grew through continued snow accumulation, the pressures at the base of the ice sheet would start to increase. The ice sheets would still creep toward the coast, but they would do so slowly as they scratched their way across bedrock. Eventually the pressures would get so high that the ice attached to the bedrock would start to liquefy. Now lying on a lubricated surface, large quantities of the ice sheet could surge seaward for two hundred and fifty to five hundred years. The amount of fresh water eventually released in a Heinrich Event upon the melting of the ice in the ocean would be about 0.16 million cubic metres per second. That's like slamming the brake on the conveyor by hosing the North Atlantic with an Amazon River for two hundred and fifty to five hundred years.

Heinrich Events, appearing about every ten thousand years or so, occur at the end of a sequence of D-O oscillations during a prolonged cold period. The sequences of D-O oscillations tend to follow a sawtooth cycle (now termed a Bond Cycle after the late Gerard Bond from Lamont-Doherty Earth Observatory in the United States, who noted this pattern in marine sediments), with successive D-O oscillations involving progressively colder warm phases. The Bond Cycle is terminated by a Heinrich Event, after which a rapid warming occurs in association with the re-establishment of the Atlantic meridional overturning circulation because of the widespread reduction or cessation of iceberg calving from the surrounding continents. The whole process begins anew (see "D-O Oscillations, Heinrich Events, and Bond Cycles").

Since the end of the Eemian interglacial one hundred and sixteen thousand years ago, there have been nine Heinrich surges into the North Atlantic. Heinrich Event 9 (H9) occurred one hundred and five thousand years ago, a time that seemed to jibe nicely with the first of several exoduses of modern humans out of Africa. Shannon Carto, an M.Sc. student at the University of Victoria, and I wondered if there may have been a relationship between the two. We decided to explore the

D-O Oscillations, Heinrich Events, and Bond Cycles

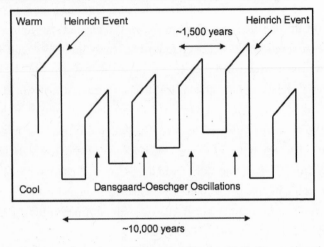

Schematic diagram of a sequence of Dansgaard-Oeschger oscillations, packaged together as a sawtoothlike Bond Cycle, and terminating with a Heinrich Event. *Adapted and redrawn from a figure originally published in Alley (1998).*

consequences of H9 on the climate of Africa. Using the UVic Earth System Climate Model, we found that the influx of fresh water to the North Atlantic associated with H9 led to a cessation of the Atlantic meridional overturning circulation as the surface waters became too fresh. This ultimately lead to the southward shift of the predominant rainfall belt across Africa and substantial changes in simulated African vegetation cover, particularly in the Sahel, which was inundated by an expanding Sahara Desert. We suggested that the overall change in climate rendered large parts of North, East, and West Africa unsuitable for human occupation, thus compelling early modern humans to migrate out of Africa.

A fascinating explosion in human ingenuity, termed the Great Leap Forward, occurred around fifty thousand years ago (see "Last Glacial Cycle in the Vostok Ice Core Record"). Suddenly it seems, humans started using more sophisticated tools and adorning themselves with primitive jewellery. Other objects of art were created, and the first signs of long-distance trade became evident. Theories for the cause of the Great Leap Forward are numerous. Some researchers even argue that the cultural evolution was not sudden but rather occurred more gradually. I find it fascinating to note that this time coincided with another major Heinrich Event in the North Atlantic (Heinrich Event 5, or H5). Could it be that this dramatic event, which we know wreaked havoc with the world's climate, stressed modern humans so that those with creative ingenuity were the ones most likely to adapt and survive? We'll never know for sure, but one thing we can say is that those early modern humans would have had a host of environmental problems to deal with. And remember, Heinrich Events, like the D-O oscillations, caused abrupt shifts in climate in just a few decades at most, well within the lifetime of an individual human.

Could these wild swings in climate happen today? The short answer is no. Dansgaard-Oeschger oscillations and Heinrich Events involved the interactions between the Atlantic Ocean and the continental ice sheets that covered much of Canada and northern Europe during the last glacial period. But this doesn't stop some from drawing the link between abrupt climate events in the past and future changes that might be in store for us as a consequence of global warming.

Busting the Imminent Ice Age Myth Once and for All

Knowing the causes of glaciation, you might ask yourself how global warming could possibly cause an ice age. Is global warming going to change the Earth's orbital configuration? Obviously not. The whole notion that global warming could cause an ice age is an example of scientific folklore that has no basis in the peer-reviewed scientific literature. But from where did this idea come?

In 1997, Stefan Rahmstorf from the Potsdam Institute for Climate Impact Research wrote an article for *New Scientist* that was given the unfortunate headline "Ice-cold in Paris." The cover showed a snow-engulfed Eiffel Tower with the caption "Global Warming's Icy Twist." While the article was well written and contained an informative, accurate review of the role of the ocean in climate change and variability, it included:

> Evidence now emerging reveals a risk that global warming could plunge most of Europe into a big chill lasting hundreds of years, bringing with it effects that could be felt right around the world.

Nowhere in the article did it claim that global warming was going to cause an ice age. However, when the above sentence is combined with the headline and the icy Eiffel photo, some might infer that an ice age was a consequence from global warming.

The following year, the connection was made in a far less subtle manner. William Calvin, a noted theoretical neurobiologist affiliated with the University of Washington, published an essay entitled "The Great Climate Flip-flop: Global warming could, paradoxically, cause a sudden and catastrophic cooling" in the highly respected and widely read *Atlantic Monthly*. He noted:

> We could go back to ice-age temperatures within a decade—and judging from recent discoveries, an abrupt cooling could be triggered by our current global-warming trend. Europe's climate could become more like Siberia's. Because such a cooling would occur too quickly for us to make readjustments in agricultural productivity and associated supply lines, it would be a potentially civilization-shattering affair, likely to cause a population crash far worse than those seen in the wars and plagues of history.

My colleagues and I spent a good deal of time responding to media calls asking us for comments on the Calvin article. The misconception that global warming could spawn an imminent ice age was spreading like an epidemic. We tried our best to contain the spread and it seemed to work. Unfortunately, another outbreak occurred April 18, 2002, when Terrence Joyce, chair of the physical oceanographic department at the Woods Hole Oceanographic Institution, wrote an opinion editorial in the *New York Times* headlined "The Heat Before the Cold."

In order to get an opinion editorial published in a newspaper, it usually has to be pegged to a recent event. Joyce used two pegs: the recent heat wave baking parts of the United States and the March 2002 collapse of the Larsen B ice shelf in Antarctica. He argued that the pegs had renewed global warming fears, but that these may in fact "be misguided." He outlined a sequence of events that he argued could cause an abrupt 3°C cooling of U.S. winter temperatures. The cooling in the northeast was to be even worse—6°C on average in the winter. Joyce was concerned that not enough was known about the ocean and ended his opinion piece by suggesting:

> A global ocean observing system would greatly enhance our ability
> to monitor changes that can spawn major, long-lasting climate
> shifts....

Joyce's concerns and call for an ocean-observing system were echoed by Robert Gagosian, the director of the Woods Hole Oceanographic Institution, in a document he prepared for a January 27, 2003, panel on abrupt climate change at the World Economic Forum in Davos, Switzerland.

The opinions of a few Woods Hole Oceanographic Institution researchers were also the subject of an extensive article written by Brad Lemley for *Discover* magazine in September 2002. The front cover of what turned out to be one of its bestselling issues warned readers of a "Global Warming Surprise. A New Ice Age." *Discover* is a very widely read, highly reputable popular science magazine and the researchers being interviewed had pretty solid track records. It's no wonder the global media picked up the story. In Canada, a full-page story appeared in the *National Post* October 4, 2002, headlined "Rumble of a coming ice age: Snap climate change," and a day later *The Gazette* (Montreal) ran a story headlined "The big chill: North America and Europe could cool dramatically in the coming decades if researchers are right about the effects of changes in ocean currents." Once more, I was inundated with media calls; this time it felt like a particularly virulent outbreak.

And then came 2004. On January 26, *Fortune* magazine published a story headlined "Climate Collapse. The Pentagon's Weather Nightmare. The climate could change radically, and fast. That would be the mother of all national security issues." The story featured a report prepared three months earlier by the Global Business Network for the U.S. Department of Defense. A *New York Times* opinion editorial headlined "Global Chilling" by Paul Epstein from the Center for Health and the Global Environment at the Harvard Medical School appeared two days later. While not the mother-of-all national security issues, this certainly was the mother-of-all outbreaks of global warming–induced ice age syndrome.

I still don't understand what happened. The Pentagon report was written three months earlier by business strategists/scenario thinkers Peter Schwartz and Doug Randall. It was a public report that was never secret, whose goal was:

> ... to imagine the unthinkable—to push the boundaries of current research on climate change so we may better understand the potential implications on United States national security.

We have interviewed leading climate change scientists, conducted additional research, and reviewed several iterations of the scenario with these experts. The scientists support this project, but caution that the scenario depicted is extreme in two fundamental ways. First, they suggest the occurrences we outline would most likely happen in a few regions, rather than globally. Second, they say the magnitude of the event may be considerably smaller.

We have created a climate change scenario that although not the most likely, is plausible, and would challenge United States national security in ways that should be considered immediately.

Why was this report suddenly newsworthy?

The news stories did not die down in the weeks that followed the publication of the *Fortune* piece. I had to cancel my Global Warming and Ice Age Google news alert as my email inbox was continually flooded with stories in the lead-up to the May 28, 2004, release of the Hollywood blockbuster *The Day After Tomorrow*.

I became frustrated and fed up. Despite my efforts to refute this claim in the media, people still believed that global warming could lead to an ice age. When I taught my undergraduate classes, I would ask my students how many of them believed that global warming could cause an ice age. Each year, about a third of the class would put up their hands. I would respond that I hoped they would see why this was not possible by the end of this unit. I remember one student becoming very upset with me. "How dare you say this is not possible," she said aggressively. "My biology prof taught me this already. What makes your opinion more valid than his opinion?" I was taken aback and simply asked, "On what basis was the claim made? Could you please point me to the scientific literature that supports that contention?" Of course, there was none. Much like the imminent ice age that scientists were apparently calling for back in the 1970s, the only mention of global warming causing an ice age occurred in a few opinion editorials, newspaper stories, and popular magazine articles.

A colleague and friend, Claude Hillaire-Marcel, a paleoclimatologist from the Université du Québec à Montréal, and I decided to try to publish two articles addressing the impossibility of global warming causing an ice age in the peer-reviewed scientific literature. I confess that it is somewhat unusual in science to disprove something that is not actually accepted by the scientific community. However, the editors and reviewers clearly believed that the submissions were timely and contributed new advances in scientific understanding. The first was entitled "Global warming and the next ice age" and appeared in the international journal *Science*, whereas the second, entitled "Ice growth in the greenhouse: A seductive paradox but unrealistic scenario," appeared in the Canadian journal *Geoscience Canada*.

Ironically, these two articles were well received by the global warming denial industry. Suddenly I was being invited to participate in talk shows hosted by well-known right-wing commentators. But these talk show hosts didn't get what they expected; they thought I would start down the path of denial, but instead I pointed out to an audience that would not normally be listening to a climate scientist that global warming was the most important issue facing humanity. There were many consequences of warming that would stretch the adaptive capabilities of human infrastructure and natural ecosystems. An imminent ice age, however, was not something we need be concerned about. On May 14, 2004, I was even invited by the George Marshall Institute to join an assorted gathering of global warming naysayers for a panel discussion at the National Press Club in Washington, D.C. I declined.

In these articles, we pointed out an historical basis for the misunderstanding. The ice and sediment core records of the last glacial cycle revealed a rich pattern of variability on the millennial timescale. The abrupt D-O transitions were known to cause dramatic cooling in the North Atlantic. They were also known to be associated with changes in the intensity of the North Atlantic conveyor as a consequence of significant fresh-water discharge into the North Atlantic. Consequently, a sequence of events was postulated along the following lines. If global warming were to boost the hydrological cycle by enhancing low-latitude evaporation and hence high high-latitude precipitation, then eventually the surface waters of the North Atlantic might become too fresh to sink. One might even throw in a bit of Arctic sea ice melt, increased river runoff, and some Greenland ice sheet melting. This could lead to a shutdown of the conveyor, a reduction in the oceanic transport of heat northwards, and hence downstream cooling over Europe, leading to the slow growth of glaciers and the onset of the next ice age; or at least so the newspaper and popular magazine articles would surmise.

But we have a relatively solid understanding of glacial inception. Orbital configurations that lead to cooler summers and warmer winters are those that are conducive to northern hemisphere glacial growth. The small change in seasonally distributed radiation must then be amplified within the climate system. The orbital properties of the Earth are so well understood that they can be predicted thousands of years into the future. This is precisely what Belgian scientists André Berger and Marie-France Loutre did in 2002 when they showed that the onset of the next ice age, if it is to occur at all in light of our high greenhouse gas levels, would not be expected for another thirty thousand years—hardly imminent by any stretch of the imagination.

It is certainly true that were the conveyor to become inactive, there would be significant short-term cooling, especially in the winter, in western Europe. Such conditions were envisioned by the 1997 Rahmstorf article in *New Scientist* before this idea was mutated into the notion of an impending ice age. However, it is important to emphasize that no climate model assessed in the IPCC's Fourth Assessment Report found a collapse of the conveyor during the twenty-first century. It is also important to emphasize that unlike glacial times, there are no Laurentide or Fennoscandian ice sheets over North America or Western Europe respectively. As such, it's difficult to imagine where you can get enough fresh water to cause an abrupt cessation of sinking in the North Atlantic and hence a shutdown of the conveyor.

The projection of future climate from the models developed around the world share many commonalities. First, every climate model finds that warming is amplified at high latitudes because of the feedback associated with the melting of sea ice and snow cover. As the surface becomes darker, more solar energy is absorbed and less is reflected. Also, as sea ice melts back, the atmosphere is exposed to the warmer ocean and so can be further heated from below. This also amplifies surface warming. Second, all models show an intensification of the hydrological cycle. That is, there is enhanced high-latitude precipitation and low-latitude evaporation. Both the high-latitude warming and freshening tend to make the surface waters lighter and hence try to weaken the strength of the conveyor. Indeed, virtually every climate model simulation finds the conveyor weakens over the twenty-first century; a few show no change, and none shows an increase in its strength. Temperature changes are more important than changes in fresh water in causing this weakening. Warming still occurs downstream over Europe because the warming associated with increases in carbon dioxide dominates over the slight cooling associated with the weakening in northward ocean heat transport. At the same time, no model finds a shutdown of the conveyor.

We summarized this in the IPCC's Fourth Assessment Report: "… it is very likely that the Atlantic Ocean Meridional Overturning Circulation (MOC) will slow down during the course of the 21st century.… It is very unlikely that the MOC will undergo a large abrupt transition during the course of the 21st century. At this stage, it is too early to assess the likelihood of a large abrupt change of the MOC beyond the end of the 21st century."

The reason we were hesitant to provide a firm assessment beyond 2100 was because of large uncertainties in the emissions pathways and rate of Greenland and Antarctica melting well into the future. Southern hemisphere melting acts to strengthen the conveyor, opposing a weakening induced by northern hemisphere melting. With that said, even if we take the 1993 to 2003 average rate of Greenland melting, which gives a global sea level rise equivalent to 0.21 ± 0.07 (0.14 to 0.28) millimetres per year and multiply it by 10, the amount of water is still small compared with what is required to stop the conveyor in climate models. Raising sea level by 3 millimetres per year corresponds to about 0.03 million cubic metres of fresh water being dumped in the North Atlantic per second. That's a little less than two Mississippi Rivers or one-fifth of the Amazon River.

While much has been made in the media of global warming potentially leading to the next ice age, it's simply not possible. Most models find a reduction of the conveyor during the twenty-first century, which leads to a negative feedback to human-caused warming in and around the North Atlantic. That is, through reducing the transport of heat from low to high latitudes, sea surface temperatures are cooler than they would otherwise be if the conveyor were left unchanged. As a consequence, warming is reduced over and downstream of the North Atlantic. I reiterate, warming still occurs downstream over Europe.

Global warming is offering decision makers and society as a whole many important challenges that need to be assessed and addressed, including the possibility of a reduction in the strength of the conveyor or the remote possibility of its cessation. One thing they need not concern themselves with is global warming triggering the next ice age.

The Last Twenty-one Thousand Years
of Earth's History

At its maximum extent twenty-one thousand years ago, the Laurentide ice sheet turned Canada into a barren wasteland by burying it under as much as three kilometres of ice from coast to coast. The Fennoscandian ice sheet over northern Europe wreaked havoc on the landscape there as well. Globally averaged temperatures were perhaps 3.5°C to 5.0°C cooler than today, and the atmospheric carbon dioxide concentration was only about 180 ppm (see "CO_2 Record Since the Last Glacial Maximum"). The massive quantities of water stored as ice on land caused global sea

CO_2 Record Since the Last Glacial Maximum

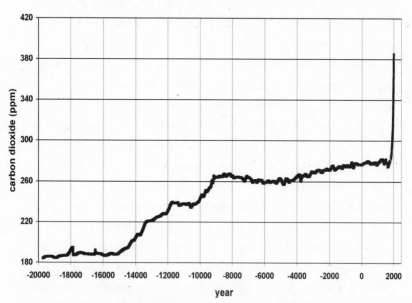

Atmospheric carbon dioxide level over the last 21,503 years. *The data from 1777 to 19,726 BC are from Monnin et al. (2004) while the data from 1832 to 1978 are from Etheridge et al. (1996). Both of these are from Antarctic ice cores. The data between 1959 and today are from the famous Mauna Loa record in Hawaii as archived by NOAA.*

level to drop by one hundred and twenty metres, exposing vast areas of the world's continental shelves to the atmosphere.

We still feel the effects of those enormous glaciers in Canada today. Think of what happens when you lie on a waterbed. You sink as the water under you is pushed away; the water level around you also rises as your body displaces the water beneath you. As an ice sheet starts to grow, it begins to depress the surface of the earth below it. The mantle below begins to flow away, just like the water in your waterbed but much more slowly as it's extremely viscous. Once the ice sheet melts away, the crust begins to return to normal, just as the water level in your waterbed does when you stand up.

Today the land is still rising in large parts of Canada, but it is falling in other parts through a process known as *post-glacial* or *isostatic rebound*. Richard Peltier and his group in the Department of Physics at the University of Toronto have calculated that peak rates of isostatic uplift are about 1.5 centimetres per year and occur in the middle of Hudson Bay; the town of Churchill, Manitoba, is rising out of the water by about 1.2 centimetres per year. Similarly, Lake Superior's northern shores are rising by 3 to 4 millimetres per year, affecting shorelines there; at the same time, the southern shore of Lake Michigan is sinking by about 1 millimetre per year. Isostatic rebound spells bad news for parts of coastal British Columbia and the Maritimes, since any rise in sea level associated with global warming will be compounded by the fact that the land is subsiding. For example, Halifax, St. John's, Victoria, and Richmond all have coastlines that are sinking by about 1 millimetre per year solely as a consequence of the long-ago melting of the Laurentide ice sheet. Of course, isostatic rebound will not go on forever, but it will certainly continue for centuries to come.

Antarctic ice core records also contain valuable information about the relationship among temperature and carbon dioxide and methane. It's only during the slow deglaciation process, however, that sufficient resolution is available to allow scientists to explore the statistical relationship between temperature and carbon dioxide. Several groups around the world have independently examined a number of different Antarctic ice cores and found that during deglaciation, the local changes in Antarctic temperature led changes in carbon dioxide by about 800 ± 600 years. That is, temperatures changed first and then greenhouse gas levels followed, precisely as one would expect. The greenhouse gases act to amplify the otherwise small changes in seasonality associated with very long timescale variations in the Earth's orbital configuration. Feedbacks act to amplify the level of carbon dioxide, methane, and water vapour in the atmosphere. These cause further warming.

So the next time you hear your favourite global warming naysayer point out that carbon dioxide lags temperature by eight hundred years in the glacial record, don't be surprised. That's exactly how it must be. There were no coal-burning plants twenty-one thousand years ago spewing carbon dioxide into the atmosphere. Carbon dioxide levels increased in response to warming, thereby amplifying this warming further. Remember that changes in the Earth's orbital configuration affect seasonality—not the total amount of radiation the Earth receives from the sun in any given year. By itself, a change in the Earth's orbital configuration does not cause global warming or cooling; the small signal must be amplified, and this is precisely what changes in surface albedo, carbon dioxide, methane, and water vapour do. That is, it doesn't matter whether you put carbon dioxide in naturally or unnaturally, the fact remains that it is a greenhouse gas and traps outgoing longwave radiation. And we've known this for more than one hundred years. Cold climates can't be maintained without a depletion of greenhouse gases, and warm climates can't be maintained without an excess of greenhouse gases.

The climate of the last eleven thousand years has been exceptionally stable when viewed in the context of the longer term record. There have been no D-O oscillations with their wild climate swings or Heinrich surges of ice into the ocean. Sea levels have changed gently, ice sheets have not grown over vast swaths of land, and globally averaged temperature variations have been small. This doesn't mean that there weren't large regional changes in climate but rather, that when averaged over the globe, they tended to cancel out.

The beginning of the Holocene also marked the onset of agriculture and the domestication of animals for the production of food. Once relying exclusively on hunting and gathering, humans could now settle and produce food locally. It is no coincidence that this occurred at the beginning of eleven thousand years of relative climate stability. In fact, no other such period exists in the history of modern humans. During this time, atmospheric carbon dioxide levels have only slightly increased from 260 ppm to 280 ppm prior to industrialization. Look again at "Carbon Dioxide Record Since the Last Glacial Maximum." In just one hundred and fifty years, humans have taken carbon dioxide levels from 280 ppm to 385 ppm. That's more than the change from the depths of the last ice age to pre-industrial times (180 ppm to 280 ppm). And then add all of the other human-produced greenhouse gases. Of course, now the rate of increase is so fast that the climate system has not had time to equilibrate to these higher levels of greenhouse gases. There is warming in store, no matter what we do. The real question is how much warming are we as a global society willing (or able) to deal with.

• • •

RECONSTRUCTING GLOBAL or hemispheric averages of past climates is a challenging task. The longest instrumental record anywhere in the world dates back to 1659 for central England ("Central England Temperature Record"). Most meteorological observing stations started more than two hundred years later. In order to reconstruct past temperatures, scientists must appeal once more to proxy records.

Central England Temperature Record

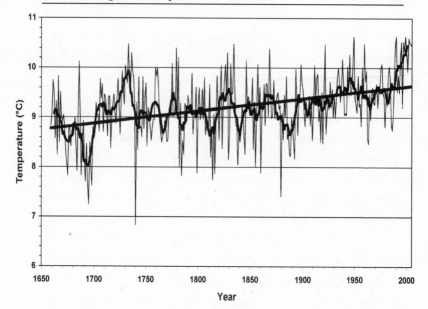

Annual mean temperatures from 1659 to 2006 from the central England temperature record. A smoothed curve using a nine-year centred running mean is also drawn as is a linear trend line.

There are many more options available to researchers wanting to reconstruct temperatures over the last one thousand years instead of one hundred thousand years. Not only can they examine ice, lake sediment, ocean sediment, and soil records, but they can also explore information contained within trees. The growth rate of trees is stored within the width of their rings. Trees grow more in some years than in other years, as is evident from their more widely spaced rings. By carefully selecting trees whose growth rate is limited by temperature (as opposed to precipitation) and by boring a small hole and extracting a core from that tree, researchers can infer temperatures at the time the tree grew. Of course, trees don't grow in the winter, so temperatures inferred in this manner typically represent growing season or summer conditions.

Several groups around the world have attempted to reconstruct northern hemisphere summer or annual mean temperature conditions over the last thirteen hundred years (see "Northern Hemisphere Temperature Reconstructions"). Different groups have combined different proxy records using different statistical techniques. Only one global reconstruction is available, but this is for the summer and extends back only to 1600. All curves show the same overall pattern; a slow cooling trend from about 700 to about 1850, interrupted by a warming between about 900 and 1100 AD (the so-called Medieval Warm Period), and finishing with a dramatic swing toward warmer temperatures starting around 1850. In fact, one of the curves has been cutely referred to as the "hockey stick." Some within the denial movement have even put forward the absurd notion that the theory of global warming is based on this "hockey stick." As they try to make the hockey

Northern Hemisphere Temperature Reconstructions

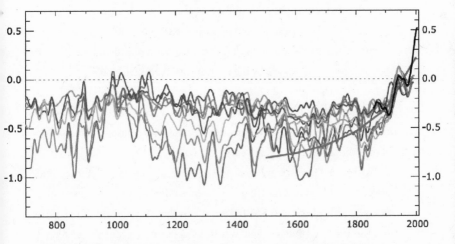

Reconstructions of northern hemisphere surface temperature anomaly relative to the 1961 to 1990 average for the last thirteen hundred years from twelve different studies using multiple proxies. The black line shows the instrumental record. *Reproduced with permission from Figure 6.10 of Jansen et al. (2007).*

stick a global warming icon, they are busy attempting to prove that it has fatal flaws. And if they can then find and expose these flaws, they are confident that public belief in the reality of global warming will come tumbling down. It strikes me as entirely disingenuous to focus on the hockey stick, on the one hand, and leave out the other eleven sticks that make up the hockey team.

The magnitude and extent of the Medieval Warm Period varies between the different reconstructions. It was during this time, around 984 AD, that the first Viking settlement in southern Greenland was created. Shortly thereafter, a second settlement on the coast of western Greenland was established. While the western settlement was abandoned first, the Vikings hung on in the south until around the 1420s, by which time the climate became so cold that crop failure began to occur. But were these Medieval Warm Period temperatures really that anomalous? This question was specifically addressed in the IPCC's Fourth Assessment Report, which concluded:

> The warmest period prior to the 20th century very likely occurred between 950 and 1100, but temperatures were probably between 0.1°C and 0.2°C below the 1961 to 1990 mean and significantly below the level shown by the instrumental data after 1980.

Today the same sites inhabited by the early Vikings are populated by modern Greenlanders. They grow food and raise animals just like the Vikings did a thousand years earlier.

"Northern Hemisphere Temperature Reconstructions" shows that between about 700 and 1850 AD, average hemispheric temperatures varied by only about ± 0.5°C from a mean that was about 0.5°C colder than the 1961 to 1990 average. But this doesn't mean that there weren't larger regional variations. Rather, what it implies is that there is no evidence to infer that events prevalent in the European historical record, including the Medieval Warm Period, were characterized by large-amplitude, global-scale phenomena.

While human civilization as a whole has flourished over the last eleven thousand years in our relatively stable climate, there have been casualties. The collapse of the great Maya civilization was linked in part to extended droughts that occurred around 810, 860, and 910 AD. Many other empires and societies are also believed to have collapsed, at least partially, because of regional climate changes. The Akkadian Empire in Mesopotamia, the area between the Tigris and Euphrates Rivers (now part of Iraq), ended around 2200 BC, coinciding with widespread cooling and drought in the region. Moche coastal communities in northern Peru were decimated around 600 AD following thirty years of extended drought. Moche society survived but had to develop new agricultural practices. The pre-Incan Tiahuanaco Empire, which flourished around Lake Titicaca in Peru and Bolivia, abruptly collapsed around 1100 AD in association with a climatic shift toward more arid conditions that started around 1040 AD. Even in North America, as noted by Jared Diamond in *Collapse: How Societies Choose to Fail or Succeed,* the Anasazi Empire in the southwestern United States ended in the twelfth century partially due to drought.

It is certainly true that climate has always varied and it will continue to do so. But while past mechanisms of global climate variability and change have nothing to do with humans, this doesn't mean that we can't affect the future climate. By simple analogy, we know that trees grow and die naturally; that doesn't mean I can't come along and chop one down and perhaps replace it with a parking lot. Over the last one hundred and fifty years, the Earth has made a transition from the past, when its climate affected the evolution of humans and their societies, to the present, in which humans are affecting the evolution of the climate and its weather. Today we are at a pivotal moment in human history; one generation will be responsible for deciding what path our future climate will take.

4

The Human Footprint

OUR SINGLE GREATEST OBSTACLE in dealing with global warming is the seemingly endless growth in world population. Since 1700, global population has increased tenfold and more than doubled since 1960 (see "World Population"). Every day there's an additional 210,000 people; that's like adding a city the size of Calgary *every five days*. Growth in some of the less developed nations is staggering, with China increasing daily by about 22,000 people and India by about 50,000 people. Canada's growth rate is only about 800 people per day (with the lion's share sustained through immigration), while the United States grows by about 7375 people each day. Countries such as Russia, Ukraine, Japan, and South Africa actually have declining populations, losing about 1875, 850, 300, and 550 people a day respectively.

While all people use energy, not all people use the same amount of energy at the same rate—not everyone has equally contributed to the predicament we are now in. From 1900 to 2002, nearly 80% of all carbon dioxide emissions came from more developed nations (representing only 20% of the world's population). And a large fraction of the emissions in less developed nations came from industries extracting resources and making products for more developed nations. Here's a surprising fact: Between 1900 and 2002, cumulative Canadian emissions of carbon dioxide have been about 22.6 billion metric tonnes. This is almost the same as the 23.1 billion metric tonnes of carbon dioxide emitted by India, even though its population is *thirty-four times* greater than ours. Equity issues come into play: The consequences of global warming are global, yet the major source of the problem is more developed nations, including Canada. But the atmosphere doesn't care from where it gets its carbon dioxide. Both less and more developed nations need to curb their emissions.

Around the time of James Watt's 1769 patent revolutionizing the steam engine, Britain began a major technological transformation: the industrial revolution. The manufacturing and transportation sectors

World Population

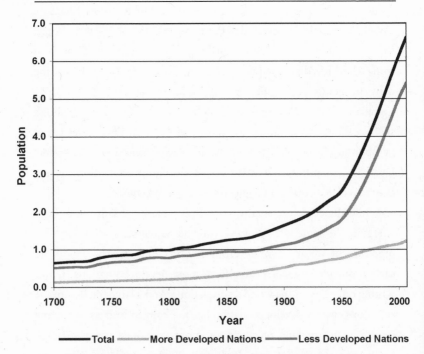

Estimated world population in billions of people since 1700. The total is broken down into the sum of population in more developed and less developed nations.

exploded with innovation, and productivity increased dramatically. Over the next hundred years, the industrial revolution spread to all corners of the globe—and it required energy. Initially we used wood as our primary energy source; the great forests of Europe were cut down and burned to generate power and to clear land for food production. Slowly but surely wood was replaced by coal (see "U.S. Energy Percentage Market Share Since 1800"). By the 1920s, oil started to replace coal as the fuel of choice, with natural gas displacing more of coal's market share shortly thereafter. It wasn't until the 1970s that nuclear power cut into the fossil fuel–dominated energy sector.

U.S. Energy Percentage Market Share Since 1800

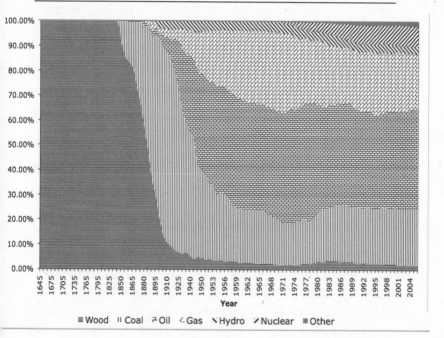

Estimated percentage of total energy consumption in the United States from 1800 to 2005 by primary energy source. *Data acquired from the U.S. Energy Information Administration, of the U.S. Department of Energy http://www.eia.doe.gov/emeu/aer/.*

The combustion of fuel follows a simple chemical formula:

Fuel + Oxygen = Carbon Dioxide + Water Vapour + Heat

The amount of carbon dioxide released is determined by the amount of carbon in the fuel (expressed as the carbon-to-hydrogen [C/H] ratio in any molecule making up that fuel). Coal has a C/H ratio of 2. Each coal molecule contains twice as many carbon atoms as hydrogen atoms. While there are many different forms of wood, it has an equivalent C/H of about 10. Oil, propane, and natural gas have C/H ratios of .5, 0.375, and 0.25 respectively. The smaller the C/H ratio, the more energy released upon combustion. So not only is there less carbon dioxide produced, but there is more energy produced as well. Throughout the last hundred and fifty years, as wood was replaced by coal, and then by oil and finally natural gas, the C/H ratio dropped from 10 to 0.25. This natural path toward decarbonization eventually leads to a C/H ratio of 0. That is, the fuel would end up being hydrogen gas, which when combusted produces nothing more than water and heat. The natural path toward the decarbonization of our global energy market seemed to stall, however, around 1980.

At first glance, "U.S. Energy Percentage Market Share Since 1800" suggests that we have greatly reduced our coal consumption. In 1910, coal dominated the U.S. energy market with 77% of the market share; in 2006, it was only 22.5%. But the energy market has itself grown dramatically over this time. More coal must be burned each year just to maintain a 22.5% share of the increasing energy market.

Compare "World Population" with "Estimated Global Production of Coal Since 1800." Do you see any similarities? The unbounded growth curve in each should be a signal that something needs to change.

What's particularly concerning is that unlike oil, and to a lesser extent natural gas, coal reserves seem limitless. In its *Statistical Review of World Energy 2007*, British Petroleum reported that proven global

Estimated Global Production of Coal Since 1800

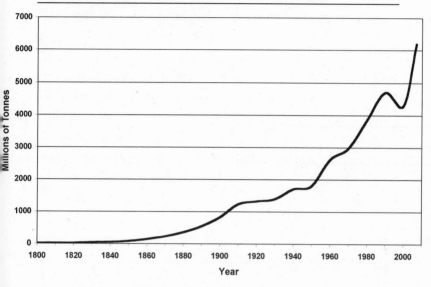

Estimate of global production of coal in millions of tonnes.

coal reserves would allow for a further 147 years of production at current rates. Gas could only meet current production for another sixty-three years, and oil would last for another forty or so years. These numbers should not be misinterpreted to mean that we are soon going to exhaust our fossil fuel reserves. In fact, in 1986, known oil reserves could only have met 1986 production rates for twenty-nine more years. At the current rate of oil extraction, those reserves would only have lasted for twenty-two years, meaning that 2008 would have been the year we ran out of oil. Instead, we have another forty more years of oil. We are continually exploring for new oil and gas reserves, and as they are discovered, their production replaces depleting reserves elsewhere. With coal, we don't have to do much exploring, as it's readily available in vast quantities all over the world. In fact, one of the cheapest ways of producing electricity is to find such a deposit, build a power plant on top of it, and burn the coal.

British Petroleum further noted that coal production was 5.2% higher in 2006 than in 2005, which in turn was 5.4% higher than in 2004, which in turn was 7.7% higher than in 2003. Global carbon emissions have been increasing at a rate of 3.3% per year when averaged between 2000 and 2006. Actual 2006 carbon dioxide emissions were 9.9 billion tonnes of carbon. And since 1850, a total of 488 billion tonnes of carbon have been emitted to the atmosphere, of which a little more than two-thirds came from fossil fuel combustion and cement production and a little less than one-third arose from deforestation and land use changes. That's a pretty strong footprint, so let's see how the climate system has responded.

Global Surface Temperature Record

Perhaps the easiest way to illustrate the effects of global warming to date is through the globally averaged record of annual mean temperatures at the Earth's surface (see "Earth's Surface Temperatures, 1880 to 2007"). Several international groups have independently compiled observations collected since the late nineteenth century by meteorological instruments around the world, including at sea. In "Earth's Surface Temperatures, 1880 to 2007"—which illustrates results from the U.S. NOAA National Climate Data Center in Asheville, nestled in the Blue Ridge Mountains of North Carolina—several features stand out.

First, a warming trend of 0.68°C over the last hundred years has occurred. However, the rate of warming has increased dramatically since the 1970s. Over the last thirty years, the globe has warmed by about 0.53°C, at a rate of 0.175°C per decade.

Second, it is evident that land is warming much faster than ocean. Since 1978, land has warmed by about 0.96°C, at a rate of 0.32°C per decade. Ocean surface temperatures have only warmed by about 0.37°C, at a rate of 0.12°C per decade.

Third, the climate system exhibits natural variability, so that each year is not always warmer than the preceding year. For example, the Earth cooled slightly in the years following the 1991 eruption of Mount Pinatubo in the Philippines.

The top ten warmest years in the 128-year surface temperature record are: 2005, 1998, 2002, 2003, 2007, 2006, 2004, 2001, 1997, and 1999. When averaged only over land, 2007 has the warmest near-surface air temperatures, being more than 1.0°C above the twentieth-century average. 2007 is followed by 2005, 2002, 1998, 2003, 2006, 2001, 2004, 1999, and 1995.

What's more, the warming is occurring beyond the Earth's surface. Satellite records reveal that the lower troposphere has warmed at a similar rate to the Earth's surface. Warming has also extended into the oceans. "Upper Ocean Heat Content" shows three estimates of changes in the heat content of the upper seven hundred to seven hundred and fifty metres of the oceans from 1955 to 2005. A distinct warming trend is observed. In fact, changes in the heat contained in the oceans have accounted for more than 80% of the change in energy contained in the Earth system as a consequence of global warming.

The Tale of the Sunspots

Have you ever visited an elaborate website put together by a well-oiled Astroturf (artificial grassroots) organization whose goal is to sow the seeds of confusion about global warming? If so, you might have heard claims that global warming is really caused by changes in solar cycles or sunspots. Perhaps you've heard your local radio talk show host tout this as a scientific fact, supported by a list of apparent scientists whom neither you (nor I) will have ever heard of. Or maybe it's been the focus of opinion in an editorial column in your favourite newspaper. Let's examine this a little more closely.

Earth's Surface Temperatures, 1880 to 2007

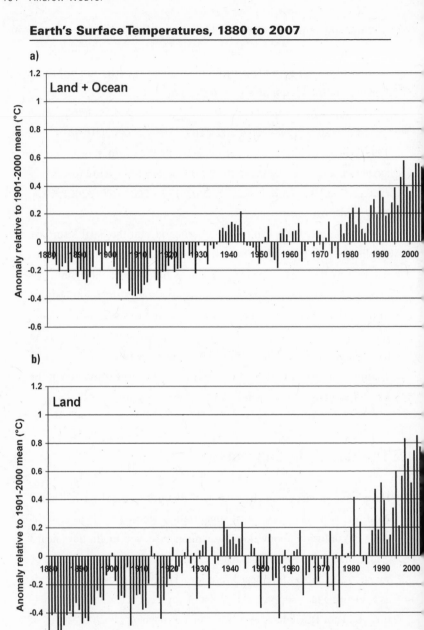

Earth's Surface Temperatures, 1880 to 2007 (*cont.*)

c)

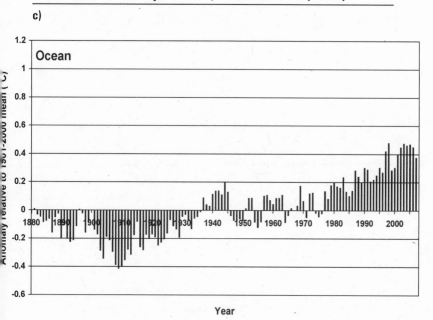

Year

Globally averaged surface temperature anomaly for the period 1880 to 2007 relative to the 1901 to 2000 average (near-surface air temperatures over land, and sea-surface temperatures over the ocean). Part a) land and ocean combined; part b) land only; part c) ocean only. Positive values indicate that conditions were warmer than the twentieth-century average, and negative values indicate that they were cooler. *Data were obtained from the U.S. NOAA National Climatic Data Center.*

Sunspots are dark blemishes on the sun's surface associated with intense magnetic activity and frequently with solar flares. They appear dark because they are much cooler (about 4000°C) than the rest of the surface (~5500°C) and range from 1500 to 50,000 kilometres in diameter (Earth's diameter is 12,700 kilometres). The number of sunspots in any given year varies; it cycles up and down with an average period of about eleven years, although longer-term undulations of this cycle also occur. Somewhat counter-intuitively, an increased number of sunspots is associated with increased solar activity. As a consequence, in years

Upper Ocean Heat Content

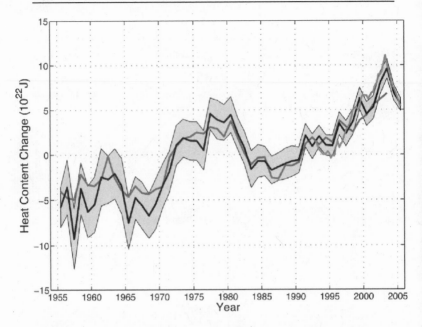

Changes in heat content of the upper seven hundred to seven hundred and fifty metres of oceans from 1955 to 2005 in tens of zettajoules (1 zettajoule = 10^{21} joules). Three different estimates are presented. The grey shading gives an error estimate for the solid black line. The two curves that span the entire range represent anomalies relative to the 1961 to 1990 average. The short curve from 1993 to 2005 represents the difference from the average of the solid black curve from 1993 to 2003. *Reproduced from Figure 5.1 of Bindoff et al. (2007).*

when there are more sunspots one might expect slightly *more* solar irradiance than in years when there are fewer sunspots. Changes in the total amount of solar radiation received at the top of the atmosphere are measurable but small throughout a solar cycle.

In 1991, Danish scientists Eigil Friis-Christensen and Knud Lassen noted the stunning *apparent* correlation between the length of the sunspot cycle and northern hemisphere temperature anomalies. Shorter sunspot cycles supposedly would mean more solar energy impinging upon the Earth's upper atmosphere than longer sunspot cycles. Anyone looking at "Solar Cycle Lengths" can't help but be impressed by the apparent relationship between temperature and the solar cycle length. No wonder the denial industry is so keen on dredging up this figure from the archives to ensure its wide dissemination more than fifteen years after it first appeared. If they can pin global warming on the sun, then there's nothing humans can do about it.

However, the curve showing the length of the solar cycle in part a) is an artifact of the way the points 1 to 4 were added to the end of the record. This was elegantly illustrated by Paul Damon and Peter Laut in an article in the *EOS Transactions of the American Geophysical Union* in 2004. Rather than smoothing the curve in a systematic manner, the end points were added on with either no smoothing or partial smoothing. How the initial reviewers of the original article missed this is beyond me. After correction of subsequent additional arithmetical errors, a corrected curve was produced by Damon and Laut, as show in part b). This curve is now just a little less impressive.

Why in 2008 would someone still show you a curve, let alone one that is known to contain an error, that stopped in 1980—especially when we have twenty-seven more years of data and several decades of high-precision direct satellite measurements of solar intensity? Well, the answer is obvious. Check out what you find if you plot the whole record of solar cycle length and northern hemisphere temperatures, as shown in part c). There is no longer any correlation—but that's hard to spin.

As U.K. scientist Mike Lockwood and Swiss scientist Claus Fröhlich concluded in their article in the July 2007 *Proceedings of the Royal Society*:

> … over the past 20 years, all the trends in the Sun that could have had an influence on the Earth's climate have been in the opposite direction to that required to explain the observed rise in global mean temperatures.

Solar Cycle Lengths

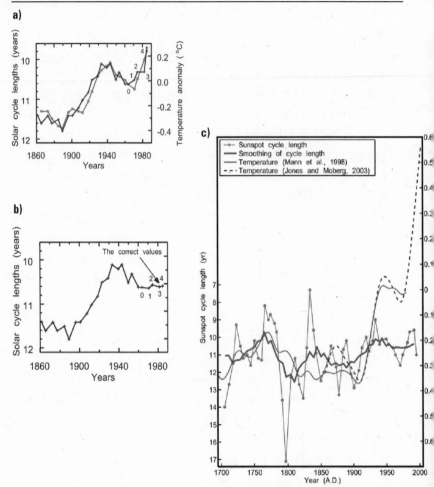

Part a) length of the solar cycle in years from 1860 to 1980 (black) as originally published by Friis-Christensen and Lassen (1991), as well as a record of northern hemisphere surface temperature anomalies (grey). Part b) length of the solar cycle in years from 1860 to 1980 after the points 1 to 4 were smoothed in the same manner as the other points on the curve and a few small arithmetic errors were fixed. Part c) the complete raw (dotted) and smoothed (thick dark grey) solar cycle record from 1700 to 2000, as well the instrumental surface temperature record from Jones and Moberg (2003; dashed) supplemented with a proxy reconstruction from Mann et al. (1998; thin light grey). *Taken from Damon and Laut (2004) and reproduced with permission of American Geophysical Union.*

Wouldn't it be convenient if the sun were entirely to blame for global warming? Then there's nothing we could do about it. Maybe that's the reason why the denial industry is so intent on trying to convince the public that it's all because of the sun. They don't want us to take measures to mitigate against global warming. Our addiction to fossil fuels, along with the profits for the companies producing and delivering them to you, would remain the status quo.

The Regional Pattern of Global Warming

The spatial pattern of the annually averaged warming trend since the beginning of the twentieth century is shown in the top panel of "Annual Mean Warming Trends." The bottom panel shows the warming trend since 1979. Several features stand out. First, there have been greater rates of warming over land than over oceans. Second, there is more warming in the northern hemisphere than in the southern hemisphere. Third, the warming rates are typically stronger in the middle of the continents or on their leeward coasts than on their windward coasts. Fourth, the warming rates at high latitudes are greater than those at low latitudes. Fifth, there have actually been some localized regions of cooling.

When we examine the seasonal patterns of warming, we also find that in the northern hemisphere, warming rates have generally been greatest in the winter for North America and Europe, and in the spring for Asia (see "Seasonal Mean Temperature Trends, 1979 to 2005"). All of these general patterns are straightforward to understand.

The specific heat of a substance is defined as the amount of heat required to raise the temperature of 1 gram of that substance by 1°C. The specific heat of water is about five times greater than the specific heat of sand or soil (it takes five times as much energy to warm 1 gram of water by 1°C than it does to warm 1 gram of sand). Most of us have

Annual Mean Warming Trends

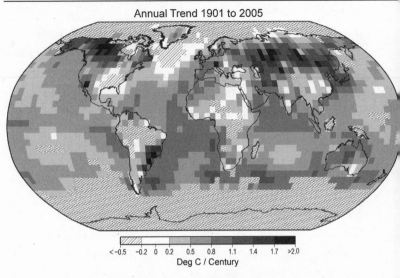

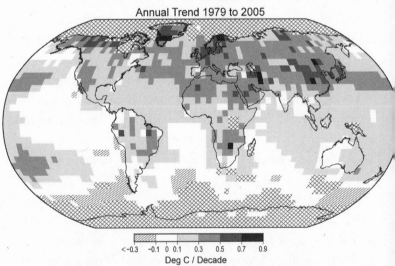

Top: Trend in annual mean temperatures over the period 1901 to 2005 in °C per century. Grey shaded regions indicate warming trends; single-hatched regions indicate a cooling trend. **Below:** Trend in annual mean temperatures over the period 1979 to 2005 in °C per decade. Grey shaded regions indicate warming trends; single-hatched regions indicate a cooling trend. In both figures, cross-hatched regions indicate areas for which there were not enough data available to determine a trend reliably. *Redrawn from Figure 3.9 of Trenberth et al. (2007).*

Seasonal Mean Temperature Trends, 1979 to 2005

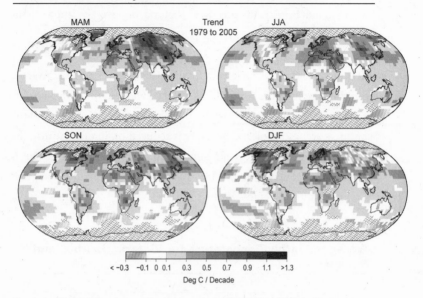

Trends in seasonal mean temperatures over the period 1979 to 2005 in °C per decade. Grey shaded regions indicate warming trends; single-hatched regions indicate a cooling trend; cross-hatched regions mean that there were not enough data available to determine a trend reliably. Results are shown for the seasons spring (March, April, May: MAM), summer (June, July, August: JJA), autumn (September, October, November: SON), and winter (December, January, February: DJF). *Redrawn from Figure 3.10 of Trenberth et al. (2007).*

experienced this directly. When you walk barefoot along a beach on a sunny summer's day, the sand feels warm (or maybe even hot) on the soles of your feet, but when you walk into the water, everything feels much cooler. This is because the water takes a lot longer to warm up (and conversely cool down) due to its larger specific heat. Water possesses thermal stability relative to the land, as it reacts much more slowly to heating and cooling.

So it comes as no surprise that warming has been greater over land than over oceans. And you would expect more warming in the northern hemisphere than the southern hemisphere because there is more land in the northern hemisphere. This is precisely what has occurred.

This simple property of water has profound effects on the climate over land that borders the oceans. In Victoria, our average January temperature is 3.8°C and our average July temperature is 16.4°C. Compare this to Winnipeg, with a bone-chilling average temperature of −17.8°C in January and an average July temperature of 19.5°C (see "Average Monthly Temperature for Victoria, Halifax, and Winnipeg"). Not only are the winters substantially warmer in Victoria than Winnipeg, but the summers are also cooler; seasonality is reduced or, in other words, the Victoria curve exhibits less of a hump than the Winnipeg curve. This is a direct consequence of the fact that Victoria is on the coast and Winnipeg is in the middle of the continent.

Average Monthly Temperature for Victoria, Halifax, and Winnipeg

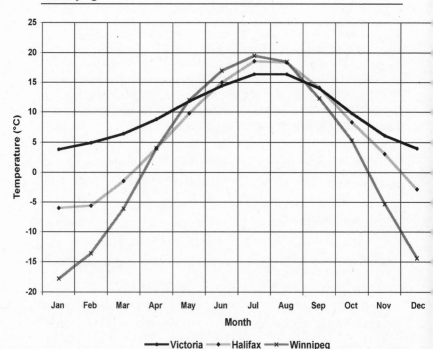

But how would this explain that Halifax's temperatures show strong seasonality, albeit not as strong as those in Winnipeg? July temperatures in Halifax average 18.6°C and the average is −6°C in January. The answer is quite simple. At the latitudes of Victoria, Winnipeg, and Halifax, the prevailing winds typically blow from west to east. Victoria's climate is strongly influenced by air that originated over the Pacific Ocean, whereas Halifax's climate is strongly influenced by continental air masses that blew eastward. As a result, Halifax has a climate somewhere between the climates of Winnipeg and Victoria.

As a response to global warming, one would expect faster warming rates in the middle or on the leeward coasts of continents than the windward side of continents. The more influenced the climate is by the ocean, the slower one would expect it to respond to a radiative forcing.

The warming is amplified at high latitudes rather than low latitudes because that's where the feedbacks are strongest. As the extent of snow and sea ice retreats northward in response to warming, the Earth's surface becomes darker. Less incoming solar radiation is reflected back to space and the warming is amplified. In addition, sea ice insulates the atmosphere from the ocean. When it melts, the atmosphere is warmed through heat loss from the now-exposed ocean waters below, thereby providing an additional amplification to the warming. These two feedbacks are most powerful in the spring and winter when snow and sea ice are generally abundant. Once more, the pattern of warming observed over the last hundred years is precisely what one would expect to see from elementary first principles of physics involving specific heat and albedo.

Average Winnipeggers are probably asking why they should care. They might think that a couple of degrees of warming in the winter would be a good thing. They might further point to evidence that the number of days with frost has already dropped and that the growing season has lengthened by up to two weeks in middle latitudes.

My response is threefold. First, climate refers to the statistics of weather, including the likelihood of occurrence of any particular weather event. An annually averaged warming of a few degrees should be viewed in the context of "Temperature Distribution," where the distribution of weather events is shifted. That is, the increased likelihood of several consecutive days of record-breaking warmth in the height of summer is what one might be more concerned about. In fact, the IPCC's Fourth Assessment Report noted that evidence already existed for "an increase in the number of warm extremes and a reduction in the number of daily cold extremes" over most of the globe. In addition, cold nights have become rarer and warm nights more common. Take the August 2003 heat wave in Europe, which led to at least thirty-five thousand deaths. While we will never be able to prove that humans were its ultimate cause, we can estimate to what extent humans increased the likelihood of such an event. In an article in *Nature* in 2004, U.K.-based scientists Peter Stott, Dáithí Stone, and Myles Allen showed that human contributions to global warming have already doubled the likelihood of another event similar to the 2003 European heat wave.

Second, warming would also be associated with changes in precipitation, drought, storm activity, soil moisture, ecosystem health, and myriad other phenomena. Northward and upward (in elevation) shifts in flora and fauna and a host of other ecosystem responses to twentieth-century warming have already been documented. Third, unchecked global warming is going to lead to global instability on a scale unparalleled in human history. There may be some short-term winners, but over the longer term, we will all be losers.

Other Observed Changes in the Climate System

Changes in our climate have not been limited to temperature. The amount, intensity, frequency, and type of precipitation have also changed noticeably over large regions of the globe. In the atmosphere, the specific humidity of a volume of air is defined as the ratio of the mass of water vapour to the total mass of the air containing that water vapour. When the air becomes saturated, condensation will typically occur. We define the saturation specific humidity as the specific humidity of the volume of air at saturation. A measure of how close the air is to saturation is then given by the ratio of the specific humidity to the saturation specific humidity and is known as the relative humidity. A relative humidity of 100% means the air is saturated and it may be cloudy, foggy, or misty; a relative humidity of 0% means there is no water vapour in the air.

The Clausius-Clapeyron equation (named after the nineteenth-century physicists Rudolf Clausius from Germany and Benoît Clapeyron from France) determines the saturation specific humidity (a measure of the water-holding capacity of the atmosphere) at any given temperature and pressure. As a rule of thumb, for every 1°C increase in temperature, there is a 7% increase in the water-holding capacity of the atmosphere. For example, if it's only a brisk 10°C in the bathroom when you shower, you'll see the formation of mist and condensation on mirrors and other cool objects. Before your next shower, increase the room temperature to 25°C and let the room acclimatize. You will find that much less mist and condensation form, because the water-holding capacity of the air has gone up. Conversely, if you're inside a warm house, you typically cannot see your breath when you breathe out. If you walk outside into chilly −5°C air, in all likelihood you would see mist when you breathed out. Your moist breath mixes with the cold air and the mixed air mass becomes saturated.

It should come as no surprise that significant increases in surface specific humidity have been observed in association with global warming. But if there's more moisture in the air, then there's more water available for precipitation. It should also come as no surprise that there have been increases in heavy precipitation events throughout the globe. When it rains or snows, there is·a greater probability for the rain or snow events to be heavier. However, since it has warmed, one would expect (and indeed it has been observed) that the likelihood of rain falling instead of snow has gone up. Of course, this is beginning to cause problems for those regions relying on meltwater from snowpacks to provide water resources in the warm summer months.

A tendency has been observed for greater annually averaged precipitation in the middle and high latitudes and less precipitation in tropical latitudes. The likelihood of drought has also increased, as warming air temperatures enhance evaporation and drying of the land surface. At the same time, decreasing snowpacks and less precipitation in the form of snow versus rain exacerbate reductions in soil moisture. Overall, there has been an increased risk of flooding when it rains due to the tendency for rainfall events to be heavier, and at the same time, there has been an increased risk of drought.

Changes have also been observed in both mid-latitude and tropical storms. By definition, hurricanes are tropical storms formed in the Atlantic or eastern Pacific oceans with winds exceeding 119 km/hr. Hurricanes in the northwest Pacific are called typhoons, and in the Indian and southwest Pacific oceans they are called tropical cyclones. There are five different categories of hurricanes according to the Saffir-Simpson Hurricane Scale. Category 1 hurricanes have wind speeds between 119 and 153 km/hr. Wind speeds increase to between 154 and 177 km/hr in category 2 hurricanes, to between 178 and 209 km/hr in category 3 hurricanes, and to between 210 and 249 km/hr in category 4 hurricanes. Category 5 hurricanes have winds in excess of 249 km/hr. Hurricane Katrina, which devastated New Orleans in 2005, was a category 1 hurricane when it crossed southern Florida, intensified to a category 5 hurricane in the Gulf of Mexico, and made landfall as a category 3 hurricane. Hurricane Andrew made landfall on the east coast of Florida as a category 5 hurricane in August 1992.

The IPCC's Fourth Assessment Report reveals that overall there has been a 75% increase in the number of category 4 and 5 hurricanes since 1970, even though the total number of hurricanes has decreased slightly. While hurricanes are occurring slightly less often, when they do form there is a greater likelihood they will be stronger and last longer than before. Warming sea surface temperatures have been strongly implicated as driving this observed change in hurricane activity.

In middle to high latitudes (which includes Canada), there has been a general poleward shift in the predominant storm tracks. The paths taken by typical mid-latitude storms are further to the north than they used to be. As in the case for hurricanes, evidence suggests that stronger storms are becoming more frequent, even though the total number of storms has dropped slightly.

More than 80% of the heat being added to the climate system is being absorbed by the oceans. As a consequence, sea levels must rise, since water, like air, expands when it is warmed. This thermal expansion accounts for about half of the 3.3 millimetres per year of global sea level rise since 1993, the remainder of which comes from the melting of glaciers and the ice sheets over Greenland and Antarctica. The rate of sea level rise has accelerated in the last decade or so, from the observed rate of 1.7 millimetres per year averaged over the twentieth century (see "Mean Sea Level Changes, 1870 to 2006"). From 1993 to 2003, melting of the Greenland and Antarctic ice sheets both contributed to sea level rise at a rate of a little over 0.2 millimetres per year; melting of ice caps and smaller glaciers contributed about 0.8 millimetres per year. These numbers may not seem like much in any given year, but if you consider changes over longer timescales, they start to add up.

Particularly disturbing are the recent satellite observations of Greenland ice sheet melting. On September 21, 2006, several months after the publication cut-off date for consideration by the IPCC's Fourth Assessment Report, University of Colorado scientists published

Mean Sea Level Changes, 1870 to 2006

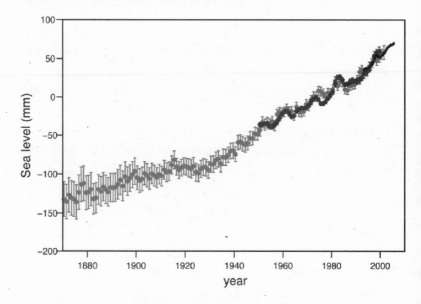

Global mean sea level change reconstruction from 1870 to 2006 relative to the 1961 to 1990 average. The solid curve is from satellite data and the black circles are from coastal tide gauges. *Reproduced with permission from Figure 5.13 of Bindoff et al. (2007).*

a study in *Nature* documenting an acceleration of Greenland ice sheet melting from April 2002 to April 2006. They found that melting of the ice sheet was now contributing more than 0.5 millimetres per year to global sea level rise. A week later, University of Texas scientists published a similar study in *Science*. It was frustrating for the IPCC scientists, since they were fully aware that these results had been published but were not allowed to include them in their assessment. As a result, the IPCC was eventually criticized for being too conservative in its assessment of future sea level projections.

The cryosphere describes the collective aspects of the Earth system that include water in its solid form—ice. Snow, glaciers, sea ice, ice sheets, and permafrost are all components of the cryosphere. Not surprisingly, the observed twentieth-century warming has left a mark on all aspects of the cryosphere, and it's not only sea ice extent that has been declining (see "Changes in the Cryosphere Since 1960"). Snow coverage has declined in both hemispheres, and most of the world's glaciers are in retreat. (In Canada, we can see melting glaciers on an inevitable path to extinction by visiting the Columbia Icefields. Any one of its six outlet valley glaciers—Athabasca, Castleguard, Columbia, Dome, Saskatchewan, and Stutfield—offers a close-up look at the landscape once buried under ice.) Peak discharge rates of many of the world's rivers fed by snow or glacier melt now arrive earlier in the spring. Communities relying on fresh water from these rivers will be in for some tough times as we move into the twenty-first century. And this includes Calgary, Edmonton, and Fort McMurray lying on the Bow, North Saskatchewan, and Athabasca rivers, all of which in the summer months are fed by the melting of glaciers and deep snowpacks.

While the interior of the Greenland ice sheet has been growing, there has been an acceleration of melting and glacial flow at the margins, which more than compensates for this increase. In 2007, areas of Greenland above two thousand metres set a new melting record. Best estimates suggest that the East Antarctic ice sheet is growing, but that this growth is more than offset by melting of the West Antarctic ice sheet. The net result is a contribution to global sea level rise of a little over 0.2 millimetres per year.

There is no significant trend observable in Antarctic sea ice extent. Perhaps this is not surprising, since Antarctica is a small island surrounded by vast amounts of water, whereas the Arctic is a small ocean surrounded by vast amounts of land. And oceans respond less rapidly than land to warming because of their thermal stability.

As with Arctic sea ice, the amount of year-round frozen soil (permafrost) has also been decreasing. Typically, most regions in our far north have a soil layer above the permafrost that undergoes a seasonal freeze/thaw cycle. The depth over which this freeze/thaw cycle occurs is

Changes in the Cryosphere Since 1960

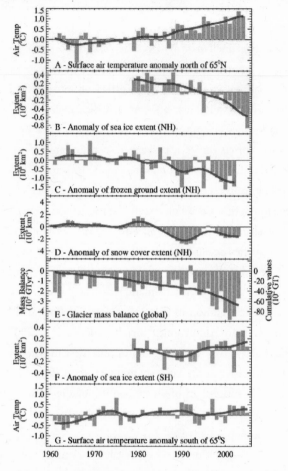

Indicators of change in the cryosphere since 1960. Anomalies, or differences from the long-term average, of A) Arctic surface air temperatures (°C); B) sea ice extent in the northern hemisphere (millions of square kilometres); C) extent of frozen soil in the northern hemisphere (millions of square kilometres); D) snow cover extent in the northern hemisphere (millions of square kilometres); E) globally averaged glacier mass balance in hundreds of billions of tonnes of ice per year with cumulative loss measured in hundred of billions of tonnes of ice (positive values mean glaciers are growing and negative values mean they are melting); F) sea ice extent in the southern hemisphere (millions of square kilometres); G) Antarctic surface air temperatures (°C). *Reproduced with permission from FAQ 4.1, Figure 1 of Lemke et al. (2007).*

the active layer. Freeze/thaw cycles also occur in areas where there is no permafrost. As one would expect with a warming climate, there have been observations of a deepening of the active layer and a northward and upward (to higher elevation) shift of permafrost zones as the climate has warmed. The area encompassing seasonally frozen ground has also decreased over the twentieth century, especially in the spring when this area has been reduced by 15%. It takes some time for heat to penetrate the ground and melt the deep permafrost. Nevertheless, permafrost warming has been observed over much of the north. As permafrost thaws, slumping of the terrain can occur in an irregular fashion, wreaking havoc on local infrastructure or habitat. Such ground instability is already being found in parts of Alaska and Siberia. Coastal erosion of exposed permafrost is also becoming a problem in coastal areas surrounding the Arctic Ocean.

No matter what policy path we choose in the next several decades, it appears that there is nothing we can do to stop the Arctic from becoming seasonally ice-free this century. This damage is in the pipeline.

Climate Models

Are these changes in the climate system over the last century unusual or just natural climate variability? And if unusual, are humans the cause?

In climate change detection studies, the goal is to use sophisticated statistical techniques to determine whether an aspect of the climate has changed beyond what one would normally expect from natural climate variability. In attribution studies, the goal is to attribute the change to a specific cause. For example, we may wish to examine whether the cause is related to the release of greenhouse gases and aerosols into the atmosphere by humans. We would need to show that the observed change is consistent with the response one expects from human and natural drivers of the climate system. We would also need to show that the observed change is inconsistent with the response one would expect from only natural drivers of the climate system.

Unfortunately, we have only one planet at our disposal. We can't use additional nearby planets to undertake parallel controlled experiments with and without human influences. As a result, we must appeal to the results obtained from climate models.

Climate models involve the numerical solution of complicated mathematical equations governing the physics of the climate system. These equations represent the conservation of energy, mass, and momentum, and include parameterizations (simplified representations) for unresolved physical processes (such as turbulence or clouds). Climate models also include detailed representations of chemical and biological interactions within the climate system. The equations are too complicated to be solved with a pencil and paper. They require a computer.

Think of a scaled replica of the Earth, its ocean, and overlying atmosphere made from Lego bricks. Each rectangular brick has a surface area that scales up to one-degree latitude by one-degree longitude. The twenty layers of bricks representing the atmosphere have different thicknesses from the twenty layers of bricks representing the ocean. In total, there are approximately two million bricks making up the atmosphere and ocean.

The Lego replica is a visual representation of the numerical grid of a coupled atmosphere-ocean general circulation model (climate model). The next stage is to simplify the equations governing the conservation of mass, energy, momentum, and water (for example) to reflect that our replica is made of Lego bricks. Each brick is in contact with a number of neighbouring bricks, and each of these bricks is in turn in contact with other bricks. Our simplified equations now represent how mass, energy, water, and momentum move from one box to the next; there are millions of these equations. At the bottom of the atmosphere, we have to add several layers of bricks to represent the land surface, its subsurface properties, and any glaciers or ice sheets that may be present. Similarly, sea ice requires another few layers of bricks sandwiched between the atmosphere and ocean. All of these bricks also exchange and conserve physical properties (such as heat and moisture) within the climate system.

A climate model starts with a set of equations governing the dynamics of the climate system and translates those equations onto a model grid that represents the Earth. Each of the subcomponents (atmosphere, ocean, land surface, cryosphere) interacts and exchanges heat, moisture, and momentum. The resulting system is then driven by specified radiative forcings, including energy from the sun and emissions of human-produced greenhouse gases (see "Interactive Components of the Earth System").

Climate Research in Canada

Building a climate model involves incorporating the work of thousands of scientists around the world in various sub-disciplines. Some scientists have made a career out of carefully measuring carbon and moisture fluxes among plants, soils, and the atmosphere. Others have studied how friction from the land surface affects the overlying winds. Still others have studied heat conduction and water flow within soils. By combining this work, other scientists have developed equations and parameterizations that represent the interaction between the atmosphere and the land surface, including the biosphere. But representing the land surface's interaction with the atmosphere is only one small part of a climate model. A similar process is involved in building the ocean, atmosphere, and sea ice components of a climate model.

Needless to say, climate models are extraordinarily computer-intensive, which is one of the reasons there are only a few dozen climate

Interactive Components of the Earth System

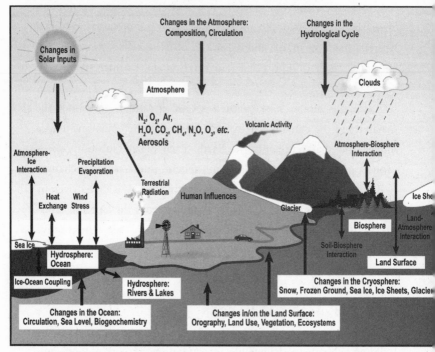

Schematic diagram of the Earth system including the various interactions among its individual components. These are the interacting subcomponents that are represented within a climate model. *Reproduced with permission from FAQ 1.2, Figure 1 of Le Treut et al. (2007).*

modelling groups around the world. It's simply too expensive for governments to support more than one or two groups. They need to provide extensive computer resources and support staff as well as numerous scientific staff with cutting-edge expertise in various aspects of the climate system. Canada's focal point for climate modelling research is the Canadian Centre for Climate Modelling and Analysis (CCCma), a division of Environment Canada, with which my research group is co-located on the University of Victoria campus. The CCCma is small compared to many of the international modelling groups, yet it is one of the most respected.

In 2000, the U.S. government undertook a national assessment enti-tled *Climate change impacts on the United States: The potential conse-quences of climate variability and change.* They analyzed projections of future climate in the United States from two climate models: the United Kingdom Meteorological Office model developed at the Hadley Centre and the Canadian model developed by the CCCma. At the time, U.S. climate modelling efforts were lagging behind those of Canada, France, Germany, and the United Kingdom. That's no longer the case: The two U.S. climate modelling groups based at the NOAA Geophysical Fluid Dynamics Laboratory in Princeton, New Jersey, and the National Center for Atmospheric Research in Boulder, Colorado, are leaders internationally along with the United Kingdom. Canada is now strug-gling to remain at the forefront.

It is no coincidence that Canada and the United Kingdom emerged early as leaders on the international climate modelling scene. This was a direct consequence of specific initiatives brought forward by Conservative governments led by Margaret Thatcher in the United Kingdom and Brian Mulroney in Canada. Thatcher held a bachelor's degree in chemistry from the University of Oxford and had been well aware of the potential dangers of global warming. On May 25, 1990, she opened the Hadley Centre for Climate Prediction and Research, one of the world's leading climate research centres, to provide her government with the best possible scientific information to develop informed cli-mate policy. On December 11, Mulroney announced Canada's Green Plan, in which money was set aside to establish the Canadian Climate Research Network, whose goal was also to provide sound science to inform decision makers. The network became operational in 1993 under the leadership of John Stone, who most recently served as vice-chair of the IPCC's Working Group II. Dealing with global warming should not depend on whether you are Conservative, Liberal, New Democrat, or Bloc Québécois. We may remember Jean Chrétien and his environment minister, David Anderson, for committing Canada to the

Kyoto Protocol, but do we remember Brian Mulroney and his environment minister, Lucien Bouchard, for giving us Canada's Green Plan?

The Canadian Climate Research Network was a brilliant, cost-effective initiative designed to harvest the wealth of climate-related expertise in universities and government laboratories all across Canada. Several research nodes were established, consisting of teams of scientists who focused their efforts on particular aspects of the climate system. One node looked at land surface processes, another examined carbon cycle modelling, others looked at Arctic or upper atmosphere processes. Research funds were almost exclusively used to support training of graduate students and recently graduated Ph.D. scientists (post-doctoral fellows). In each case, improving Canada's climate model maintained at the CCCma was the ultimate goal. Canada soon rocketed to international prominence in climate science.

The Canadian Climate Research Network thrived through Green Plan funding that worked its way through the Meteorological Service of Canada until 2001. At that time, it was subsumed by the Canadian Foundation for Climate and Atmospheric Sciences (CFCAS), an autonomous foundation established in 2000 by Jean Chrétien's government with an important mandate:

> CFCAS enhances Canada's scientific capacity by funding the generation and dissemination of knowledge in areas of national importance and policy relevance, through focused support for excellent university-based research in climate and atmospheric sciences.

The success of the Canadian Climate Research Network inspired Natural Resources Canada to establish a Canadian Climate Impacts and Adaptation Research Network (C-CIARN) in 2001, with the objective:

> ... of promoting and encouraging research on climate change impacts and adaptation, as well as promoting interaction between researchers and stakeholders.

Unbeknownst to anyone working in the C-CIARN, it had apparently "met the mandate that it was given when it was created in 2001" and was shut down in 2007, a year after the Stephen Harper government came to office. At the same time, CFCAS requests for funding renewal have been ignored. As Gordon McBean, chair of the CFCAS board of directors, said in a Canwest News Service interview November 9, 2007:

> [the Conservatives] have never allowed us to give them a briefing on what we do ... They don't acknowledge our requests.

When Environment Minister John Baird was confronted with these observations, Canwest reported:

> He said they are sponsoring projects such as $150 million in funding for Arctic research for the International Polar Year and more than $1.5 billion in spending for new technologies.

First, if you wanted to receive research funding from the Natural Sciences and Engineering Council for the International Polar Year program, you had to submit a proposal by November 28, 2005. The Government of Canada call for science and research proposals for the International Polar Year was issued December 19, 2005. It's all very well for the Conservatives to take credit for these funding opportunities, but the fact of the matter is they had nothing to do with them as they only were elected January 23, 2006.

Second, responding to a question about cuts to climate research with a list of new spending initiatives on energy technologies is like me complaining to you about cuts to medical research and you replying, "But we are spending a record amount building bridges." What have new technologies got to do with climate impacts and adaptation research? Nothing. Any effective climate policy must address both mitigation (which requires new technologies) and adaptation (which requires understanding our vulnerabilities and how climate will change in the future). No matter what we do, a certain amount of climate change is already in the pipeline as the Earth system tries to equilibrate to existing levels of greenhouse gases.

The 2007 Conservative government policies of cutting or not renewing research grant funding for climate studies in Canada were either vindictive (as climate scientists have been quite outspoken about the need to deal with global warming) or just plain stupid. Frankly, I believe it's the latter, as I am convinced that the Harper government got dragged kicking and screaming into dealing with global warming. They spent years in opposition throwing mud on any government initiative designed to curb emissions and now they have to change their tune. Their knee-jerk reaction was to cancel programs set up by the Liberals and come up with their own. Perhaps a wiser course of action would have been to consult with their own departments to determine which programs have been effective and which have not, prior to shutting them all down.

Evaluating the Climate Model

Before a climate model can be used to project possible scenarios of future climate, it must be evaluated extensively against contemporary observations. These observations not only include annually averaged fields such as temperature or precipitation, but also their seasonal variation, their extremes, and their interannual variability. In fact, each of the individual subcomponents of a climate model—such as the ocean, sea ice, and land surface models—must also be individually evaluated against observations prior to their inclusion in the climate model. And the parameterizations of unresolved processes, such as clouds and turbulence, must in turn be carefully tested before they are used. It takes years to build a climate model, and they are continually improved as the international scientific community learns more about the fundamental physics, chemistry, and biology of the Earth system.

You have to specify initial conditions before you can integrate (run forward in time) a model to get an equilibrium climate. For example, if I ask you to tell me the street number of the house a hundred metres down the road from there, you would probably ask, "Where is there?" I would need to give you an initial starting point. The same thing is true for climate models. For the UVic Earth System Climate Model (ESCM), the starting point is an atmosphere that contains no moisture and has a uniform temperature. The ocean is initialized with a constant temperature. There is no sea ice, no moisture in the soils, and the land is barren with no vegetation. As I want to obtain a pre-industrial climate, I use the orbital configuration (from Milankovitch theory) for the year 1800 and set the atmospheric carbon dioxide level to 284 ppm. The entire system is driven by energy from the sun.

The UVic ESCM is now integrated for ten thousand simulated years with the solar forcing, orbital configuration, and atmospheric carbon dioxide levels fixed. This takes seven weeks of real time, twenty-four hours a day, using one of the world's fastest computers. During this spin-up phase, the deep ocean cools and the ocean circulation begins, sea ice forms and carbon is taken up by the ocean, including its sediments, growing vegetation, and soils. Eventually an equilibrium is reached where year after year the same seasonal cycle occurs. But this equilibrium is for the year 1800, and it's pretty hard to evaluate your model with observations from that time as they are so few and far between.

The next step is to integrate the model forward in time from 1800 to 2000 but also including transient changes in radiative forcing. These include changes in volcanic emissions, the solar constant, and the orbital configuration (natural forcings), as well as changes in greenhouse gas emissions, aerosol emissions, and land use changes (human-caused or anthropogenic forcings). When the simulation of the present-day climate is finally realized, it's possible to evaluate the resulting climate through comparison with observations (see "ESCM 2000").

Parts a) and b) of "ESCM 2000" show the surface air temperature simulated by the UVic model (part a)) and inferred from the observational record (reanalysis data; part b)). Parts c) and d) show analogous plots for precipitation. While there are some differences between the simulated and reanalysis data, overall the agreement is very good. Parts e) through g) show the simulation of sea surface temperature, fraction of land covered by needleleaf trees, and the amount of sea ice coverage in September from the UVic model. Sea surface temperatures are about what they should be, sea ice extent is well captured, by and large the needleleaf trees grow where they should and not where they shouldn't. The boreal forest in the northern hemisphere is visible as the band of needleleaf trees across high northern latitudes. And remember, these results were obtained by only specifying the radiative forcing. The climate model was not constrained to reproduce the contemporary climate but rather reproduced this climate by solving the mathematical equations that govern the physics of the climate system.

Available information from past climates is also used in the evaluation of climate models. If we drive these models with the radiative forcing appropriate for the Last Glacial Maximum (LGM) twenty-one thousand years ago, we would end up with a simulated LGM climate that we could check against available proxy observations. Obviously this is more difficult than for the present climate because of the more limited availability of data and the need to use proxy records instead of direct observations. Nevertheless, paleoclimate modelling provides a stringent test of our knowledge of climate processes. For example, proxy records

ESCM 2000

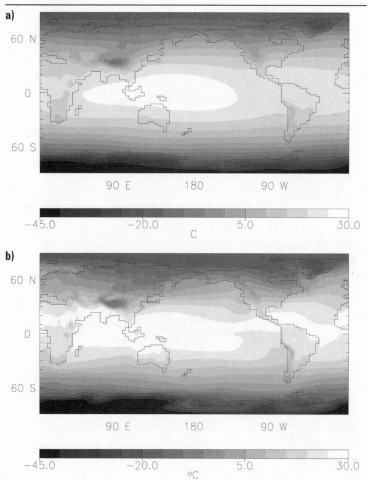

a)

b)

ESCM 2000 (*cont.*)

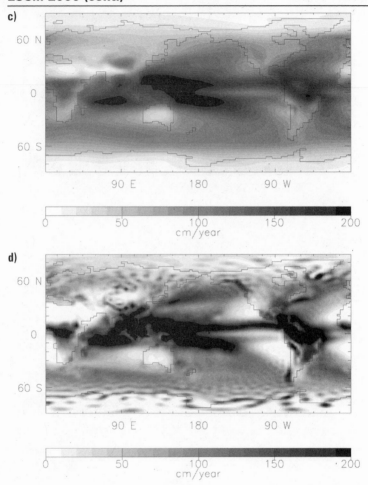

ESCM 2000 (*cont.*)

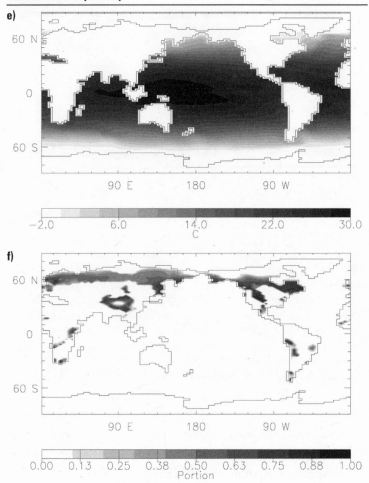

ESCM 2000 (*cont.*)

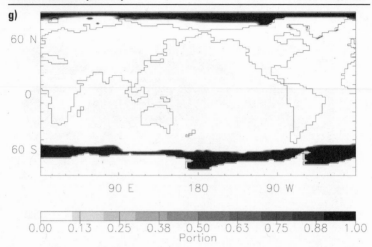

UVic Earth System Climate Model (ESCM) simulation of the present-day (year 2000) annually averaged a) surface air temperature (°C); c) precipitation (cm/year); e) sea surface temperature (°C); f) fractional coverage by needleleaf trees; g) September fractional sea ice coverage. Black indicates complete ice coverage in g). U.S. National Centers for Environment Prediction (NCEP) reanalysis product present-day b) surface air temperature (°C) and d) precipitation (cm/year). NCEP uses a weather forecast model to dynamically interpolate between meteorological station, balloon, and satellite observations. Some of the noise in the NCEP precipitation field at high latitudes is a consequence of the dynamical interpolation procedure.

for the LGM climate suggest that the North Atlantic conveyor circulation was weaker and shallower than today and that the Sahara Desert was more extensive; our model would need to simulate this.

It's also necessary to ensure that the time-evolving twentieth-century climate is adequately reproduced by the climate model. In part a) of "ESCM Global Mean Surface Temperature Anomalies, 1800 to 2005," three of the simulations force the model only with the observed changes in a component of the natural radiative forcing (orbital, solar, volcanic emissions); four of the simulations use a component of the anthropogenic radiative forcings (sulphate aerosols, land cover change,

ESCM Global Mean Surface Temperature Anomalies, 1800 to 2005

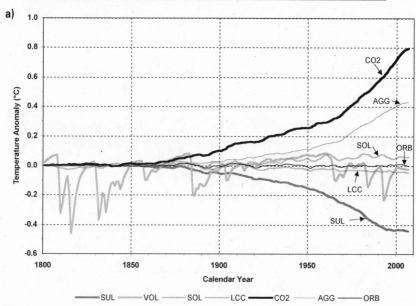

a)

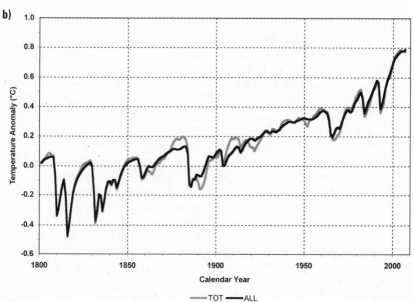

b)

ESCM Global Mean Surface Temperature Anomalies, 1800 to 2005 (*cont.*)

c)

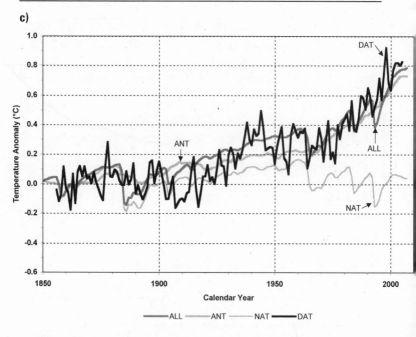

Global mean surface temperature anomalies relative to 1800 as simulated by the UVic Earth System Climate Model from 1800 to 2005. Part a) Integrations of the UVic model are driven by changes in only one external forcing at a time. SUL: sulphate aerosols; VOL: volcanic emissions; ORB: Milankovitch orbital configuration; SOL: incoming solar radiation; LCC: changing land cover and use; CO2: carbon dioxide; AGG: additional greenhouse gases. Part b) As in part a) but for the TOT curve representing the addition of the SUL, VOL, ORB, SOL, LCC, CO2, and AGG curves. The ALL curve shows the result of integrating the UVic model with changes in all external forcings. Part c) The results from only three integrations are shown. NAT represents the case when the UVic model is driven with changes in natural forcings (VOL, ORB, and SOL). ANT is the corresponding simulation with only human-caused forcing (SUL, LCC, CO2, AGG). ALL is the same as in part b). The curve labelled DAT represents the observed Jones and Moberg (2003) surface temperature record.

carbon dioxide, additional greenhouse gases). Part b) shows the results of a simulation using all of the radiative forcing (ALL) and compares it to the result obtained by adding together the curves from all the individual simulations (TOT). If the climate system responded *linearly* to radiative forcing, then we would expect ALL to equal TOT. They are close, but they do not match up exactly.

From part a), the changes in volcanic emissions and land cover (deforestation) have small cooling effects on the climate system. Orbital changes have negligible effects, since the timescale associated with these changes is so much longer than the two hundred years simulated here. Solar changes have a small net warming effect. The single biggest contribution to warming comes from carbon dioxide, whereas the warming contributed from all other greenhouse gases is nearly cancelled by the cooling associated with sulphate aerosols. But in the years ahead, as we curtail sulphate aerosols emissions due to air quality and acid rain concerns, this cancellation effect will be reduced and the overall warming will be compounded.

Part c) shows the simulated global mean temperature anomaly that results when the natural (NAT) or the anthropogenic (ANT) forcings are combined together to drive the UVic model. I also include the results from the ALL simulation. It should be pretty clear that the late twentieth-century warming in the observed temperature record cannot be explained by any natural forcing mechanism. However, variations in solar activity and volcanic emissions are important in explaining some of the change in the earlier part of the twentieth century. When added together, the ALL curve does a very good job of reproducing the observed global mean temperature record since pre-industrial times.

The UVic ESCM was built to resolve as many processes and feedbacks as possible that affect climate sensitivity and oceanic heat uptake on long timescales. As a consequence of its design, the UVic ESCM includes a simple representation of the atmosphere and so is not designed to simulate individual storms or other aspects of atmospheric variability. Climate models used by international modelling groups, including the CCCma in Victoria, have more complex atmospheric subcomponents. Typically they would undertake several simulations (known as an ensemble) of the twentieth-century climate. Due to the chaotic nature of the atmospheric noise, they would look to ensure that the observed global mean temperature record falls within the area spanned by the ensemble of twentieth-century simulations.

If during the evaluation process it turned out that the present-day, twentieth-century, or paleoclimate comparisons with observations were unacceptable, this would mean that some component of the climate system was poorly represented. We would spend several weeks narrowing down possible causes through a detailed analysis of the climate model's output. We would have to start re-examining our parameterizations of unresolved processes, re-evaluating the individual subcomponents of the model, and then move through the entire evaluation process again. It's no wonder it took us more than a decade to build the UVic ESCM.

Climate Change Detection and Attribution

To determine whether some aspect of the climate system has changed beyond what one would expect from natural climate variability—and attributing that change to a specific cause—requires a climate model. First, climate simulations are conducted from pre-industrial times to the present under the influence of only natural forcing (NAT), anthropogenic forcing (ANT), and combined forcing (ALL). In fact, if you want to detect the signature of a particular component of the radiative forcing, such as greenhouse gases or sulphate aerosols, you would conduct additional simulations as I did with each of the individual forcing agents (part a) of "ESCM Global Mean Surface Temperature Anomalies, 1800 to 2005"). Next, the time evolution of the simulated spatial pattern of change since pre-industrial times is determined for each of the simulations. A similar time-evolving pattern of change is obtained from the observational record. The next step is to decide whether the observed time-evolving pattern can be explained, in a statistical sense, by, and only by, anthropogenic forcing. To do this, we must rule out unforced internal climate variability as an explanation for the observed change. Here, climate models are again used, but now the observed pattern of change is compared with thousand-year-long simulations without anthropogenic or natural forcings.

The first climate change detection and attribution studies appeared in the mid-1990s. Attention was focused on global temperature patterns. Scientists found that the pattern of change in the observed temperature record could not be explained by natural causes and that it could only be explained when human-caused radiative forcing was accounted for. In addition, the signal of human-caused climate change had now risen above the background of natural, internal climate variability.

The IPCC's Second Assessment Report (1996) summarized these findings with the apparently innocuous statement: "The balance of evidence suggests a discernible human influence on global climate." And even this was difficult to get through, as Kuwaiti and Saudi Arabian delegates to the IPCC's final plenary in Madrid in 1995, supported by a consortium of U.S. oil and coal interests, questioned every word in the "Summary for Policymakers." This statement was so important because it was the first time the IPCC had formally implicated humans as a contributor to the warming climate. Ultimately, the Second Assessment Report played an important role in getting nations to adopt the Kyoto Protocol December 11, 1997.

The observed warming trends since the turn of the twentieth century and the start of the satellite era are shown in the top panels of "Observed and Simulated Temperature Trends." Around the world, nineteen different modelling groups contributed combined forcing (ALL) simulations of the twentieth-century climate to the IPCC assessment project.

Observed and Simulated Temperature Trends

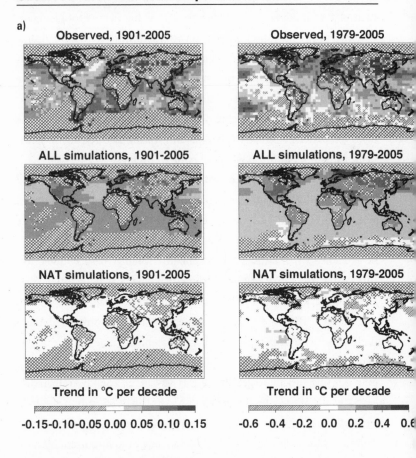

a)

Observed, 1901-2005

Observed, 1979-2005

ALL simulations, 1901-2005

ALL simulations, 1979-2005

NAT simulations, 1901-2005

NAT simulations, 1979-2005

Trend in °C per decade

Trend in °C per decade

-0.15 -0.10 -0.05 0.00 0.05 0.10 0.15

-0.6 -0.4 -0.2 0.0 0.2 0.4 0.6

Most of the modelling groups actually produced several simulations, each with slightly different initial conditions. The second row shows the resulting trends when all fifty-eight simulations were averaged together. Needless to say, where data exist, the observed and simulated trends are quite similar.

The third row shows the analogous results from the international modelling groups when, instead of combined forcing, only the natural forcing (volcanic emissions and changes in solar activity) was used. The

Observed and Simulated Temperature Trends (*cont.*)

b)

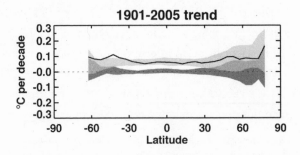

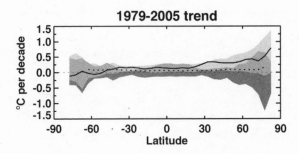

Part a), first row: Observed trends in surface air temperature from 1901–2005 (left) and from 1979 to 2005 (right) in °C per decade. The scale is given near the bottom of the figure. Grey shaded regions indicate warming trends; single-hatched regions indicate a cooling trend; cross-hatched regions mean that there were not enough data available to determine a trend reliably. **Second row:** As in the first row but from the average of fifty-eight simulations using fourteen different climate models driven by observed changes in both natural and anthropogenic radiative forcing. **Third row:** As in the first row but from the average of nineteen simulations using five different climate models driven exclusively by observed changes in natural radiative forcing. **Part b):** Surface air temperature trends as a function of latitude. The light grey shading represents the 90% range of estimates from all fifty-eight simulations used to produce the second row in part a). The dark grey represents the 90% range of estimates from all nineteen simulations used to produce the third row in part a). The solid black line gives the observed trend obtained by averaging the first row along lines of latitude. All available climate simulations were used; some international groups had not yet conducted simulations exclusively with natural radiative. *Reproduced with permission from Figure 9.6 of from Hegerl et al. (2007).*

observed trends shown in the top row look nothing like the simulated trends shown in the third row. In fact, since the turn of the twentieth century, the overall simulated response shows very little warming, whereas a distinct warming trend has been observed. Since 1979, natural forcing has actually acted to cool the planet, as one would have expected from the Lockwood and Fröhlich study.

In the IPCC's Third Assessment Report (2001), a far stronger statement on detection and attribution was included by Working Group I:

> There is now new and stronger evidence that most of the warming observed over the last 50 years is attributable to human activities,

and, as one would expect, in 2007 the analogous statement became even more forceful:

> Most of the observed increase in global averaged temperatures since the mid-20th century is very likely due to the observed increase in anthropogenic greenhouse gas concentrations.

> Discernible human influences now extend to other aspects of climate, including ocean warming, continental-average temperatures, temperature extremes and wind patterns.

The signature of global warming is now detectable on every continent except Antarctica, where observations are few and far between. In fact, if you look even at subcontinental scales, detectable warming is emerging that is attributable to human activities.

Canadian researcher Dáithí Stone, a former Ph.D. student from my lab now at Oxford University, decided to look at how all fifty-eight simulations from the nineteen international climate modelling groups fared when they simulated twentieth-century temperatures in twenty-two subcontinental-scale regions. The striking results are shown in

"Regional Climate Change Detection," a figure for which Dáithí won an unofficial "best figure" award from the IPCC's Working Group I, as well as a more formal "outstanding contributing author" award. In every one of the regions, the observed surface temperature record, indicated by the solid black line, falls within the area spanned by the light grey shading. But that area represents the range simulated by the models driven by combined anthropogenic and natural radiative (ALL) forcing. In all but one of the twenty-two cases, the observations are inconsistent with the range of possible outcomes simulated under only natural radiative forcing (changes in volcanic emission and solar forcing). This means that the regional signature of global warming is now detectable in twenty-one of the twenty-two regions examined.

The effects of global warming have now been formally detected above the background of natural variability in many other features of the climate system. We can now say that human combustion of fossil fuels has led to warming of the lower atmosphere and upper ocean, sea level rise, a decrease in Arctic sea ice extent, increased glacier melt, changes in temperature extremes (a decrease in the frequency of days with frost and an increase in the occurrence of warm nights), increased frequency of heat waves, decreased frequency of extreme cold periods, surface pressure changes, increased specific humidity, increased precipitation (amount and extremes), increased likelihood of drought and forest fires, and increased frequency of the most intense tropical cyclones. The list grows monthly.

The scientific community has no doubt that we have already started to see the pervasive effects of human-caused global warming. Not only can changes in solar forcing and volcanic emissions not explain the warming, they have actually been acting to cool the planet in recent decades. And finally, warming is now starting to be felt throughout the world's natural ecosystems. They have one of two options: adapt or become extinct.

Regional Climate Change Detection

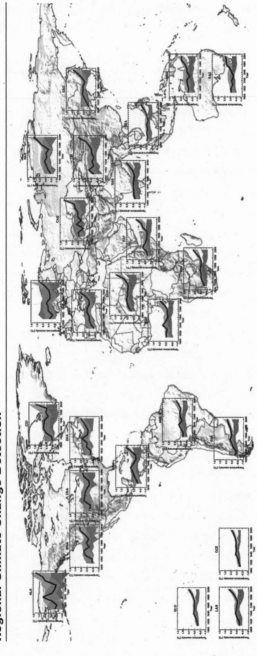

Average of all twentieth-century simulations from all models using combined anthropogenic and natural radiative forcing (light grey) and only natural radiative forcing (dark grey). The comparison with observations is conducted over twenty-two different subcontinental regions. In the bottom left are the respective global-, land-, and ocean-averaged curves. The grey shading represents the 90% range of estimates from all the simulations and the solid black line gives the observed twentieth-century warming. The combined (ALL) forcing simulations are anomalies from the 1901 to 2000 average. The natural forcing simulations (NAT) are anomalies from the averages of their respective ALL simulations. *Reproduced with the permission of Dr. Dáithí Stone.*

5

Turbulent Times

On November 20, 2007, I was proud to be a citizen of British Columbia. The day began as usual: responding to emails, reading a scientific paper, creating a few graphs for this book. Then I was off to the legislature for the launch of the Climate Action Team—a think tank of province-wide experts from industry, academia, First Nations, government, and non-government organizations—whose mandate is to advise the B.C. government on interim greenhouse gas reduction targets for 2012 and 2016. Six colleagues from federal research laboratories based in British Columbia were also invited to be part of the team. Now, I've become accustomed to the federal government's incompetence in every aspect of the climate portfolio, but even this one surprised me. Federal scientists were not allowed to attend without ministerial approval. And that approval only came once the event was in progress, so federal scientists were not present.

I suspect that you are skeptical: another committee, another set of recommendations. This time, however, there was a difference. After the launch, a number of us went to the public gallery to watch the legislative assembly debates. The Honourable Barry Penner, B.C. minister of environment, introduced the first reading of the Greenhouse Gas Reduction Targets Act, which puts into law British Columbia's

2020 reduction target of 33% and a new 2050 reduction target of 80% relative to 2007 levels. The act also requires carbon neutrality for the public sector, including universities, schools, hospitals, Crown corporations, and the government by 2010. These are the kinds of numbers we're after.

This is a bold step for British Columbia. In 2004, the province produced only 8.9% of Canada's greenhouse gas emissions and Canada only 2.2% of global carbon dioxide emissions. So while British Columbia may represent a drop in the proverbial bucket of international greenhouse gas emissions, the government has recognized the importance of showing leadership. And dealing with global warming also represents an economic opportunity. If the rest of North America follows the lead of British Columbia in Canada and California in the United States, emissions will be curtailed and the worst consequences of global warming will be avoided.

Estimating Future Emissions

Projecting future climate requires making assumptions about future emissions of human-produced greenhouse gases and sulphate aerosols. In climate change projections, about half of the overall scientific uncertainty arises from uncertainty in the future emissions pathways. That's why the IPCC produced thirty-five different possible trajectories representing a breadth of socio-economic assumptions including population growth, social behaviour, economic growth, energy use, and technology change. It's virtually impossible for international climate modelling groups to conduct century-long simulations using all thirty-five future scenarios, so typically only a subset are used. These six "illustrative markers" span the range of possible trajectories mapped out by the broader suite of scenarios. The resulting carbon dioxide emissions are shown in "Projected Total CO_2 Emissions, 1990 to 2100."

Projected Total CO$_2$ Emissions, 1990 to 2100

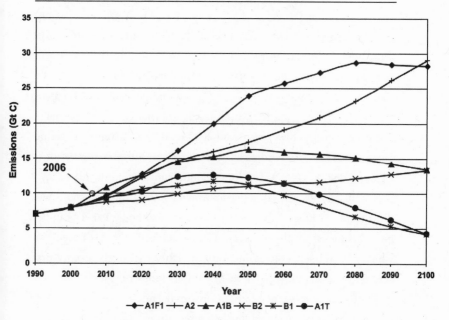

Six illustrative markers showing projected total emissions of carbon dioxide measured in gigatonnes (billions of tonnes) of carbon arising from human activities, including the combustion of fossil fuels, cement manufacturing, and land use change. For reference, 2006 emissions are also shown.

Some of the illustrative scenarios shown here are more fossil fuel intensive (A1F1) than others (A1T). Some have population growth that peaks mid-century at about 8.7 billion people and then declines thereafter (B1). Others have population that continues to grow throughout the twenty-first century (B2), reaching about 10.4 billion people by 2100. The most disturbing feature of these curves is that the 9.9 gigatonnes of carbon emitted in 2006 lies outside the most extreme scenario put forward by the IPCC in 2000. As is so typical of what has transpired in the physical climate system to date, the actual emissions have been greater than any of the projections.

Global Temperature Is Increasing

Let's first examine what will happen to global mean temperature over the course of this century. I turn once more to the IPCC's Fourth Assessment Report and in particular to the chapter for which I was a lead author. The projected range of global temperature change spanning all models around the world using all scenarios is 1.1°C to 6.4°C warming averaged over the period 2090 to 2099 relative to the period 1980 to 1999 (see "Projected Global Mean Surface Temperature Change, 2090 to 2099"). The lower bound comes from the least sensitive models under the B1 scenario, which assumes that emissions will drop below 1990 levels sometime between 2070 and 2080. The upper bound comes from the most sensitive model using the A1F1 scenario, which has emissions increasing until the latter part of the twenty-first century, at which time they level out at four times 1990 levels.

These increases in temperature may not seem like a lot, but remember that global mean temperatures were only 3.5°C to 5.0°C cooler than pre-industrial times at the depth of the last ice age when most of Canada was buried under ice. Warming of more than 2.0°C would create temperatures that have not existed on Earth in the last 2.6 million years defining the Quaternary period; and this would occur on the timescale of a century. In fact, the projected rate of change in temperature over the next two centuries has no analogue in at least the last fifty million years.

"Projections of Surface Temperatures" shows the spatial pattern of warming for the B1, A1B, and A2 scenarios and the probability distributions for warming averaged over the periods 2020 to 2029 and 2090 to 2099. A number of features stand out. First, there will generally be greater rates of warming over land than over oceans. Second, there is more warming in the northern hemisphere than in the southern hemisphere. Third, the warming rates are typically stronger in the middle of the continents or on their leeward coasts than on their windward

Projected Global Mean Surface Temperature Change, 2090 to 2099

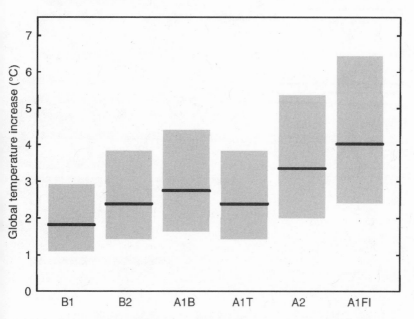

Projected global mean surface temperature change averaged over the period 2090 to 2099 relative to the period 1980 to 1999, using the six illustrative scenarios shown in "Projected Total CO$_2$ Emissions, 1990 to 2100." The horizontal black lines represent the average from global climate models. The shading represents an error range estimated as the mean plus 60% and minus 40%. This represents greater certainty on the lower bound and less certainty on the upper bound. *Redrawn from Figure 10.29 of Meehl et al. (2007).*

coasts. Fourth, the warming rates at high latitudes are greater than those at low latitudes. Do you recognize these words? They are exactly how I described the observed pattern of warming to date. The only difference is that there are no cooling regions. This simple pattern is easy to explain from elementary first principles of physics involving specific heat and albedo. In essence, the pattern of warming that has already occurred will continue, with warming greater in the winter than in the

Projections of Surface Temperatures

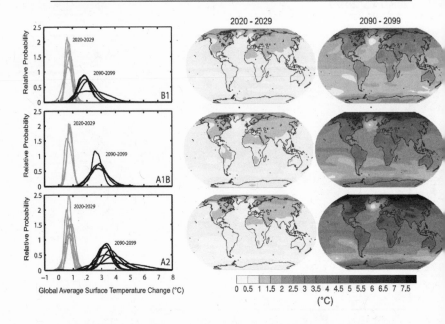

Projected global and annual mean surface temperature change averaged over the periods 2020 to 2029 and 2090 to 2099 relative to the period 1980 to 1999 using the B1, A1B, and A2 illustrative scenarios shown in "Projected Total CO_2 Emissions, 1990 to 2100." The results shown are derived by averaging simulations from ensembles using twenty-two different climate models. The left panels show various estimates of the probability distribution of warming averaged over the period 2020 to 2029 and 2090 to 2099. *Reproduced with permission from Figure TS.28, page 72 of IPCC 2007.*

summer. But now the magnitude of warming is much greater. Canada, as a northern hemisphere, high-latitude nation, is particularly affected.

The probability distributions shown on the left of "Projections of Surface Temperatures" indicate the likelihood of a particular globally averaged temperature when averaged over 2020 to 2029 (grey) or 2090 to 2099 (black). These distributions have been estimated a number of different ways, with each independent estimate corresponding to a different curve. Small values of relative probability imply unlikely outcomes, and large values imply more probable outcomes. The most probable temperature corresponds to the peak of the distribution curve.

A key result relevant to policy making can be extracted from the probability curves shown here. Regardless of the scenario or the means by which the probability distribution is estimated, the curves representing the period 2020 to 2029 are all very similar. This is important, as it means all emissions trajectories project a warming of about 0.2°C per decade over the next two decades. This is the level of global warming to which we must adapt, regardless of our emissions trajectory. Even if we held greenhouse gas levels fixed at 2000 levels, there would be about 0.1°C per decade warming over this period. There is a warming commitment arising from the fact that we have yet to equilibrate to the existing levels of greenhouse gases.

By the end of the century, things are different. Now there is a much wider spread between both emissions scenarios and individual probability curves. By 2090 to 2099, the most probable warming estimates relative to 1980 to 1999 range from 1.8°C for the B1 scenario to 4.0°C for the A1F1 scenario (see "Projected Global Mean Surface Temperature Change, 2090 to 2099"). And even if we immediately stabilized greenhouse gases at 2000 levels, the Earth would realize about 0.6°C of its overall warming commitment by 2100. That is, we have 0.6°C warming in store, about as much as we have seen since pre-industrial times, no matter what we do.

Suppose you placed a pot of room-temperature water on the stove and then turned the element on. Does the water immediately boil? Of course not; it takes time for it to heat up and eventually boil. Remove the pot from the stove and turn the element off. Does the water cool to room temperature immediately? No, it slowly loses its heat to the surrounding air. It's the same with the climate system. When you turn on the radiative forcing, it takes a while for the oceans to warm up and respond; unfortunately, when you turn off the radiative forcing, it also takes a while for the oceans to cool down. The bad news is that recent research led by Michael Eby in my group at the University of Victoria indicates that surface air temperature anomalies last for a very long time. In fact, we found that if known fossil fuel reserves are burnt, these temperature anomalies last 60% longer than human-caused carbon dioxide; two-thirds of the temperature anomaly will persist for more than ten thousand years.

The Sea Level Is Rising

As with temperature, projected changes in other aspects of the climate system are advancing in the same direction. While there will always be ice in the depths of winter when the Arctic is veiled in darkness, summer sea ice will disappear sometime this century. There is probably nothing we can do about it, as there is already enough committed warming to take us to an ice-free summer Arctic. Antarctic sea ice also starts to melt away. Most of the world's glaciers and ice caps are in dramatic retreat and will all but disappear over the next several centuries.

The IPCC's Fourth Assessment Report projected a globally averaged sea level rise of between eighteen and fifty-nine centimetres averaged over the period 2090 to 2099 relative to the period 1980 to 1999 (see "Projected Global Mean Sea Level Rise, 2090 to 2099") when the six illustrative scenarios were used. About 70% to 75% of the rise was associated with thermal expansion, with the rest coming from the melting of glaciers on land and a small contribution from the Greenland ice sheet. In determining its projected range, the IPCC relied on published estimates of ice sheet growth and decay over the twenty-first century. As a consequence, Antarctica was actually projected to grow because of increased snow accumulation on the East Antarctic ice sheet dominating melting elsewhere. This is clearly at odds with what's going on today. The East Antarctic ice sheet is growing, but this growth is more than offset by melting of the West Antarctic ice sheet. There is a net

Antarctic contribution to global sea level rise of a little over 0.2 millimetres per year. The Fourth Assessment Synthesis Report's "Summary for Policymakers" specifically stated:

> Because understanding of some important effects driving sea level
> rise is too limited, this report does not assess the likelihood, nor
> provide a best estimate or an upper bound for sea level rise.

Gordon McGranahan, director of the Human Settlements Group at the International Institute for the Environment and Development in London, England, and two U.S. colleagues recently calculated that

Projected Global Mean Sea Level Rise, 2090 to 2099

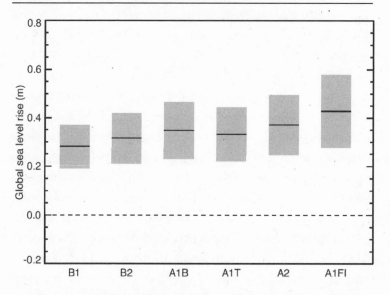

Projected global mean sea level rise in metres averaged over the period 2090 to 2099 relative to the period 1980 to 1999, using the six illustrative scenarios from "Projected Total CO_2 Emissions, 1990 to 2100." The horizontal black lines represent the best estimate, with the shading giving an estimated error range. *Redrawn from Figure 10.33 of Meehl et al. (2007).*

634 million people in the world live on the coast less than ten metres above sea level. Of these, a whopping 466 million are in Asia, including 144 million in China and 63 million in each of Bangladesh and India. The United States ranked in eighth place, with only 23 million people, albeit many in Florida, living less than ten metres above sea level. Future sea level rise is of particular concern to coastal communities when viewed in combination with storm surges that may occur at high tide. The devastation associated with Hurricane Katrina is a case in point. Another striking example happened in November 2007 when a five-metre storm surge caused by a category 4 cyclone inundated parts of low-lying Bangladesh. At least 3500 people died, the worst disaster to hit the region since 1991 when a similar event killed 143,000 people.

In May 2006, Jonathan Gregory and Philippe Huybrechts published an influential study in *Philosophical Transactions of the Royal Society*. They expanded upon earlier studies to show that if as little as 1.9°C global warming from pre-industrial times occurs (a further 1.2°C from today since we've warmed by about 0.7°C already), then the Greenland ice cap passes the point of no return. If this happens (we are on track for it to occur this century), we are committed to an inevitable seven metres of additional sea level rise. This rise doesn't happen overnight, but rather takes many centuries to occur, as the ice sheet slowly but inevitably melts away. And there's large uncertainty in the timescale for this melting since scientific understanding of the fundamental processes involved is still in its infancy. Early indications are that the West Antarctic ice sheet is also losing mass, although the East Antarctic ice sheet appears to be growing. It's too early to determine with confidence the quantifiable point of no return for the West Antarctic ice sheet and a concomitant five-metre additional sea level rise, although some early estimates have it as low as 2°C warming from pre-industrial times.

On September 22, 2007, I was quoted in an Associated Press wire story that appeared around the world:

> We're going to get a meter and there's nothing we can do about it…. It's going to happen no matter what—the question is when.

One metre is about the amount of sea level rise that we are committed to even if we immediately stabilized greenhouse gas levels. What we certainly don't want to do is warm the Earth beyond the threshold of the Greenland ice sheet. The 634 million people living less than ten metres above sea level would probably agree with me.

Precipitation and Extreme Weather

No aspect of our climate system will be untouched by global warming. As the Earth warms, the number of days with frost decreases, the area covered by snow decreases, and the growing season lengthens. At the same time, heat waves will become more likely, more extreme, and longer lasting. Let's suppose that temperatures reach 32°C once every twenty years at Vancouver airport (the twenty-year return event). Let's further suppose that Vancouver warms by 3°C on average in the summer over the course of the twenty-first century. The best prediction for the twenty-year return event at the end of this century is 35°C. The distribution of extreme warm events shifts with the change in summer temperatures, and that's true for much of the globe.

Averaged over the globe, the likelihood of extreme cold periods decreases 30% to 40% faster than the rate at which extreme warm periods increase. And temperatures also generally warm more quickly at night than in the daytime, which, together with increasing atmospheric humidity, compounds human discomfort levels in the more frequently occurring heat waves.

Overall, precipitation is expected to increase in middle to high latitudes and some tropical regions and decrease at subtropical latitudes

(see "Projected Annual Mean Change in Precipitation, 2080 to 2099").
In middle to high latitudes, that increase is in winter—not summer—
with an increasing likelihood of rain instead of snow. At the same time,
there is a greater likelihood of summer drought. Precipitation intensity
and the interval between precipitation events will also increase
throughout the globe. It rains less often, but when it does rain, there is
more of it. Viatcheslav Kharin and Francis Zwiers from the Canadian
Centre for Climate Modelling and Analysis based in Victoria, B.C.,

Projected Annual Mean Change in Precipitation, 2080 to 2099

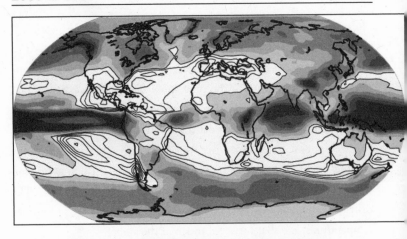

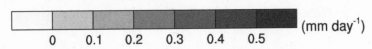

Projected annual mean change in precipitation in millimetres per day averaged over
the period 2080 to 2099 relative to the period 1980 to 1999 using the A1B scenario
from "Projected Total CO_2 Emissions, 1990 to 2100." 0.1 millimetres per day
corresponds to 3.65 centimetres per year. Grey shaded regions indicate more rain
while white regions indicate less rain. The white regions are contoured with a
contour interval of 0.1 millimetres per day. *Produced by and reproduced with
permission from Julie Arblaster at the Australian Bureau of Meteorology Research
Centre.*

determined that, averaged over the globe, by mid-century the twenty-year return event will typically occur once every 11.5 years for the A1B scenario and by the end of the century it will occur once every 8.6 years.

As the difference between high latitude and subtropical temperatures shrinks due to amplification of global warming at high latitudes, the overall number of mid-latitude storms will decrease. At the same time, the paths these storms take (storm tracks) shift poleward in both hemispheres. But the likelihood of strong storms with intense wind speeds goes up. So there are fewer overall storms, but when they occur, they have a greater chance of being stronger. The consequences for wave height, coastal erosion, natural habitats, and human infrastructure are profound. A similar trend is in store for tropical cyclones (hurricanes in the Atlantic Ocean). Best estimates suggest that the total number may decrease (although there is large uncertainty in this), but that the number of category 4 and 5 storms will increase.

In Canada, overall precipitation will increase, but it will come in fewer, more extreme events, interspersed between longer periods of little or no precipitation. There will be an increased risk of flooding. The precipitation will be skewed to the winter, with a greater likelihood of rain instead of snow as the century progresses. And summer drought will become more common. These changes pose significant challenges for communities as they attempt to meet future water demands. There will be lots of water around, but it will come at times when it's not needed and not at times when it is needed. Global warming will create an issue of water storage, not water availability, for Canadian communities.

How Climate Change Affects Us

When thinking of the future impacts of climate change, people often focus on changes in the physical climate system. What really matters, however, is the impact on natural ecosystems and human infrastructure.

The IPCC's Fourth Assessment Report assessed the vulnerability of natural ecosystems to future warming, noting that for a further 0.9°C warming from today's temperatures, between 9% and 31% of the world's species become committed to extinction. This number rises to between 15% and 37% for global warming of 1.5°C above today's temperatures. Not surprisingly, it rises still farther to between 21% and 52% once global temperatures rise 2.2°C above those of today. It's around this level that the global warming poster animal, the polar bear, becomes extinct, along with most of the world's coral ecosystems. And if global temperatures exceed about 3.3°C warming beyond today's temperatures (about 4.0°C above pre-industrial values), the best estimate is that between 40% and 70% of the world's species become extinct.

Water availability is already affecting parts of the world. The southwestern United States is experiencing persistent drought conditions, while the southeastern United States had its worst drought on record in decades. Conditions were so dire in Georgia that on October 20, 2007, the governor declared a state of emergency. In the summer of 2007, Greece experienced extensive drought, and Australia continues to have its worst drought on record. Clashes between ethnic groups in the Darfur region of the Sudan, initially over dwindling water resources, have led to human atrocities of monumental proportions. Tensions will surely rise as Lake Chad—spanning Niger, Nigeria, Chad, and Cameroon—slowly but surely dries up. And these conditions are only likely to worsen as the pattern of projected precipitation changes shown in "Projected Annual Mean Change in Precipitation, 2080 to 2099" comes to fruition.

In Canada, we have and will continue to have ample water resources. But global warming poses a water storage rather than water availability challenge. This isn't the case for much of the southern and central United States, and it's pretty clear our water will be in high demand south of the border. The great High Plains Aquifer that covers an area of four hundred and fifty thousand square kilometres buried under

Colorado, Kansas, Nebraska, New Mexico, Oklahoma, South Dakota, Texas, and Wyoming is being discharged, primarily for agricultural purposes, at between twelve and forty times the rate at which it is being naturally recharged. Obviously this is unsustainable, and if one of the world's greatest agricultural regions is to sustain itself, water will have to be found elsewhere. A quick look at "Projected Annual Mean Change in Precipitation, 2080 to 2099" shows that it's not going to come from increased rain; conditions are expected to dry further in the central United States as the climate warms, thereby exacerbating water shortages. The only place left is north of the forty-ninth parallel. So, rather than waiting a few decades for our neighbours to come asking for water, it's probably best we start engaging in cross-border discussions now. I very much doubt the United States will take no for an answer in the near future; it's a lot wiser to enter international negotiations long before the situation becomes one of crisis management.

Global warming will take a toll on every continent, with semi-arid and arid regions particularly hard hit initially. What's disturbing is that these hardest hit areas will likely have the least economic ability to adapt to the changes in store. In Canada, you might even be able to imagine a few short-term positive benefits of global warming associated with a longer growing season, fewer mortalities due to exposure to cold, and enhanced plant growth due to fertilization with higher levels of atmospheric carbon dioxide. But what about the people of Africa already suffering from economic hardship? Their agricultural production is projected to be severely compromised in the years ahead.

Even in Canada, an increase in crop yield has to be viewed in terms of the utter devastation of the lodgepole pine forests of British Columbia. Natural Resources Canada estimates that if the current rate of mountain pine beetle infestation continues, 50% of British Columbia's mature lodgepole forests will be dead by 2008 and 80% by 2013. The pesky little pine beetle has recently jumped into Alberta's lodgepole trees, and if it takes hold in the Jack pine, prevalent throughout Canada's boreal forest, we will have an ecosystem collapse of biblical proportion. For good measure, add a greater likelihood of forest fires to a landscape covered by dead trees. I think you get the picture.

British Columbia's coastal salmon fisheries, already hard hit by over-fishing and stream degradation from past forest management practices, will receive an additional kick from global warming. As temperatures warm, salmon that make it to the river mouth will have increasing mortality rates as they struggle upstream to their spawning grounds. In southern regions, there will also be less water in these streams during the summer and early fall as glaciers retreat and more precipitation comes in the form of rain instead of snow. With an increased likelihood of drought, the autumn rains will have a greater chance of being delayed. As a consequence, fewer fish will spawn. Flooding and its disturbance of stream beds following the increasingly likely extreme precipitation events spell bad news for the eggs buried under the gravel. Fewer juvenile salmon will hatch. Either the salmon move northward or they face dramatic declines. This is already occurring and salmon are becoming more common in the Arctic Ocean. British Columbia has received a rejuvenation of Pacific sardines as they moved northward along with the warming ocean. In the future, we'll probably be getting more tuna and mackerel, along with other warmer water species.

An increase of salmon in the Arctic and an open Northwest Passage may seem like good things. However, one of the most ironic, and frankly depressing, consequences of Arctic warming is that it is opening up vast new areas for the exploration of oil and natural gas. Already there is a feeding frenzy in the north as oil companies clamber over one another for exploration rights. But there is trouble lurking down the road; it will be difficult to get there by land. The north is experiencing a decreasing season for viable ice roads. Moreover, much of the northern infrastructure, including current and any future pipelines, is built on permafrost. One thing we can count on: Warming temperatures will lead to a reduction in permafrost. The consequences are ugly for infrastructure and surface vegetation as the ground slumps in regions where permafrost melts. Even more disquieting from a climate perspective is the amount of carbon trapped in this frozen soil.

As permafrost melts and the depth of the active layer deepens, more organic material can now start to decay. If the surface is covered with water, methane-producing bacteria break down the organic matter. But these bacteria can't survive in the presence of oxygen. Instead, if the thawed soils are exposed to air, carbon dioxide–producing bacteria are involved in the decay process. In either case, it's a positive feedback to global warming. In fact, this feedback represents one of the most important unknowns in the science of global warming, as it hasn't been accounted for in any of the IPCC projections. We know the sign of the feedback—it's positive—but we don't know its magnitude. What's particularly disconcerting is that there's an awful lot of carbon that can potentially be released from these frozen soils—somewhere between three hundred and fifty and nine hundred and fifty billion tonnes' worth. And whether this carbon comes out in the form of carbon dioxide or methane matters, because on a molecule-per-molecule basis, methane is twenty-one times more potent as a greenhouse gas than is carbon dioxide over a hundred-year time horizon.

It strikes me as a rather urgent matter for the scientific community to reduce the uncertainty involved in estimating the potential release of carbon dioxide or methane from the thawing of northern soils. To put this into perspective, let's suppose it turns out that the reserve is nine hundred and fifty billion tonnes of carbon. Let's further suppose that sometime in the near future we start to release 1% of this carbon every year. That amount translates to 9.5 billion tonnes of carbon per year, which is almost identical to the current estimate of carbon emissions from all human activities, including fossil fuel combustion, agriculture, cement manufacturing, and land use changes. In other words, from this example we see that thawing of the northern soils would double total carbon emissions to the atmosphere. That's not a good thing, especially if the carbon were released as methane instead of carbon dioxide.

Global Warming's Impact Around the World

Rather than attempt to provide a comprehensive list of all the potential impacts of global warming around the world, I include the examples summarized in Table SPM.2 of the "Summary for Policymakers" from the IPCC's Fourth Assessment Synthesis Report (November 17, 2007):

Projected Regional Impact Examples

Region	Projected Examples
	Reproduced with permission from Table SPM.2 on pages 11 to 12 of the "Summary for Policymakers" of the IPCC AR4 Synthesis Report available at www.ipcc.ch/ipccreports/ ar4-syr.htm
Africa	• By 2020, between 75 and 250 million people are projected to be exposed to increased water stress due to climate change.
	• By 2020, in some countries, yields from rain-fed agriculture could be reduced by up to 50%. Agricultural production, including access to food, in many African countries is projected to be severely compromised. This would further adversely affect food security and exacerbate malnutrition.
	• Towards the end of the 21st century, projected sea level rise will affect low-lying coastal areas with large populations. The cost of adaptation could amount to at least 5 to 10% of Gross Domestic Product (GDP).
	• By 2080, an increase of 5 to 8% of arid and semi-arid land in Africa is projected under a range of climate scenarios.
Asia	• By the 2050s, freshwater availability in Central, South, East and South-East Asia, particularly in large river basins, is projected to decrease.
	• Coastal areas, especially heavily populated megadelta regions in South, East and South-East Asia, will be at greatest risk due to increased flooding from the sea and, in some megadeltas, flooding from the rivers.

- Climate change is projected to compound the pressures on natural resources and the environment associated with rapid urbanisation, industrialisation and economic development.
- Endemic morbidity and mortality due to diarrhoeal disease primarily associated with floods and droughts are expected to rise in East, South and South-East Asia due to projected changes in the hydrological cycle.

Australia and New Zealand	• By 2020, significant loss of biodiversity is projected to occur in some ecologically rich sites, including the Great Barrier Reef and Queensland Wet Tropics.
	• By 2030, water security problems are projected to intensify in southern and eastern Australia and, in New Zealand, in Northland and some eastern regions.
	• By 2030, production from agriculture and forestry is projected to decline over much of southern and eastern Australia, and over parts of eastern New Zealand, due to increased drought and fire. However, in New Zealand, initial benefits are projected in some other regions.
	• By 2050, ongoing coastal development and population growth in some areas of Australia and New Zealand are projected to exacerbate risks from sea level rise and increases in the severity and frequency of storms and coastal flooding.
Europe	• Climate change is expected to magnify regional differences in Europe's natural resources and assets. Negative impacts will include increased risk of inland flash floods and more frequent coastal flooding and increased erosion (due to storminess and sea level rise).
	• Mountainous areas will face glacier retreat, reduced snow cover and winter tourism, and extensive species losses (in some areas up to 60% under high emissions scenarios by 2080).
	• In southern Europe, climate change is projected to worsen conditions (high temperatures and drought) in a region already vulnerable to climate variability, and to reduce water availability, hydropower potential, summer tourism and, in general, crop productivity.
	• Climate change is also projected to increase the health risks due to heat waves and the frequency of wildfires.
Latin America	• By mid-century, increases in temperature and associated decreases in soil water are projected to lead to gradual replacement of tropical forest by savanna in eastern Amazonia.

Semi-arid vegetation will tend to be replaced by arid-land vegetation.

- There is a risk of significant biodiversity loss through species extinction in many areas of tropical Latin America.

- Productivity of some important crops is projected to decrease and livestock productivity to decline, with adverse consequences for food security. In temperate zones, soybean yields are projected to increase. Overall, the number of people at risk of hunger is projected to increase (medium confidence).

- Changes in precipitation patterns and the disappearance of glaciers are projected to significantly affect water availability for human consumption, agriculture and energy generation.

North America	• Warming in western mountains is projected to cause decreased snowpack, more winter flooding and reduced summer flows, exacerbating competition for over-allocated water resources.

- In the early decades of the century, moderate climate change is projected to increase aggregate yields of rain-fed agriculture by 5 to 20%, but with important variability among regions. Major challenges are projected for crops that are near the warm end of their suitable range or which depend on highly utilised water resources.

- Cities that currently experience heat waves are expected to be further challenged by an increased number, intensity and duration of heat waves during the course of the century, with potential for adverse health impacts.

- Coastal communities and habitats will be increasingly stressed by climate change impacts interacting with development and pollution.

Polar Regions	• The main projected biophysical effects are reductions in thickness and extent of glaciers, ice sheets and sea ice, and changes in natural ecosystems with detrimental effects on many organisms including migratory birds, mammals and higher predators.

- For human communities in the Arctic, impacts, particularly those resulting from changing snow and ice conditions, are projected to be mixed.

- Detrimental impacts would include those on infrastructure and traditional indigenous ways of life.

- In both polar regions, specific ecosystems and habitats are projected to be vulnerable, as climatic barriers to species invasions are lowered.

Small Islands

- Sea level rise is expected to exacerbate inundation, storm surge, erosion and other coastal hazards, thus threatening vital infrastructure, settlements and facilities that support the livelihood of island communities.

- Deterioration in coastal conditions, for example through erosion of beaches and coral bleaching, is expected to affect local resources.

- By mid-century, climate change is expected to reduce water resources in many small islands, e.g. in the Caribbean and Pacific, to the point where they become insufficient to meet demand during low-rainfall periods.

- With higher temperatures, increased invasion by non-native species is expected to occur, particularly on mid- and high-latitude islands.

This brief excerpt only skims the surface of global warming impacts. For the Arctic alone, a 2005 Arctic Climate Impact Assessment put together by the intergovernmental Arctic Council and the International Arctic Science Committee of what's in store from global warming filled 1042 pages. And that's a lot to digest.

At What Price?

Humans have an established track record of recovering from adversity. If our homes are destroyed, we rebuild or move elsewhere, provided that we have the economic wherewithal to do so. If we don't, we look to others for help. Humans are remarkably resilient. We live throughout the world in both warm and cold climates, and we freely move among every different climatic zone on the planet. For us, adapting to a warm or cold climate in our travels means changing the clothes we wear and the amount of heating or cooling in our buildings. Unfortunately, it's not that easy for the world's natural ecosystems.

When asked what I believe will be the most serious consequences of global warming, I always reply with the same two answers. The first concerns the effect of global warming on the world's natural ecosystems; the second involves global security and political instability. These aren't the answers people expect. Rather, people usually want to know how global warming will affect their daily lives. Some ask if they will be able to grow the same crops. Others want to know what trees to plant today so that they will thrive in the future. From a city planning side, I've been asked whether storm drains would need to be redesigned to handle the increased likelihood of more extreme precipitation events and whether building codes would need to be changed. I've been asked about the ski industry, tourism, vector-born diseases, parasites, and even whether one should purchase waterfront property. All of these are valid questions and concerns, but in my mind they are not what we should be most troubled about.

If global warming remains unchecked, many species on land and in the oceans will become extinct. Of course, fundamentally it is the rate of climate change that is the problem and the fact that humans are so prevalent throughout the world. If an ecosystem on land collapses in one place, it's pretty difficult for it to re-establish in another place if that area is already occupied by humans. Working Group II of the IPCC's Fourth Assessment Report pointed out that with a further 3°C warming from today's temperatures, 50% of all nature reserves will no longer be able to fulfill their conservation mandate. A question we need to answer as a society is whether we value our natural ecosystems. What cost do we assign to their extinction? Is it simply the lost tourism revenue, or is there some moral and aesthetic cost that is hard to quantify? Does it really matter if there are no more hippopotami, gorillas, tigers, orang-utans, or polar bears? Do we really need the biodiversity in our tropical rainforests? What about lost opportunities, or the so-called unknown unknowns, in which some undiscovered naturally occurring substance may provide unrealized human benefit?

The consequences of global warming will be distributed unevenly and will be largest in some of the world's most impoverished regions. It's well known in economic circles, dating back to work by the late Dutch economist Henri Theil at the University of Florida, that the distance from the equator is a strong indicator of a country's per capita gross domestic product. Obviously there are notable exceptions, such as the bustling economy of Singapore, but most of us would immediately look to the lower latitudes when asked to locate the poorest countries. These are precisely the regions where climate stresses will be greatest. Many of these areas already suffer from chronic water shortages, yet these shortages will only get worse. It's pretty clear that the world's most impoverished nations have contributed negligibly to the cumulative 488 billion tonnes of human-produced carbon emissions. Yet they will still pay the price. These same nations have neither the technological nor the economic ability to adapt to global warming. Developed nations have sown the seeds of discontent, and these seeds could grow to resentment and hostility. Or, if we take appropriate international steps both to mitigate global warming and to assist developing nations in adapting to its effects, these seeds could blossom into a mechanism for creating global stability.

As we move forward into the twenty-first century, the world will have to deal with displaced people, or global warming refugees. As water resources become harder to acquire in subtropical latitudes, millions of people will likely be forced to move in search of food and water. And this will spark regional tensions. Low-lying coastal areas under pressure from rising sea levels will likely be a source of millions more displaced people. How will individual nations respond? Will they open their borders and allow the refugees in or build barriers to keep them out? Already the government of the tiny Pacific islands of Tuvalu has entered into negotiations with New Zealand about the possibility of relocating their twelve thousand residents should the need arise. At the same time, the U.S. government is grappling with what to do with the three hundred and ninety inhabitants of the town of Kivalina, Alaska, while it erodes and sinks into the ocean as the underlying permafrost melts away.

The economic dependence of many major western countries on foreign oil is also problematic. Some of the most productive oil-producing nations also represent some of the most turbulent and unstable regimes. In short, dealing with global warming is about dealing with domestic and global security.

Let's suppose my neighbour doesn't have a job and is struggling to make ends meet. Suppose that I live an affluent lifestyle, and every week I pick up the garbage around my house and dump it over the fence into my neighbour's yard. What would he think? Perhaps he might ask me politely to stop. After a while, if I continued to ignore his pleas, I suspect he might get upset. He may choose to take legal action, or he might take matters into his own hands. I suspect the latter, as I would be able to afford far better lawyers than he would.

Now suppose that instead of household garbage, the junk I threw into his yard made it impossible for him to live in his house. It destroyed his sources of food and water, and his children became deathly ill as a result. I suspect that he'd now become extremely upset. I created the problem, yet he has to pay the consequences with the health and livelihood of his family.

You might imagine one of three possible outcomes. The first scenario is that my neighbour might take his family and quietly go away and die somewhere. Since he was poor and unemployed, his lifetime earnings wouldn't add up to much. As a consequence, there would be little cost to the economy since his life wasn't worth much anyway. Somehow I doubt my neighbour would choose this option.

The second outcome is that he would fight back. I might have seen this coming and hired a brawny mercenary or two to occupy my neighbour's property while he lived there. I would keep my neighbour at bay and let him suffer without bothering me directly. Of course I would have to pay and feed the guards, but that would be a cost I'd willingly incur to ensure my security. Nevertheless, I would still live in fear that one day my neighbour might overpower the guards.

In the third scenario, I might apologize to my neighbour and invite him to live with me.

Suppose instead that I had dealt with the garbage myself. While my neighbour would still be poor and unemployed, at least he wouldn't have to cope with me destroying the environment in which he lived. And how much would it cost for me to deal with the garbage? A few dollars a week to have it picked up and taken to the landfill.

Bringing us back to global warming, for far too long humans have treated the atmosphere as an unregulated dumping ground. We would not tolerate people throwing their garbage all over the neighbourhood; we create a fuss when our streams, rivers, and oceans are loaded with trash; yet we tolerate throwing our waste into the atmosphere. Of course, by using the atmosphere as a dumping ground, our problem becomes someone else's problem.

Defining Dangerous

The objective of the United Nations Framework Convention on Climate Change (UNFCCC) is:

> ... stabilization of greenhouse gas concentrations in the atmosphere at a level that would prevent dangerous anthropogenic interference with the climate system. Such a level should be

achieved within a time frame sufficient to allow ecosystems to adapt naturally to climate change, to ensure that food production is not threatened and to enable economic development to proceed in a sustainable manner.

A question naturally arises as to what exactly defines *dangerous anthropogenic interference*. The UNFCCC objective gives us a clue by suggesting that steps should be taken to ensure that:

1) ecosystems can adapt naturally;
2) food production is not threatened;
3) economic development can proceed in a sustainable manner.

But nowhere does the UNFCCC actually define *dangerous*.

Any definition of dangerous involves value judgments that would vary from person to person, city to city, region to region, and country to country. What I consider to be a dangerous level of global warming in Victoria would be quite different from what someone in Bangladesh, Tuvalu, or Australia might consider to be dangerous. People in drought-stricken southwestern U.S. cities would likely assess danger differently than those in the eastern seaboard communities. It would be virtually impossible to come up with a quantifiable definition of dangerous that would be agreeable to all. And the scientific community would not be able to resolve the issue since assessing value judgments is ultimately a socio-political as opposed to a scientific issue.

Rather than trying to define what constitutes dangerous anthropogenic influence, a general consensus appears to be emerging that global warming should be limited to less than 2°C relative to pre-industrial times (about 1.3°C from today). This is close to the lower bound of warming estimates beyond which the Greenland and perhaps the West Antarctic ice sheet pass the point of no return. While widespread species extinctions will still occur, many of the worst projected ecosystem responses will be avoided. To be sure, the consequences of global warming will be felt everywhere and throughout the economy, but at least the 2°C number appears to be attainable if international policy measures to limit greenhouse gas emissions are implemented immediately. On January 10, 2007, the European Commission, the executive body of the European Union, communicated a suite of actions to limit global warming to no more than 2°C, which was then endorsed by the European unit of Greenpeace. The commission concluded:

> By 2050 global emissions must be reduced by up to 50% compared to 1990, implying reductions in developed countries of 60–80% by 2050. Many developing countries will also need to significantly reduce their emissions.

In 2006, Malte Meinshausen, based at the Potsdam Institute for Climate Impact Research in Germany, assessed the likelihood of limiting global warming to under 2°C for a range of greenhouse gas stabilization scenarios. He based his analysis on what is called equivalent carbon dioxide (CO2e). Each of the six greenhouse gases regulated under the Kyoto Protocol—carbon dioxide, methane, nitrous oxide, HFCs, PFCs, and sulphur hexafluoride—has a different global warming potential. On a molecule-per-molecule basis, all these gases affect the Earth's outgoing longwave radiation differently. Equivalent carbon dioxide represents the combined radiative forcing of all the Kyoto-regulated gases in terms of an equivalent carbon dioxide concentration. Today, CO2e is about 440 ppm (455 ppm, if you count greenhouse gases such as CFCs and ozone not included in the Kyoto Protocol). The positive radiative forcing of all greenhouse gases other than carbon dioxide is almost exactly cancelled out by the negative radiative forcing associated with human-caused aerosols. That is, the current net human-caused radiative forcing is about 385 ppm CO2e, which is the present-day carbon dioxide concentration.

Meinshausen found that if the atmospheric concentration of human-produced greenhouse gases was stabilized at CO2e levels of 550 ppm, then there was a 63% to 99% chance of breaking the 2°C warming threshold. Those aren't the kind of odds you would bet against. He and his Dutch colleague Michel den Elzen found that to keep global warming less than 2°C with a 60% probability, atmospheric CO2e would need to be stabilized at 450 ppm or less. But we are already at 455 ppm CO2e, and we're increasing at 2 ppm per year. If it were not for the cooling effects of human-produced aerosols, we would actually be feeling the full brunt of this 455 ppm CO2e. Nevertheless, these aerosols have very short atmospheric lifetimes, as they are continually rained out.

The 2°C threshold originally entered the public arena shortly after the IPCC released its Second Assessment Report and prior to the establishment of the Kyoto Protocol. In 1996, the Council of the European Union concluded:

> The Council recognizes that, according to the IPCC S.A.R., stabilization of atmospheric concentrations of CO2 at twice the pre-industrial level, i.e. 550 ppm, will eventually require global emissions to be less than 50% of current levels of emissions; such a concentration level is likely to lead to an increase of the global average temperature of around 2°C above the pre-industrial level.

And:

> Given the serious risk of such an increase and particularly the very high rate of change, the Council believes that global average tem-

peratures should not exceed 2 degrees above pre-industrial level
and that therefore concentration levels lower than 550 ppm CO2
[carbon dioxide] should guide global limitation and reduction
efforts. This means that the concentrations of all greenhouse gases
should also be stabilized. This is likely to require a reduction of
emissions of greenhouse gases other than CO2 in particular CH4
[methane] and NO2 [sic; nitrous oxide].

It seems confusing that on the one hand, the EU Council was advocating for carbon dioxide to be stabilized at or below 550 ppm with
emissions eventually dropping to less than 50% of 1996 levels, while on
the other hand, it was arguing for the 2°C threshold not to be exceeded.
Not exceeding the 2°C threshold with a 60% probability requires
atmospheric CO2e to be stabilized at or below 450 ppm and carbon
dioxide emissions eventually going to zero. We've learned a lot about
the carbon cycle since the Council of the European Union released its
recommendations in 1996.

A Declaration on Global Warming

On October 30, 2007, I received an email from Matthew England, a col-
league based at the University of New South Wales (UNSW) in Sydney,
Australia, inviting me to sign the Bali Climate Declaration by Scientists,
for release at the 13th Conference of Parties to the UNFCCC in Bali,
Indonesia, from December 3 to 14. England, Andy Pitman (also from
UNSW), Richard Somerville (University of California, San Diego),
Stefan Rahmstorf (Potsdam Institute for Climate Impact Research in
Germany), and a few others had put together a declaration for which
they were:

> ... seeking signatures from a limited number of climate scientists
> from around the world. This list might ramp up to approx. 80–100
> signatures over the coming weeks. We are inviting national leads
> to sign—the goal is quality not quantity.

They were selective in their distribution, and we were asked not to forward the email on to a wider community since:

> signing is password-protected ... We have done this to ensure that
> the list of signatures is manageable and focused. This declaration
> would gather 100,000 signatures if we let it loose on the wider
> community.

The declaration quickly picked up signatures from more than two hundred leading climate scientists from around the world—a who's who of climate science. It's truly remarkable that a global scientific community would unite in an urgent call for action. This was not done under the auspices of any national or international organization; rather, it was a spontaneous grassroots initiative to essentially plead with governments to take action on global warming. Our climate science community is extraordinarily concerned about the consequences of escalating greenhouse gas emissions. The Bali declaration is a testament to that concern.

The Bali Climate Declaration by Scientists was released at a press conference December 6, 2007. It was reported upon by media outlets all over the world. Did governments listen? (See Chapter 6.)

2007 Bali Climate Declaration by Scientists

This consensus document was prepared under the auspices of the Climate Change Research Centre at the University of New South Wales in Sydney, Australia.

The 2007 IPCC report, compiled by several hundred climate scientists, has unequivocally concluded that our climate is warming rapidly, and that we are now at least 90% certain that this is mostly due to human activities. The amount of carbon dioxide in our atmosphere now far exceeds the natural range of the past 650,000 years, and it is rising very quickly due to human activity. If this trend is not halted soon, many millions of people will be at risk from extreme events such as heat waves, drought, floods and storms, our coasts and cities will be threatened by rising sea levels, and many ecosystems, plants and animal species will be in serious danger of extinction.

The next round of focused negotiations for a new global climate treaty (within the 1992 UNFCCC process) needs to begin in December 2007 and be completed by 2009. The prime goal of this new regime must be to limit global warming to no more than 2°C above the pre-industrial temperature, a limit that has already been formally adopted by the European Union and a number of other countries.

Based on current scientific understanding, this requires that global greenhouse gas emissions need to be reduced by at least 50% below their 1990 levels by the year 2050. In the long run, greenhouse gas concentrations need to be stabilised at a level well below 450 ppm (parts per million; measured in CO_2-equivalent concentration). In order to stay below 2°C, global emissions must peak and decline in the next 10 to 15 years, so there is no time to lose.

As scientists, we urge the negotiators to reach an agreement that takes these targets as a minimum requirement for a fair and effective global climate agreement.

Dear Prime Minister

Closer to home, the Canadian atmospheric and climate science community rallied together April 18, 2006, when Gordon McBean from the University of Western Ontario, Ken Denman from the Department of Fisheries and Oceans, and I sent an open letter to Prime Minister Stephen Harper urging the government "to develop an effective national strategy to deal with the many important aspects of climate that will affect both Canada and the rest of the world in the near future." We were inspired to act after an earlier open letter to Prime Minister Harper, signed by sixty climate change naysayers (including most of the familiar names from around the world), was published in the *National Post* April 6, 2006.

We were incensed by the outlandish scientific statements contained in the April 6 letter; among other things it proposed "comprehensive public-consultation sessions be held so as to examine the scientific foundation of the federal government's climate-change plans." Within just over a week, we collected ninety signatures representing virtually the entire Canadian climate and atmospheric science community. I am still amazed at how quickly our scientific community responded; in fact, we moved so fast that a couple of our colleagues missed the opportunity to sign and berated us about this later.

We were not prescribing policy options but rather urging the government to develop them. This is an important distinction, since as a group our expertise is science and not policy; we know what the problem is, but ultimately developing solutions to the problem requires broader input.

An Open Letter to the Prime Minister of Canada on Climate Change Science

April 18, 2006

The Right Honourable Stephen Harper, P.C., M.P.
Prime Minister of Canada
Ottawa, ON K1A 0A3

Dear Prime Minister:

As climate science leaders from the academic, public and private sectors across Canada, we wish to convey our views on the current state of knowledge of climate change and to call upon you to provide national leadership in addressing the issue. The scientific views we express are shared by the vast majority of the national and international climate science community.

We concur with the climate science assessment of the Intergovernmental Panel on Climate Change (IPCC) in 2001, which has also been supported by the Royal Society of Canada and the national academies of science of all G-8 countries, as well as those of China, India and Brazil. We endorse the conclusions of the IPCC assessment that "There is new and stronger evidence that most of the warming observed over the last 50 years is attributable to human activities" and of the 2005 Arctic Climate Impact Assessment that "Arctic temperatures have risen at almost twice the rate of those in the rest of the world over the past few decades".

Climate variability and change is a global issue and the international IPCC process for assessment of climate science, with its rigorous scientific peer review processes, is the appropriate mechanism for assessing what is known and not known about

climate science. Many Canadian climate scientists are participating in the preparation of the IPCC Fourth Assessment Report
which will be completed in 2007.

The following points emerge from the assessments and ongoing
research by respected Canadian and international researchers:

- There is increasingly unambiguous evidence of changing climate in Canada and around the world.

- There will be increasing impacts of climate change on Canada's
  natural ecosystems and on our socio-economic activities.

- Advances in climate science since the 2001 IPCC Assessment
  have provided more evidence supporting the need for action
  and development of a strategy for adaptation to projected
  changes.

- Canada needs a national climate change strategy with continued investments in research to track the rate and nature of
  changes, understand what is happening, to refine projections
  of changes induced by anthropogenic release of greenhouse
  gases and to analyse opportunities and threats presented by
  these changes.

We have supplied justification and more detail for each of these
points in the accompanying documentation.

We urge you and your government to develop an effective national
strategy to deal with the many important aspects of climate that
will affect both Canada and the rest of the world in the near
future. We believe that sound policy requires good scientific input.

We would be pleased to provide a scientific briefing and further support, clarification and information at any time.

Yours sincerely:

Signed by 90 Canadian climate science leaders from the academic, public and private sectors across the country

Unfortunately, our letter was ignored; instead, Canada has developed a policy of inaction on the climate portfolio. Not only that, our country has played a major role in obstructing international efforts to reduce greenhouse gas emissions.

Target 2050

Both before and after the 2007 release of the IPCC's Fourth Assessment Report, individual cities, states, provinces, and countries began discussing, and in some cases passing, legislation requiring specified reductions in greenhouse gas emissions over the next several decades. One of the key targets emerging from policy discussions is the emission reduction promised by 2050. Examples from several cities, states, provinces, and countries are listed in "Emissions Reduction Targets for 2050."

On March 23, 2007, the city of Toronto released a framework leading to 80% greenhouse gas emission reductions relative to 1990 levels by 2050. Of the American states that have already passed legislation, California has the most aggressive target; states setting 2050 targets such as Illinois, New Mexico, New Jersey, Oregon, and Washington have proposed more modest reductions (ranging from a 50% cut relative to 1990 levels in Washington to an 80% cut relative to 2006 levels in New Jersey). At the national level, three pieces of U.S. legislation have been proposed that call for cuts ranging from 65% relative to 2000 levels to 80% relative to 1990 levels. In Canada, the federal government initially proposed 45% to 65% reductions relative to 2003 levels but later increased this to 60% to 70% relative to 2006 levels; the Official Opposition has called for a 60% to 80% reduction relative to 1990 levels by 2050. Draft legislation has also been introduced in the United Kingdom for a 60% reduction of greenhouse gas emissions relative to 1990 levels by the year 2050, while Greenpeace is calling for a minimum 50% global reduction by this time.

On March 21, 2006, Al Gore testified to the joint hearing by the House Committee on Energy and Commerce's Subcommittee on Energy and Air Quality and the House Committee on Science and Technology's Subcommittee on Energy and Environment and argued for a 90% reduction in greenhouse gas levels by 2050 relative to 1990. Prime Minister Jens Stoltenberg went even further April 19, 2007, declaring that Norway would be carbon neutral (100% emission reduction) by this time. At the G8 meeting in Heiligendamm, Germany, in June 2007, leaders (including the United States) agreed to "consider seriously the decisions made by the European Union, Canada and Japan which include at least a halving of global emissions by 2050." Finally, British Columbia introduced its Greenhouse Gas Reduction Targets Act (Bill 44) on November 20, 2007, setting an 80% reduction relative to 2007 levels as its target. This bill came into force when it received royal assent from the lieutenant-governor November 29, 2007.

Let's have a further look at the internal consistency of proposed global emissions reductions, potential policies aimed at limiting the magnitude of warming, and atmospheric levels of greenhouse gases. Once more, I'll use results from the UVic Earth System Climate Model to illustrate my analysis. A few years ago, Tom Wigley from the U.S. National Center for Atmospheric Research in Boulder, Colorado, assessed the climate implications of the modest greenhouse gas reductions agreed to under the Kyoto Protocol. When averaged over all developed nations, the Kyoto target was a 5.2% emissions reduction averaged over 2008 to 2012 relative to 1990 levels. Not surprisingly, Wigley found that meeting the Kyoto targets had very small effects on global warming during the twenty-first century.

Starting from a pre-industrial equilibrium climate, I force the UVic model with observed natural and human-caused radiative forcing until the end of 2005. After 2005, future trajectories in emissions must be specified. Each of the post-2005 scenarios I use assumes that contributions to radiative forcing from sulphate aerosols and greenhouse gases other than carbon dioxide remained fixed throughout the simulations. An alternative way of looking at this is that any increase in human-produced, non-carbon dioxide greenhouse gases is assumed to be balanced by an increase in sulphate aerosols (or some other negative radiative forcing). This assumption should be viewed as extremely conservative, since most future emissions scenarios have decreasing sulphate emissions and increasing emissions of non-carbon dioxide greenhouse gases.

We'll start by examining the effects of a hypothetical international policy option that linearly cuts emissions by some percentage of 2006 levels by 2050, and maintains emissions constant thereafter until the year 2500 (see "Projected Climatic Response to 2050 Policy Options"). Of course, my baseline case of constant 2006 emissions is substantially more optimistic than the IPCC scenarios, some of which have 2050 emissions at more than double 2006 levels (see "Projected Total CO_2 Emissions, 1990 to 2100"). The various pathways in emissions lead to atmospheric carbon dioxide levels in 2050 ranging from 407 ppm to 466 ppm, corresponding to warming relative to 1800 of between 1.5°C and 1.8°C (parts c) and e) of "Projected Climatic Response to 2050 Policy Options" and "Projected Warming and Carbon Dioxide Levels in Response to 2050 Policy Options"). As the twenty-first

Emissions Reduction Targets for 2050

Government/NGO	2050 reduction:	Relative to:
British Columbia	80%	2007
City of Toronto	80%	1990
California	80%	1990
Illinois	60%	1990
New Mexico	75%	2000
New Jersey	80%	2006
Oregon	75%	1990
Washington	50%	1990
U.S. Proposed (Waxman)	80%	1990
U.S. Proposed (Jeffords)	80%	1990
U.S. Proposed (Kerry)	65%	2000
Canada (Conservative)	45–65%	2003
Canada (Conservative)	60–70%	2006
Canada (Liberal)	60–80%	1990
United Kingdom	60%	1990
France	75%	2000
Germany	80%	1990
Sweden	50%	2004
Greenpeace	50%	1990
Western Australia	60%	2000
South Australia	40%	1990
New South Wales	60%	2005
Al Gore (U.S. Senate)	90%	1990
Norway	100%	n/a
G8	50%	2007

Proposed or legislated 2050 emissions reduction targets relative to a particular year.

century progresses, the atmospheric carbon dioxide levels and warming begin to diverge between scenarios, and by 2100 the range is 394 ppm to 570 ppm, with a warming of between 1.5°C and 2.6°C. None of the emissions trajectories lead to an equilibrium climate and carbon cycle in 2500, although the 90% and 100% sustained 2050 emissions reductions have atmospheric carbon dioxide levels that are levelling off. Of particular note is that by 2500, the scenario depicting a 100% reduction in emissions leads to an atmospheric carbon dioxide level below that in 2006, although global mean surface air temperature is still 0.5°C warmer than in 2006 (1.5°C warmer than 1800). This is the warming commitment in action.

All simulations that have less than a 60% reduction in global emissions by 2050 eventually break the threshold of 2°C warming this century. Particularly disturbing from a policy perspective is that even if emissions are eventually stabilized at 90% less than 2006 levels globally (1.1 billion tonnes of carbon emitted per year), the 2°C threshold warming limit is eventually broken well before the year 2500. This implies that if a 2°C warming is to be avoided, direct carbon dioxide capture from the air, together with subsequent sequestration, would eventually have to be introduced in addition to 90% reductions in global carbon emissions.

I purposely kept emissions constant after 2050 in my idealized scenarios to illustrate that cutting emissions by some prescribed amount by 2050 is in and of itself not sufficient to deal with global warming. Even if we maintain global carbon dioxide emissions at 90% below current levels, we eventually break the 2°C threshold. This is because the natural carbon dioxide removal processes can't work fast enough to take up the emissions we spew into the atmosphere year after year. Any solution to global warming will ultimately require the world either to move toward carbon neutrality or contemplate geo-engineering projects, such as artificially seeding the atmosphere with reflective particles

Projected Climatic Response to 2050 Policy Options

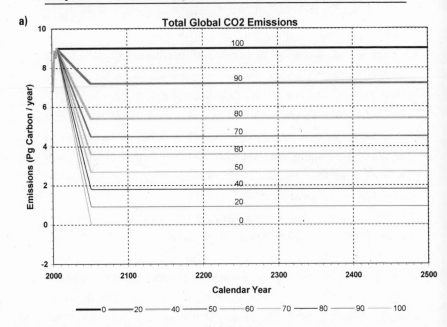

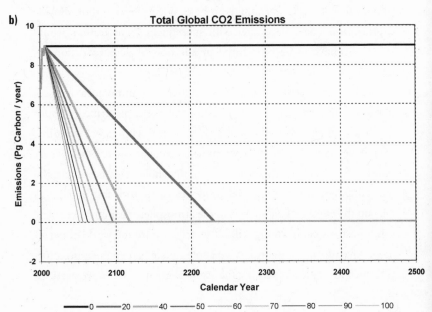

Projected Climatic Response to 2050 Policy Options (*cont.*)

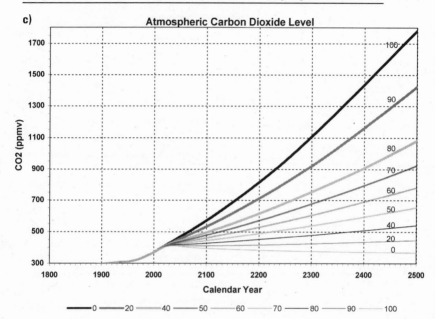

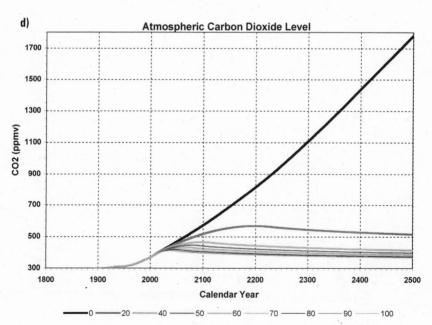

Projected Climatic Response to 2050 Policy Options (*cont.*)

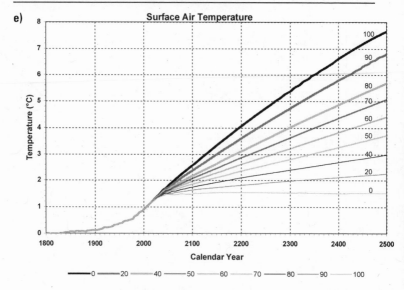

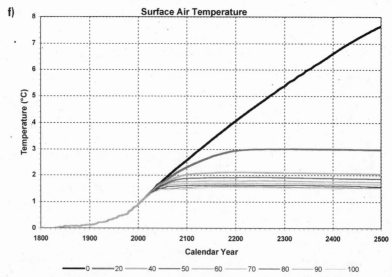

Part a): Specified emissions of carbon dioxide from 2006 onward. The trajectory involves a linear reduction of 0 to 100% of 2006 levels by 2050. From 2050 onward, emissions are held constant. Part b): As in part a) but continuing the linear decrease until zero emissions are reached. Parts c) and d): Atmospheric carbon dioxide. Parts e) and f): Surface air temperatures arising from the emissions shown in parts a) and b) respectively. Prior to 2006, the grey curve in parts c) to e) shows the model response to historical emissions.

or putting reflectors in space, which have their own pitfalls. And frankly, in my mind these pitfalls far outweigh any potential benefit.

The effects of another hypothetical international policy option are worth examining. We start from the results obtained in the previous suite of experiments at 2050 but continue to linearly decrease emissions at the same rate until zero emissions are reached. The resulting emissions are shown in part b) of "Projected Climatic Response to 2050 Policy Options" and the date at which emissions fall to zero is given in "Year Carbon Neutrality is Reached." If we keep emissions on a linearly decreasing emissions path to carbon neutrality, in the UVic model about 45% or greater reductions are required by 2050 if we do not wish to break the 2°C threshold. And peak atmospheric carbon dioxide levels reach a little over 450 ppm before settling down to slightly above 400 ppm.

Year Carbon Neutrality Is Reached

Reduction scenario	Year emissions drop to zero
0%	—
10%	2455
20%	2230
30%	2155
40%	2118
50%	2095
60%	2080
70%	2070
80%	2062
90%	2056
100%	2050

The year at which emissions go to zero for the profiles shown in part b) of "Projected Response to 2050 Policy Options." Each of the experiments consists of a linear reduction in emissions from 2006 levels to the end of 2050. The 2050 percentage reduction is shown in the first column. The emissions continue to be reduced at the same rate until zero emissions are reached.

Projected Warming and Carbon Dioxide Levels in Response to 2050 Policy Options

Year	Reduction scenario	Linear reduction of emissions to 2050; constant emissions thereafter			Linear reduction of emissions to 2050; continuation to zero emissions thereafter		
		Emissions GtC/year	Atmospheric carbon dioxide (ppm)	Global Warming (°C)	Emissions GtC/year	Atmospheric carbon dioxide (ppm)	Global Warming (°C)
2006	—	9.0	380	1.0	9.0	380	1.0
2050	0%	9.0	466	1.8	9.0	466	1.8
2050	20%	7.2	454	1.7	7.2	454	1.7
2050	40%	5.5	442	1.6	5.5	442	1.6
2050	50%	4.6	436	1.6	4.6	436	1.6
2050	60%	3.7	430	1.6	3.7	430	1.6
2050	70%	2.8	424	1.6	2.8	424	1.6
2050	80%	2.0	419	1.5	2.0	419	1.5
2050	90%	1.1	413	1.5	1.1	413	1.5
2050	100%	0.2	407	1.5	0.2	407	1.5
2100	0%	9.0	570	2.6	9.0	570	2.6
2100	20%	7.2	532	2.4	5.2	515	2.3

Year							
2100	40%	5.4	495	2.2	1.5	465	2.0
2100	50%	4.5	477	2.1	0.0	441	1.9
2100	60%	3.6	460	2.0	0.0	424	1.8
2100	70%	2.7	443	1.9	0.0	413	1.7
2100	80%	1.8	426	1.7	0.0	405	1.6
2100	90%	0.9	410	1.6	0.0	399	1.5
2100	100%	0.0	394	1.5	0.0	394	1.5
2500	0%	9.0	1779	7.7	9.0	1779	7.7
2500	20%	7.2	1421	6.8	0.0	514	3.0
2500	40%	5.4	1080	5.7	0.0	414	2.1
2500	50%	4.5	924	5.1	0.0	398	1.9
2500	60%	3.6	780	4.4	0.0	387	1.8
2500	70%	2.7	652	3.7	0.0	380	1.7
2500	80%	1.8	540	3.0	0.0	374	1.6
2500	90%	0.9	445	2.3	0.0	370	1.6
2500	100%	0.0	367	1.5	0.0	367	1.5

Year 2006, 2050, 2100, and 2500 emissions in billions of tonnes of carbon per year (GtC/year), atmospheric carbon dioxide concentration (ppm), and global warming relative to 1800 (°C). Columns 3 to 5 give results from simulations that are forced by a linear reduction in emissions from 2006 levels to the end of 2050, with emissions held fixed thereafter at 2050 levels (columns 6 to 8 assume that after 2050, emissions continue to be reduced at the same rate as they were prior to 2050 until zero emissions are reached.

How Much More Can We Burn?

Another way of helping policy-makers determine what measures must be taken to ensure that global warming is kept below 2°C (or any other agreed-upon value) is to calculate the total cumulative amount of carbon that humans may emit before this threshold is broken. Due to the very long timescales associated with the draw down of human-produced carbon dioxide, all such policy measures need to end up with zero emissions. Nevertheless, I believe that setting policy discussions in a cumulative emissions framework allows for easier international agreement on future emission reduction targets.

Kirsten Zickfeld and Michael Eby (researchers in my laboratory), Damon Matthews (a former Ph.D. student from my lab and now a faculty member at Concordia University), and I further examined these cumulative emissions restrictions using the UVic Earth System Climate Model.

Climate sensitivity is the equilibrium surface warming that occurs in response to a doubling of carbon dioxide. The IPCC's Fourth Assessment Report found that the climate sensitivity was likely in the range 2.0°C to 4.5°C, with a most likely value of 3.0°C and that "values substantially higher than 4.5°C cannot be excluded." In the latest version of the UVic model, complete with its fully interactive carbon cycle model, the climate sensitivity is 3.6°C. Using this version, it turned out that regardless of the emissions pathway, the 2°C threshold was never broken if human emissions from the year 2001 onward were limited to less than 716 billion tonnes of carbon. But humans have already emitted 55 billion tonnes of carbon between 2001 and 2006. This leaves a total of 661 billion tonnes of allowable carbon emissions from 2007 onward if we don't wish to pass the 2°C warming threshold.

To put this number in perspective, humans have emitted about 488 billion tonnes of carbon since pre-industrial times and are currently adding about 10 billion tonnes each year. Rather than going down, the annual emissions are increasing year after year. Even under the B1 emissions scenario (see "Projected Total CO_2 Emissions, 1990 to 2100"), the 661 billion tonnes of allowable carbon will be exhausted by 2070. In most scenarios, we use up our carbon allotment much earlier. And when that happens, we are committed to breaking the 2°C threshold.

I recognize that I've just shown numbers from one model with a single climate sensitivity and haven't provided a range of estimates. That's why we also examined what would happen to the allowable cumulative emissions for a number of climate sensitivities. The results for climate sensitivities ranging from 2°C to 8°C are shown in "Trajectories to Stabilize at Two Degrees Warming" and tabulated in "Allowable Cumulative Emissions." This range was not chosen arbitrarily. In 2006, Chris Forest and colleagues from the Massachusetts Institute of Technology provided an estimated probability distribution of climate sensitivity that incorporated twentieth-century observations. Consistent with the IPCC likely range of 2.0°C to 4.5°C, with a most likely value of 3.0°C and higher uncertainty in the upper bound, Forest and his colleagues determined that there was a 90% likelihood that climate sensitivity lay within the range 2.1°C to 8.9°C, with a most probable value of about 3°C. Let's look at the range of cumulative allowable emissions over this range of climate sensitivity.

For a low value of climate sensitivity (2°C), 1314 billion tonnes of carbon can be emitted to the atmosphere without breaking the 2°C threshold. Atmospheric carbon dioxide levels peak at about 578 ppm before starting to slowly decrease. For a high value of climate sensitivity (8°C), only 163 billion tonnes of carbon can be released from 2007 onwards. That's only another sixteen years at current levels of emissions. In fact, even if we linearly cut emissions by 90% of 2006 levels by 2050 (see part b) of "Projected Climatic Response to

Allowable Cumulative Emissions

Climate sensitivity (°C)	Allowable cumulative emissions (GtC/year) from 2001 to 2500	Allowable cumulative emissions (GtC/year) from 2007 to 2500	Peak atmospheric carbon dioxide concentration (ppm)
2	1369	1314	578
3	875	820	495
3.6	716	661	470
4	625	570	458
4.5	539	484	445
6	358	303	422
8	218	163	405

Allowable cumulative emissions from 2001 (column 2) and 2007 (column 3) onward for different climate sensitivities (column 1) that cannot be exceeded if the 2°C global warming threshold is not to be breached. The final column shows the peak atmospheric carbon dioxide concentration (the current level is 385 ppm).

2050 Policy Options"), continuing down to zero emissions at 2056 ("Year Carbon Neutrality is Reached"), we will have ended up emitting 220 billion tonnes of carbon, thereby committing us to a 2°C warming if the climate sensitivity turns out to be this high. Let's hope it doesn't.

Finally, let's suppose we take the upper bound of climate sensitivity from the IPCC likely range of 2°C to 4.5°C. In the IPCC terminology, likely implies a greater than 66% probability that the actual climate sensitivity falls within this range. In this case, atmospheric carbon dioxide levels peak at 445 ppm and total allowable cumulative emissions are 484 billion tonnes from 2007 onward.

I want to re-emphasize that it's not the actual emissions pathway that matters but rather the total overall cumulative emissions of carbon that counts. Stabilization of global warming at some temperature, however, requires every pathway eventually to arrive at zero emissions. If you now look back at "Projected Total CO_2 Emissions, 1990 to 2100," each IPCC

Trajectories to Stabilize at Two Degrees Warming

a)

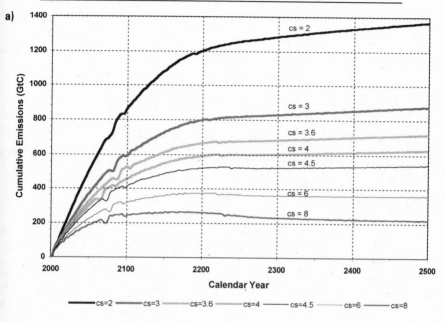

b)

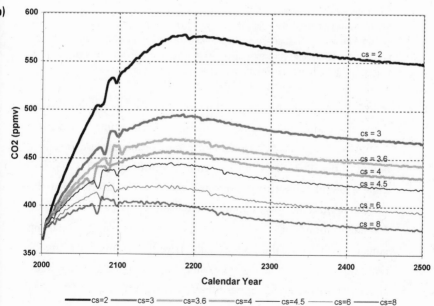

Trajectories to Stabilize at Two Degrees Warming (*cont.*)

c)

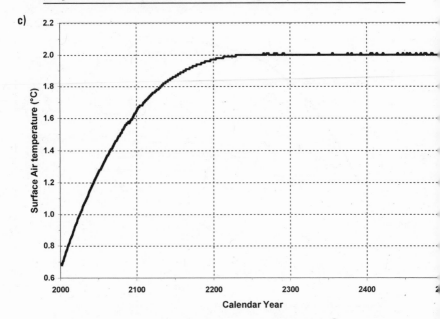

Cumulative emissions from 2001 (part a): billions of tonnes of carbon [GtC]) and resulting atmospheric carbon dioxide concentration (part b): ppmv) leading to stabilization at 2°C. The surface air temperature trajectory (°C) is shown in part c), although the total cumulative emissions required for stabilization is insensitive to this trajectory. Each different curve corresponds to a different climate sensitivity (cs).

trajectory eventually breaks the allowable cumulative carbon emission threshold (820 billion tonnes) for the most likely estimate of climate sensitivity (3°C). In fact, it would be far more prudent to use the upper bound of the IPCC likely range of climate sensitivity (4.5°C) to determine allowable cumulative emissions. So if society accepts that the 2°C threshold is the upper bound of acceptable global warming, we have 484 billion tonnes of allowable carbon emissions to play with starting January 1, 2007, until the day we finally arrive at zero emissions. And for each year we dither about deciding what to do, we lose 10 billion tonnes, at current emission rates, of our future carbon allotment.

6

Investing in the Future

Do we have any responsibility for the well-being of future generations? This fundamental ethical question underlies the debate about
what—if anything—should be done about global warming. It requires
value judgments from broad elements of society. I believe the answer is
yes; in fact, I believe that through its broader actions, society has already
accepted the inherent rights of future generations.

Although future generations are not able to contribute to our deci-
sion-making process, they will be affected by it. Some economists argue
that we should do little because future damages are difficult to cost and
would be insignificant when compared to the cost of early action. It
would be better to invest money today to be able to pay for future damages. But the problem with this argument lies in how the future costs
(social, environmental, and economic) are converted into their equivalent present-day value.

Economic arguments that suggest it's too expensive to act now to
avoid future costs may have some merit for costs associated with
weather-related disasters (flooding, the destruction of infrastructure
by strong storms, or the occasional drought), but they fall apart when
it comes to sustained, irreversible changes to our planet. Or, frankly,
the destruction of civilization as we know it. How do you cost the

commitment to extinction of 40% to 70% of all species? How do you value the cost of a life? I find these questions morally repugnant, yet life must be valued in any economic cost-benefit analysis of dealing with global warming. How do you differentiate the cost of a life between developed and developing nations? Do you use the lifetime earnings of the average individual? If so, poor people are less valuable than rich people. And poor nations are less valuable than developed nations. The world will have to deal with displaced people as water resources become scarce in subtropical latitudes. How do we cost this? Do we simply price the cost, suitably discounted, of relocating these people? Do we ignore the obvious regional tensions and global insecurity issues that will arise? Deciding whether to deal with global warming is far more complex than textbook economics.

It's a basic human instinct to want to provide for your children and to offer them a better life. Many Canadians are the offspring of immigrants who came to Canada for precisely this reason. If you have children, you would probably agree that they have as much right to enjoy our standard of living as we do; our parents would have thought the same for us. We enjoy our high standards of living today because of the hard work of previous generations. Each year on November 11 we remember those who gave their lives to ensure that we could live better and more peaceful lives.

Many of us have bought Registered Education Savings Plans to provide our children with better education; we probably have written wills to ensure they are looked after in case something happens to us. Some may have acquired an additional property as a nest egg for their children in case they can't afford housing costs down the road. As a society, we have created national parks and nature reserves to conserve our ecosystems for future generations. We have banned CFCs to preserve the ozone layer and mandated the removal of lead from gasoline. We have set standards to reduce harmful emissions. Forest companies must replant trees and mining companies must reclaim the landscapes once these resources have been extracted. We have taken steps to ensure that we don't pollute our streams, lakes, and oceans. Why? To preserve them for future generations.

Now it doesn't take a great leap of faith to believe that our children will feel the same way about their children. They would want us to preserve the environment so that their children could enjoy it. And if we care about our children, we will listen to them.

Modern society has a rich history of considering the long-term implications of its actions, whether they be environmental or financial. On February 26, 2008, with reference to paying down our national debt, Minister of Finance Jim Flaherty told Peter Mansbridge on the *CBC National News*: "The other thing about reducing public debt is it's a matter of intergenerational equity. That is, we should not be passing on debt to the next generation…." I agree. However, the same argument of intergenerational equity would imply that today's generation should not leave future generations to deal with the problems of global warming.

Sharing the Responsibility

Ignoring global warming is not an option. Pretending it's not going to happen will not make it go away. We have warming in store for many decades to come, as the climate system responds to the levels of greenhouse gases already in the atmosphere. We will need to develop adaptation strategies and take appropriate measures to reduce the costs associated with them. At the same time, we will need to determine an unacceptable level of global warming and take appropriate measures to ensure this level is not surpassed.

In the 2007 Bali Climate Declaration by Scientists, the scientific community stated that 2°C above pre-industrial levels (a number endorsed by the European Union) was an unacceptable level of global warming. If we set this number as our limit, humans may emit only about 484 billion tonnes of carbon to the atmosphere starting January 1, 2007. But how does one equitably partition those 484 billion tonnes among various nations?

Any future global agreement to meet the inevitable mandatory reductions in emissions will have to reflect several realities:

1) The atmosphere does not care who emits the carbon dioxide; its radiative effects are the same if the gas is released from China, the United States, or Botswana;

2) The global carbon cycle and the atmosphere are affected by the total cumulative carbon dioxide emissions, not just the emissions in any given year;

3) The lion's share of cumulative emissions has come from the developed nations (with less than 20% of the global population);

4) People in less developed nations aspire to increase their standard of living;

5) Any solution to global warming will necessarily involve everyone eventually reaching carbon neutrality;

and, ironically, the most controversial yet only defensible position:

6) "Every individual is equal before and under the law and has the right to the equal protection and equal benefit of the law without discrimination and, in particular, without discrimination based on race, national or ethnic origin, colour, religion, sex, age or mental or physical disability."

You should recognize the quote at the end: It's article 15(2) of the Canadian Charter of Rights and Freedoms.

The fact that everyone has to eventually eliminate their emissions and arrive at carbon neutrality makes it a little easier to construct an international policy framework. Achieving carbon neutrality is a grand challenge, but it's one that we can and must meet. The good news is that an international policy framework already exists. In the early 1990s, Aubrey Meyer, founder of the U.K.-based Global Commons Institute, developed "contraction and convergence." The concept is simple and straightforward.

First, you determine what level of global warming is tolerable and what is unacceptable. We'll use 2°C as the threshold. Second, you determine the allowable emissions that would keep you within this target. Our analysis suggests 539 billion tonnes of carbon from 2001 onward (484 billion tonnes from 2007 onward). This corresponds to the assumption of a 4.5°C climate sensitivity, the upper bound of the IPCC likely range, meaning that there is less than a 33% chance of breaking the 2°C threshold. The final contraction target is carbon neutrality, and we'll assume this occurs in 2100.

Now we must allocate the 539 billion tonnes of carbon emissions to individual countries between 2001 and 2100. This is the convergence phase. On the convergence date, the principle of global equity is evoked, and every person on Earth is given the right to emit the same amount of carbon. That is, per capita carbon emissions for all countries converge to a common number. We'll use 2075 as the convergence year, although there is no reason why it could not be the same as the contraction year, 2100. Finally, a date has to be chosen beyond which additional credits are not gained for increasing your country's population. That is, increasing your allowable emissions by increasing your country's birth rate is not to be encouraged.

Part a) of "Equitable Emissions Pathway" illustrates a sample global emissions trajectory. The model started at 2000 and allocated 539 billion tonnes of cumulative emissions. Since the model was not constrained to follow the actual emissions from 2001 to 2007, it ended up assigning annual carbon emissions that attain a value well below the 9.9 billion tonnes emitted in 2006. Nevertheless, peak global carbon emissions of 8.8 billion tonnes occur in 2020 and decline continually thereafter. But in North America, this peak occurs in 2008 (see part c)). Eastern Asia, which includes China, has peak emissions in 2029, and Central Asia, which includes India, has peak emissions in 2043. Carbon neutrality is reached in 2100. In reality, with global carbon emissions already at close to 10 billion tonnes per year, the descent to carbon neutrality would have to be steeper than that portrayed in part a).

The purpose of this example is not to argue for a particular emissions trajectory but rather to illustrate an equitable framework for allocating carbon emissions as we move toward carbon neutrality. To ensure the success of such a program, emissions rights need to be binding and tradable among individual nations. The contraction and convergence framework would eventually force per capita emissions reductions on everyone. Yet the developed nations, whose cumulative emissions are responsible for the situation we are in today, would be required to make the biggest per capita reductions initially (see part b) of "Equitable Emissions Pathway"). And these are the same nations with the economic wherewithal to do so.

So what is stopping nations from moving forward in a post-Kyoto world? To be honest, I have no idea. Our government's position is that it will only sign an international agreement with binding targets on developed nations if all nations, including China and India, are included. At the 2007 Commonwealth Heads of Government Meeting in Uganda, Canada scuttled efforts aimed at getting consensus on a strongly worded commitment to greenhouse gas reduction. Instead, the Commonwealth

Equitable Emissions Pathway

a)

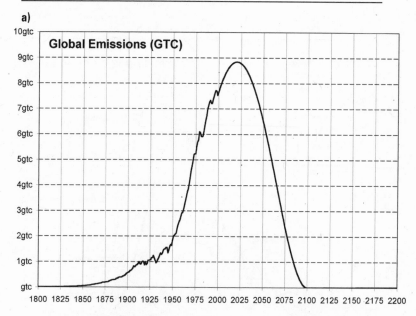

b)

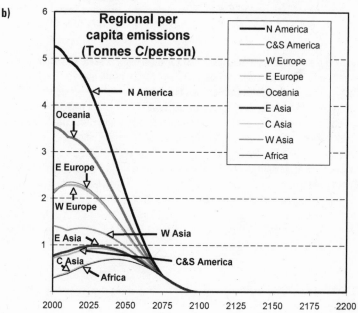

Equitable Emissions Pathway (*cont.*)

c)

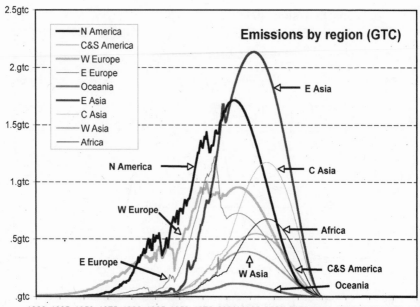

An example of an emissions pathway that could equitably allocate 539 billion tonnes of carbon to individual countries from 2001 until carbon neutrality is reached at 2100. Part a): Annual mean global carbon emissions in billions of tonnes of carbon (GtC). Part b): Annual mean regional per capita emissions in tonnes per person. Part c): Annual mean regional emissions in billions of tonnes of carbon (GtC). There are nine regions: Africa, Oceania, Central Asia (which includes India), Central and South America, Western Asia (which includes the middle east), Eastern Asia (which includes China), Eastern Europe, Western Europe, and North America (which includes Canada and the United States). The contraction and convergence approach uses a fourth-order polynomial to fit the curves. Initial and final emissions growth rates must also be specified.

leaders adopted the warm and fuzzy *Lake Victoria Commonwealth Climate Change Action Plan,* which included the statement:

> Our shared goal should be to achieve a comprehensive post-2012 global agreement that strengthens, broadens, and deepens current arrangements and leads to reduced emissions of global greenhouse gases. This should include a long term aspirational global goal for emissions reduction to which all countries would contribute.

I have no idea what *aspirational targets* are. It strikes me that this political mumbo-jumbo translates into *targets that we have no intention of achieving.*

If a horde of lemmings was running toward a cliff and you were one of those lemmings, albeit a little smarter than the rest, would you continue running with the pack toward the cliff? Or would you step aside and try to warn the other lemmings of the imminent danger? I think the answer is obvious.

Suppose that your child got into trouble for bullying a classmate. When you asked for an explanation, your child responded: "Because Bobby did it." Would you accept that excuse? Probably not. You would probably say that just because Bobby did it doesn't mean it was the right thing to do. You might even ask your child if he or she would jump off a cliff if Bobby did that too.

These simple examples illustrate the absurdity of the arguments "We will not agree to cut emissions unless everyone else does" and "We're going to keep emitting because China does." Yet these are precisely the childish arguments being put forward by Canada as a basis for international climate policy. A more defensible position would be to offer a constructive framework that would bring the world toward carbon neutrality before it's too late. In light of the broad support that already exists for contraction and convergence from China, India, the European

Union, and the Africa Group of Nations, it would not be too onerous a task. Doing so would also restore Canada's credibility as a global leader. Or are we content to remain just another obstructionist lemming?

"Stop Eating the Cheese"

Stabilization of the climate system requires carbon dioxide emissions to be eventually eliminated. The natural mechanisms for drawing down carbon dioxide on land and in oceans cannot keep up with the rate of emissions. As the climate system warms, these natural mechanisms also become less efficient. At the current rate, the terrestrial biosphere will turn from a net sink to a net source of carbon dioxide toward the end of this century. It's only after thousands of years that carbonate dissolution from marine sediments can start to increase the alkalinity of the upper ocean and allow for enhanced oceanic uptake of carbon dioxide. It takes tens of thousands to hundreds of thousands of years for chemical weathering to return the atmosphere's carbon dioxide levels back to normal. It strikes me that we have two options. The first is to eliminate carbon dioxide emissions and the second is geo-engineering.

Geo-engineering involves humans deliberately altering the climate to counterbalance the warming from increasing greenhouse gases. Many examples have been considered, including scattering tiny reflective particles in the upper atmosphere, placing satellites in orbits with retractable mirrors that could reflect solar radiation back to space on demand, and sprinkling the ocean with iron in the hope that enhanced biological activity would draw down carbon dioxide. I find all these ideas disconcerting, and they remind me of a 1965 children's book called *The King, the Mice and the Cheese* by Nancy and Eric Gurney.

A king likes cheese so much that his palace gets infested with mice. Unable to cope with the infestation, the king asks his wise men what he should do. They suggest bringing in cats to get rid of the mice. The king complies and the cats do their thing, but now the palace is infested with cats. Once more, the wise men are summoned. You guessed it. Dogs are brought in to get rid of the cats. Then lions are brought in to get rid of the dogs and finally elephants to rid the palace of the lions. Now the king is not very happy with the elephants wrecking the palace so again he seeks counsel with his wise men. The wise men decide to bring the mice back to get rid of the elephants; everyone is back at square one. The king took three days to ponder what he called "the only answer." His solution involved the mice and him agreeing to get along with one another; he would share his cheese with them and they would develop good manners.

That's the problem with geo-engineering. In trying to solve one problem, you may create an entirely different suite of problems. But that risk shouldn't entirely exclude geo-engineering options. Human ingenuity may be called upon to remove greenhouse gases that we have put into the atmosphere. Perhaps we will be able to find ways of controlling and speeding up chemical weathering. Technologies exist today that would allow us to extract carbon dioxide directly from the air, but they are very expensive. But if someone comes up with an effective and economically viable solution, they would be eligible for Richard Branson's $25-million award as part of the Virgin Earth Challenge.

When I read *The King, the Mice and the Cheese* to elementary schoolchildren at the end of visits or their field trips to my lab, I always pause just before I reveal the king's "only answer." I ask the children what *they* think the king should do. To this day I have never had a student say "share the cheese with the mice." Invariably, within seconds, they say in unison "stop eating the cheese." Funny how the adults didn't get it, but the children always do.

Emissions-Free Energy Options

Dealing with global warming requires us to fundamentally reconstruct our global energy system. We must find new ways of creating, storing, and using energy that do not produce greenhouse gas emissions. Existing energy technologies have to compete in the marketplace on a level playing field with traditional fossil fuels. This means eliminating tax subsidies for the fossil fuel industry. And it means paying the true cost of emitting greenhouse gases to the atmosphere. With the exception of airplane travel, low-emission or emission-free alternatives exist for most technological applications. With a little human ingenuity, we'll soon be flying in hydrogen-powered jets.

Ask yourself how many technologies you are aware of that have remained largely unchanged for more than a hundred years. There were no computers, televisions, satellites, cellphones, or Nintendo Wiis at the beginning of the twentieth century. Yet the internal combustion engine has remained almost the same over this entire time. Why is that? We've been able to put people on the moon since 1969, but we're still unable to advance the automobile engine beyond tiny explosions that cause pistons to move up and down. Is it really because humans lack the ingenuity and ability to design alternative technologies? Or are there other reasons? What happened to the electric trams that were prevalent in many North American cities? Were they really economically unviable? Many of them were bought up in the 1930s and 1940s by a major automobile company, working with a tire company and an oil company. They were then shut down and replaced with diesel buses.

In the early 1920s, lead was added to gasoline to reduce uneven fuel combustion known as engine knocking. For decades the auto industry vigorously defended the additive, dismissing concerns about its known toxicity to humans. Concerns over air quality arising from automobile exhaust led to U.S. emissions standards being regulated beginning in 1970. The automobile industry vehemently argued that requiring catalytic converters would kill their industry. It didn't. They have subsequently argued that mandatory seatbelts and air bags would also kill their industry. It didn't. And now they're complaining about improved fuel standards. The resistance to change continues. In fact, what is killing the North American car industry is their refusal to make cars that people want to buy. While North American car manufacturers are bemoaning their annual losses, Japanese car manufacturers rake in record profits.

But if we suddenly made fuel-efficient or, heaven forbid, zero-emission automobiles, what would we do with the massive infrastructure that extracts fossil fuels from the ground, delivers them to refineries, and transports them to our service stations? And the internal combustion engine has many moving parts that require regular maintenance. It becomes obvious why we don't produce highly efficient or zero-emission vehicles. It's not because we can't; rather it's because certain special interests need to preserve a marketplace for a commodity in which they have a vested interest. This needs to change.

In Canada, 22% of all greenhouse gas emissions come from the transportation sector; in British Columbia, it's 38%. Think about where each of us drives in any given day. We might commute to work, take our kids to school and other activities; we might go shopping, to the movies, or to visit friends. Only rarely do we go on long trips. Very few people would drive more than a few hundred kilometres in a day, well within the range of an electric vehicle. Yet I can't go to the car dealership and buy an electric vehicle even though I want to. Hydrogen fuel cell vehicles may be a technology of tomorrow, but electric vehicles are a technology we have today. Even hybrid automobiles, with their increased fuel efficiency, are only an interim technology. Why did we not go straight to the plug-in hybrid that would allow virtually all travelling to be done on electric power with gasoline only as a backup on long trips or if there were a power outage?

Moving toward zero-emission vehicles has many co-benefits for the consumer. They are quiet and do not produce toxic exhaust. They are also less costly to run and they do not require oil changes every six months. But we have to be able to buy them.

You might argue that electricity is needed to charge the batteries in an electric vehicle. And in many parts of the world that electricity is coming from coal. You would be right, which is why any global solution to global warming will also require the complete elimination of greenhouse gas emissions from electricity production. Again, there are technologies that exist.

First, there is nuclear energy. Already I can hear the groans, but think of the following. When you burn coal, the emissions are distributed globally. With nuclear power, your waste storage is local. Those who generate the power are required to deal with its by-products rather than tossing them into their neighbour's yard. And if you think nuclear waste lasts a long time, remember that if known fossil fuel reserves are burnt, 50% of the emitted carbon dioxide will stay in the atmosphere for more than two thousand years and two-thirds of the maximum temperature anomaly will persist for longer than ten thousand years. These timescales are not all that different from those associated with the decay of nuclear waste. Whatever your opinion of nuclear power, it needs to be discussed as one item in a basket of possible solutions to the global warming problem.

Second, there are the renewables such as solar, wind, geothermal, tidal, wave, hydro, and biomass, some of which are more cost effective than others. It starts to get interesting when you combine two or three of these options. Wind energy is incapable of meeting base demand since energy is only produced when it is windy. So it needs to be coupled with another form of energy that can produce electricity on demand. In Alberta, wind power production has been growing steadily. However, Alberta's backup supply of electricity is largely coal-based. It takes a long time to ramp up and turn off a coal-fired power plant. So when wind is available to generate electricity, rather than the coal plant shutting down, the burning and emissions continue but now no electricity is produced. An Alberta power utility has recently announced the construction of a massive electricity production facility that will burn natural gas, thereby alleviating this dilemma (natural gas facilities can turn on and off rapidly). Nevertheless, coupling wind energy with hydro power in places such as Manitoba and British Columbia, which are already heavily dependent on hydro electricity, would allow for better load levelling. Excess wind energy could even be used to pump water back uphill. And the more energy produced by renewables, the less we are dependent on coal-based electricity.

In recent years, clean coal has been trumpeted as a potential emissions-free solution to our energy needs. The concept involves capturing the emissions (including carbon dioxide) and storing them underground in geologic formations. While I'm tempted to label the term *clean coal* an oxymoron, I am prepared to reserve judgment until successful demonstration projects that capture 100% of carbon dioxide emissions are in place. To date, carbon capture and storage technology is only 80% to 90% efficient and very costly. It is also necessary to couple any sequestration with a long-term carbon dioxide monitoring system to ensure there are no leaks back to the Earth's surface. Carbon dioxide is heavier than air, and in large quantities, it can pool and displace oxygen and nitrogen. This is what happened between 9 and 10 P.M. on August 21, 1986, when a vast amount of carbon dioxide was released from an extinct volcano lying below Lake Nyos in Cameroon. Thousands of animals and 1746 people in the neighbouring areas died from suffocation. Escaping carbon dioxide could therefore pose a significant, albeit local, risk.

Switching from fossil fuels to emissions-free energy sources will not happen without resistance. Each new hydro project or nuclear plant will likely be opposed by well-meaning environmental groups or concerned citizens. People will complain about windmills blocking their view. The public dialogue will be riddled with outlandish and demonstrably false assertions such as windmills will devastate local bird populations or a hydro project will create more greenhouse emissions than it will displace by eliminating a coal-burning power plant. But what are the options? It's unrealistic to expect people to stop using energy. People are prepared to use energy more efficiently simply because it saves money, but they do not aspire to a declining quality of life. Until global leaders are brave enough to deal with Earth's ever-increasing human population, energy demand will continue to grow. So in the years ahead, environmental organizations and citizen groups will have to work constructively to support emissions-free energy options. Modern society has no choice but to move toward carbon neutrality if we hope to preserve our well-being. Emissions-free energy production is the only means of getting there.

Carbon Tax

So how can governments facilitate change? Voluntary measures, public education programs, and aspirational targets have resulted in two decades of failure to decrease greenhouse gas emissions in Canada and elsewhere. Even some subsidy programs have been fiercely criticized as rewarding (in the words of Jeffrey Simpson, Mark Jaccard, and Nic Rivers) free riders—those who receive a subsidy for doing something that they would have done anyway as it made economic sense to do so. Governments only have two options. First, they can legislate regulations. Second, they can use the taxation system to facilitate change.

The only way to solve the looming global warming crisis is to eliminate our dependence on fossil fuels. There are no other options. This may spell bad news for the oil, gas, and coal industry, but it will provide other economic opportunities the world has never seen before. Rather than trying to prop up a sector that we know has to change, innovative policy measures should be adopted to take advantage of the financial opportunities provided by the switch from fossil fuels.

One policy measure that has been adopted is the cap-and-trade system. Rather than a government initially assigning emission allowances to heavy emitters as they did in Europe, proponents of the cap-and-trade system argue that it is better to auction them off to industries instead. This way, a fair market price is assigned to the emission permits. The problem with this system is that it is inefficient and difficult to regulate.

Fortunately, there is an extremely efficient and readily accessible solution available to governments—the carbon tax. In the fall of 2007, seventy academic economists in B.C. universities wrote a letter to the B.C. finance minister, urging her to: "include a revenue neutral carbon tax in your upcoming budget."

Rick Hyndman, senior policy adviser for the Canadian Association of Petroleum Producers, told the *Georgia Straight* in December 2007: "The carbon tax, levy, or whatever you want to call it, is the better way to go." I have yet to meet an economist who disagrees with this assessment.

The carbon tax is simple. Governments assign a price to a tonne of carbon dioxide emissions and then add that price to the cost of energy that produced those emissions. To make the tax revenue neutral, other forms of taxation are reduced. Central to the carbon tax system is the belief that the atmosphere can no longer be treated as a free dumping ground.

Ensuring that the tax is revenue neutral is extremely important if one wishes to gain public support for the introduction of a carbon tax. There are two candidates for attaining tax neutrality. First, you could use the carbon tax to reduce or replace the provincial sales tax (PST) or the federal goods and services tax (GST). Second, you could use it to reduce income taxes. Any effort to reduce income taxes would need to be sensitive to low-income earners who might otherwise be overly burdened by the carbon tax. This could easily be accomplished by increasing basic personal exemptions or by disproportionately reducing rates in the lowest tax brackets. The beauty of the carbon tax is that it propagates throughout every aspect of the economy. This means that consumers pay the true cost of the goods and services they acquire. Consumers have more money in their pockets to spend on more carbon-friendly products. As the carbon tax is increased in the years ahead, renewable forms of energy become more competitively priced.

There are many other co-benefits to the carbon tax that are rarely discussed. As the carbon tax permeates throughout the economy, the cost of locally produced products goes down relative to the cost of those transported from faraway places. Cars built in Ontario wouldn't have to be delivered as far as those built in Japan; and if they were more fuel efficient, or emissions-free, they would be even more desirable to the consumer. Locally grown food becomes more competitive with food produced on mega-farms thousands of kilometres away. We may even wean ourselves from our dependence on cheap labour in Asia, since a carbon tax would build transportation costs into the price of those goods. In principle, a carbon tax could be used as a levy on products from countries or individual foreign factories that use high carbon energy sources and are not subject to their own national carbon taxation system.

All the while, consumers would have more disposable income. We could use our pocketbooks to drive us to carbon neutrality. But for this to occur, government decision makers need to stop listening to oil, gas, and coal industry lobbyists who have vested interests in maintaining the status quo. The sooner carbon taxes are introduced into our global economy, the sooner we make the transition to a carbon-neutral world.

A Plan to Form Yet Another Plan

The IPCC reports released throughout 2007 galvanized worldwide public opinion on the need for action to deal with global warming. There were huge expectations for a successful outcome to the 13th Conference of Parties to the UNFCCC in Bali, Indonesia, from December 3 to 14. The Bali meeting turned out to be another *Gong Show*. Rather than entering the history books as a celebrated event, it will be remembered as an historic waste of time. And true to form, Canada was an international embarrassment, winning a total of fourteen not-so-flattering Fossil of the Day awards given by the international organization Avaaz.org (see "Fossil of the Day Awards").

Fossil of the Day Awards

Country	Firsts	Seconds	Thirds	Total	Points
Canada	4	3	7	14	25
USA	3	5	6	14	25
Japan	2	3	4	9	16
Saudi Arabia	3	2	0	5	13
Australia	1	0	1	2	4
Russia	1	0	0	1	3
EU	0	0	1	1	1

Countries awarded Fossil of the Day awards by the international organization Avaaz.org at the 13th Conference of Parties to the UNFCCC in Bali, Indonesia, December 3 to 14, 2007. Each day, three awards were presented "to the countries who've done the most to block progress at the talks." *www.avaaz.org/fossils.*

Canada would only agree to binding targets if the developing world also agreed to binding targets. It then invoked the Montreal Protocol on ozone depletion as an example for the world to follow. (It makes me wonder if the Canadian delegation actually read the Montreal Protocol, since it committed the developed world to eliminate ozone-depleting substances first as they had the economic and technological wherewithal to do so.) Canada resisted all attempts to include specific reference to 25% to 40% reduction targets by 2020 proposed by the European Union and others. Our country also blocked efforts to include language calling for global emissions to peak in ten to fifteen years.

Why would the Canadian government take such an obstructionist position on the international policy scene? Perhaps it's because our current government has deep roots in Alberta and, in particular, the burgeoning tar sands sector. In 2005, Alberta oil sand production was 966,000 barrels per day, and by 2020 this is expected to increase to three million barrels per day. With oil prices over $100 a barrel, there's a great deal of money to be made by the oil sector. Preserving this future income at all costs seems to be the fundamental consideration driving the climate agenda of the Harper government.

But there's money to be made in other energy sectors as we wean ourselves from our addiction to fossil fuels. On November 27, 2007, Google announced "a new strategic initiative to develop electricity from renewable energy sources that will be cheaper than electricity from coal." Google plans to invest hundreds of millions of dollars in its new initiative. And it's not doing this to lose money. According to Google co-founder Larry Page, "We expect this would be good for business as well." These recent developments within Google, America's fifth largest company (behind Exxon Mobil, GE, Microsoft, and AT & T), are a testament to the fact that there are numerous opportunities for innovation and growth as we move to carbon neutrality.

You will often hear those averse to reducing greenhouse gas emissions say that it will be too costly and that there will be job losses. What they invariably fail to mention is that there will also be opportunities and job creation in other aspects of the economy. California, a trend-setter in terms of climate policy in North America, currently has the second lowest per capita emissions of all fifty U.S. states. Yet it also has the ninth highest gross domestic product per capita. Low emissions do not equate with a collapsing economy. Imagine if a North American car manufacturer produced plug-in hybrid vehicles. There would be a surge in demand for these emissions-free and cheap-to-run vehicles. There would be money to be made in building and selling them. And the technology exists. I have always viewed dealing with global warming as not only representing a challenge but also a huge economic opportunity, much like the internet wave of the 1990s. Google obviously thinks so too.

The Bali meeting was a colossal disappointment: 187 nations finally agreed on an Action Plan, but that plan was only to form another group, known as the Ad Hoc Working Group on Long-term Cooperative Action under the Convention. The working group is tasked with conducting a *process* in order to arrive at an *agreed outcome* and to *adopt a decision* at the 15th Conference of Parties to the UNFCCC in Denmark November 20 to December 11, 2009. Everything is vague. In fact, the only element of the Bali Climate Declaration by Scientists that ended up in the Bali Action Plan was the agreement that negotiations needed "to begin in December 2007 and be completed by 2009." Fortunately, the working group is to commence its work immediately and will report upon its progress at the 14th Conference of Parties in Poland December 1 to 12, 2008.

Nevertheless, in trying to put on a brave face, the United Nations released a press release at the conclusion of the event, stating: "UN Breakthrough on climate change reached in Bali."

The only breakthrough was that negotiations didn't completely fall apart and the countries agreed to continue meeting with the aim of eventually reaching an agreement to reduce greenhouse gas emissions. Two more years means another 20 billion tonnnes of carbon being released to the atmosphere. That leaves a margin of only 454 billion tonnes (484 billion tonnes less 10 billion tonnes per year from 2007) of carbon emissions before the 2°C warming threshold is committed to being broken with a high probability.

Break Free of Your Car

Reducing our carbon emissions will not only require technological innovation, but it will also rely heavily upon behavioural change. In North America, this may pose the most difficult hurdle to overcome as we have become so accustomed to unbounded consumption. This is obviously unsustainable on Earth with its finite resources. But behavioural change is not only possible, we've seen it happen many times before.

Take the issue of smoking. Thirty years ago you could pretty much smoke anywhere you wanted. Now it's deemed socially unacceptable, and smoking is banned in most public areas. How many of you would tolerate an adult smoking at the front entrance of your child's school while parents dropped off their children? Probably not many. As a society, we've recognized the health risks associated with second-hand smoke and our behaviour has changed accordingly. But would you care if a parent left their gas-guzzling SUV idling for ten minutes while they caught up on the latest school gossip? Probably not, even though the exhaust fumes are likely just as toxic as the second-hand cigarette smoke. And that's not even taking into account the greenhouse gases.

I recognize that I've picked on the automobile a fair amount, but I've done so for a reason. The car is a symbol of consumption, status, and affluence. It's a polluting relic from a bygone era that is at the very heart of the problem of global warming. Advertisements encourage us to buy bigger and more powerful vehicles. We drive them around our cities and towns for all our family, friends, and neighbours to admire. I look forward to the day when people look at a gas-guzzling SUV with disdain instead of admiration. Frankly, I've never understood why people would spend so much money on a depreciating asset anyway.

The Power of Change

It's a normal human reaction to resist change and instead try to preserve the status quo. Yet global warming will bring change to the world like it has never experienced in the history of humankind. But that change is not going to happen overnight. It's precisely for this reason that so many of our politicians have been reluctant to introduce policies to deal with global warming. They're elected for four-year terms and might perceive the introduction of a revenue-neutral carbon tax as a death sentence on their prospects for re-election. The public wants leadership, yet leadership is so hard to come by. When politicians—whether they be local, provincial, or national—stick their necks out to try to deal with global warming, the public, and especially environmental groups, will need to be supportive.

A beautiful example of resistance to change comes from my own neighbourhood in a suburb of Victoria, B.C. Our local transit authority proposed two new routes to be served by small community buses that only hold twenty passengers. The routes were designed to take commuters in unserviced areas to the main bus hub at the University of Victoria, the area's biggest employer. Many university students also live in secondary suites in the areas to be served. Rather than embracing the two new routes as a means of alleviating traffic congestion, noise, and unnecessary emissions, a group of concerned citizens, supported by the local residents' association, initiated a campaign to stop the new routes from being introduced. Their argument was that the neighbourhood did not have sidewalks and children walking to school would no longer be safe. The logic of this argument is mind-boggling as it implies that a professional driver operating a small community bus not much bigger than a minivan is somehow less safe than all the drivers he or she has taken off the road.

Two recent attempts at developing large plots of land in my neighbourhood with a mixture of residential and light commercial zoning were also resisted by my local residents' association over traffic concerns. They argued that commercial zoning already existed along the main street in the area, even though that was far away from where most people lived. Once more, the argument made little sense and struck me more as a fear of change. As it stands, very few can walk to a grocery store, video store, pharmacy, or restaurant—they all drive. Having distributed light commercial zoning throughout suburbs reduces, rather than increases, traffic.

I am not trying to single out my local residents' association but it's the only one that affects the community in which I live. I am sure that the same resistance to change exists throughout North America. Yet change is necessary if we wish to deal with global warming. Part of the change requires limiting the amount of energy we need to consume, whether it is through reducing our transportation requirements, or increasing the efficiency in the way we use energy. By itself, conservation will not be enough to take us to carbon neutrality, but it certainly will help us reach this target. Moreover, change can be empowering to the individual. Rather than fearing the unknown, one can view it as an opportunity for innovation and creativity. At the same time, reducing your energy consumption saves you money.

Carrots and Sticks

As I sat down November 16, 2007, to read the morning paper, two stories caught my attention. The first headline read: "Arctic Ocean could be ice-free in the summer as early as 2010." The second headline was: "Try environmental carrot first, B.C. legislature report says." The first story involved an interview with Canadian scientist Louis Fortier from the Université Laval, in which he discussed the dramatic 2007 Arctic sea ice melt. Fortier correctly pointed out that the 2007 Arctic melt back far exceeded even the most pessimistic scientific projections. He projected that the Arctic could be ice-free in the summer somewhere between 2010 and 2015.

The second story covered the release of a report from the Select Standing Committee on Finance and Government Services. This committee had just finished criss-crossing British Columbia soliciting public input, proposals, and recommendations concerning the upcoming 2008 B.C. budget. While the 102-page report contained myriad recommendations on all aspects of the economy, its second recommendation is particularly relevant:

> 2. take decisive action to reduce greenhouse gas emissions.

The third recommendation provided some additional guidance:

> 3. provide clear and concise information on programs and measures available to individuals and businesses on steps they may take to reduce greenhouse gases and incentives that are available to do so.

In the news story, Bill Bennett, the chair of the standing committee and the MLA for East Kootenay, stated that most submissions to the committee suggested using "the carrot, not the stick" and that "If the carrot doesn't work, then consider the stick."

I found it particularly ironic that the story about disappearing Arctic sea ice was directly beneath a half-page spread with the headline "Weird dinosaur with shovel-like mouth vacuumed greens through rows of teeth" along with an artist's conception of a 110-million-year-old *Nigersaurus taqueti*. Our greenhouse gas levels are on track to reach those that have not been seen since *Nigersaurus taqueti* and his sauropod cousins roamed the Earth. I hope the irony was not lost on others; it certainly made me stop and think. Unfortunately, three decades of incentives and voluntary emissions reductions targets have done nothing to curb our ever-increasing emissions.

The Business Community Call to Action

By 2009, the world's leaders will have to produce an international agreement that will take us to carbon neutrality. Voluntary measures and aspirational targets cannot form the basis of such an agreement if we hope to curb our greenhouse emissions. Canada can play a productive role in future negotiations and save face at the same time if it promotes and supports a contraction and convergence framework. Such an approach would acknowledge the leadership role that developed nations must play, yet commit all nations to eventual carbon reductions. And it would do so in an equitable fashion.

Governments have policy instruments to guide society to carbon neutrality. The most efficient and easiest to implement is the revenue-neutral carbon tax. It has the beauty of not prescribing the technological outcomes but rather driving the markets to be more innovative and develop their own solutions. Governments could supplement carbon taxes with cap-and-trade systems on heavy emitters. Of course, with time, the carbon tax would have to go up and the cap would have to go down in order to wean us from our dependence on fossil fuels.

Both the public and business leaders are ready for change. On October 1, 2007, the Canadian Council of Chief Executives (CCCE) issued a statement calling for "aggressive action to tackle climate change, drive energy innovation and strengthen economic perform-ance." The thirty-three CEOs on the CCCE Task Force on Environmental Leadership who signed the eleven-page statement rep-resented many of Canada's top corporations. The CCCE called for a national plan to deal with global warming, noting that everyone would have to accept their "share of the responsibility." They viewed curbing global warming as an economic opportunity. Perhaps most surprising is that the CCCE called for "price signals," which translate into assigning a future cost to the price of greenhouse gas emissions. And this cost, they argued, could be applied through either an environ-mental tax (another term for a carbon tax) or a cap-and-trade system.

Without knowing which CEOs signed, a cynic might suspect that they would be from companies who had something to gain if tough tar-gets for reducing greenhouse gas emissions were imposed. The list shown in "Canadian Corporations Represented on the CCCE Task Force" will surprise you. It seems the Canadian government is not only out of touch with public opinion, but also with industry.

It's not only Canadian business leaders calling for action. On November 30, 2007, leaders from one hundred and fifty of the world's largest companies issued The Bali Communiqué, which called for:

- a comprehensive, legally binding United Nations framework to tackle climate change;

- emission reduction targets to be guided primarily by science;

- those countries that have already industrialised to make the greatest effort;

- world leaders to seize the window of opportunity and agree a work plan of negotiations to ensure an agreement can come into force post 2012 (when the existing Kyoto Protocol expires).

Canadian Corporations Represented on the CCCE Task Force

Agrium Inc.	E.I. du Pont Canada Company	Pengrowth Management Ltd.
Alcan Inc.	Edco Financial Holdings Ltd.	Petro-Canada
Amaranth Resources Limited	General Electric Canada	Power Corporation of Canada
Bowater Incorporated	GreenField Ethanol Inc.	Royal Bank of Canada
Bruce Power	IBM Canada Ltd.	SNC-Lavalin Group Inc.
Canadian Council of Chief Executives	Imperial Oil Limited	Stone Creek Properties Inc.
Canadian Oil Sands Limited	James Richardson & Sons, Ltd.	Suncor Energy Inc.
Canadian Pacific Railway Company	Linamar Corporation	Teck Cominco Limited
Coril Holdings Ltd.	Manulife Financial	The Home Depot Canada
Direct Energy	NOVA Chemicals	TransAlta Corporation
Dow Chemical Canada Inc.	Palliser Furniture Ltd.	Ultramar Ltd.

Canadian corporations whose presidents or CEOs serve on the CCCE Task Force on Environmental Leadership and signed an eleven-page statement calling for aggressive action to deal with global warming.

Some countries are ahead of the game in developing technological solutions to global warming. Iceland, which already obtains most of its electricity and heating from renewable energy sources, has vowed it will become the world's first hydrogen economy. Its vision is a transportation sector dominated by fuel cell vehicles. Others apparently share this vision, since a number of car companies are using Iceland, with its progressive governmental attitude toward hydrogen power, as a testing ground for fuel cell technology.

Dealing with global warming today, when much of the developed world is democratically governed, is possible and preferable to waiting until some future time. As global warming increases, its impact will become more and more severe. Governments can easily initiate change by sending price signals to the marketplace through a carbon tax or cap-and-trade systems. Doing so might upset a few self-serving individuals or companies in certain sectors of our economy. But they'll get over it. The consequences of not limiting greenhouse gas emissions are so severe that the entire world's population will be affected. And we won't get over it. If we reach the stage of crisis management, I can't see how our western democracies will survive unless we move toward a War Measures Act or despot style of governance with centralized power in the hands of a few. I doubt many of us would want to head down that path.

• • •

EVERY SPRING, nature gives us a glimpse of one of the future possible outcomes of our current unsustainable lifestyle. During the winter months, winds stir the ocean surface, bringing nutrients up from the deeper layers. These nutrients are vital for the growth of brainless marine algae known as phytoplankton. With the arrival of sunshine in the spring, the phytoplankton start to bloom. They grow and consume exponentially until all the nutrients are used up; their population then collapses. The early inhabitants of Easter Island in the southeast Pacific Ocean fared no better. Deforestation and overconsumption led to the widespread extinction of native plants and animals, as well as to the collapse of their society. Yet this is the same path modern civilization is now on. There is still time for us to avoid the most serious consequences of global warming if we take action now. I think humans are smarter than phytoplankton.

Epilogue

A FEW DAYS BEFORE B.C. finance minister Carol Taylor delivered her February 19, 2008, budget speech, staff from the B.C. Ministry of Environment had invited me to observe from the legislature's public gallery. Staff from the Ministry of Finance had also contacted me, wondering whether I would be interested in attending the budget lock-up. Seeing as I couldn't be in two places at once, I chose to witness the budget speech in person.

The government would probably not be inviting me to the legislature if it was going to be a bad-news budget from an environmental perspective. I knew something was up; my suspicions were further heightened when I saw Taylor enter the legislature dressed in green.

After a preamble framing the context of the budget, Taylor began:

> With this budget, we are introducing a major shift in the way we levy taxes.

> Effective July 1st, we intend to put a price on carbon-emitting fuels in B.C. This carbon tax will be entirely revenue neutral, meaning every dollar raised will be returned to the people of B.C. in the form of lower taxes. Furthermore, that commitment will be enshrined in law. And we will provide additional support for lower-income British Columbians.

I was stunned. I've argued that sending a price signal to the market through a revenue-neutral carbon tax was the most efficient means of reducing emissions. The cornerstone of the B.C. budget was precisely this policy. And they enshrined the revenue neutrality in legislation.

In 2008, British Columbia will assign $10 per tonne to carbon emissions, a price that will increase by $5 per tonne in each year. What's important is not so much this initial number, but rather the signal to the market about the future increase in the cost of emissions. In British Columbia, consumers and business can now price carbon emissions into their longer term decision making.

In June 2007, Quebec announced it was going to add a small carbon tax to fossil fuel products sold in that province. Their carbon tax came into effect October 2007, but it took a fundamentally different form from the one in British Columbia. In Quebec, a fixed tax was applied to fossil fuels. Propane was taxed at 0.5 cents per litre, gasoline at 0.8 cents per litre, diesel at 0.9 cents per litre, and light heating oil at 0.96 cents per litre. It was a tax designed to generate the funds required to support public transit initiatives and other provincial projects aimed at reducing greenhouse gas emissions. The market was not being sent a signal that the price of carbon emissions was going to increase annually and the tax was not revenue neutral.

After the B.C. budget, Ontario and the federal government were quick to point out they were not considering a carbon tax. Ontario premier Dalton McGuinty told Maria Babbage of the Canadian Press on February 21 that "... we're doing something different here in Ontario that suits our economy and the direction it's pursuing." Their immediate focus was apparently attempting to shut down coal-fired electricity production plants. The federal government, on the other hand, claimed they were going to take a regulatory approach with an emphasis on large industrial emitters.

One thing you can bet on is that other jurisdictions are watching closely what transpires in British Columbia. British Columbia cleverly started off its carbon tax at a meagre $10 per tonne, with legislated increases of $5 per tonne in each of the next four years. It turns out that companies typically charge around $20 per tonne to offset your carbon emissions. From their perspective, that's the market price. By starting low, other jurisdictions can watch British Columbia's implementation and presumed success in reducing emissions associated with the escalating price of carbon. On July 1, 2010, shortly after the world has finished watching the 2010 Winter Olympics in British Columbia, the price of carbon will hit $20 per tonne. By this time I hope that numerous other North American provinces and states will have realized that costing emissions and sending a price signal to the market is ultimately the only effective way of reducing these emissions. And by July 1, 2010, I expect these states and provinces will begin joining British Columbia through the use of its groundbreaking approach to emissions reduction—the carbon tax.

Mixed Messages

As British Columbia breaks new ground with innovative policies to mitigate global warming while positioning itself to take advantage of the resulting economic opportunities, it remains a circus in Ottawa. First, the federal government opposed a patchwork of different policies being implemented in different provinces and at the federal level. On January 14, 2008, Finance Minister Jim Flaherty told the Canadian Press:

> Generally speaking, the consensus I would say is that it is desirable in Canada not to have multiple regulators in various areas of the economy.

He further argued:

> We've urged the provinces to get together on this with the government of Canada and to practice co-operative federalism so that we can work together on it and accomplish the goal.

On February 20, Environment Minister John Baird told Becky Rynor of the Canwest News Service:

> Environment is a shared jurisdiction between federal and provincial government

and that

> Every province's situation is unique.... So each province has a different reality in terms of their greenhouse gas emissions and will take different strategies.

Are you confused? So am I.

Muzzling Environment Canada

On January 18, 2008, I received an email from the Green Party of Canada inviting me to attend a February 13 reception in Ottawa to honour the Canadians involved in the Nobel Prize–winning IPCC. I politely declined. I felt uncomfortable accepting this invitation as

I expected it to come from the Government of Canada and not a party without elected representatives in the House of Commons. In the United States, President George W. Bush held such a reception for American IPCC scientists and Al Gore in November 2007.

Two weeks later, yet another email invitation arrived, but this time it was coming from the Liberal Party, New Democratic Party, Bloc Québécois, and the Green Party. Once more, I politely declined. I was dismayed by the absence of the Government of Canada on the invitation. While I was grateful to the other parties for hosting the reception, I was worried that the event would end up becoming entirely political.

The reception went forward as planned, and as expected the Tories were punished by the media for boycotting the event. Perhaps most damning was Rick Mercer's rant on the February 19 CBC *Rick Mercer Report*. He said, "… we cannot allow the government to declare war on knowledge, otherwise we all lose. Unless of course they start passing out Nobel Prizes for idiocy."

The day after the reception, Environment Minister John Baird sent all Environment Canada scientists involved in the IPCC an invitation to a March 4 reception in Ottawa designed to honour them. University-based scientists were excluded. I very much doubt the Environment Canada scientists were in any mood for a party. Just a few weeks earlier they had received directives from Ottawa that they could no longer respond to media questions concerning their science without going through media relations in Ottawa. In effect, they were muzzled.

Let's suppose that a new scientific study appears in *Nature* or *Science* and that a reporter wants to understand what's important about the work. Alternatively, let's suppose that an unusual ice storm wreaks havoc on Prince Edward Island and a reporter wants to know what caused it. In the past, a reporter would phone a local expert who would explain the science behind the study or weather event. Now the reporter would be directed to Ottawa, and the Environment Canada scientist would have to notify his or her immediate supervisor. A media relations officer would ask the reporter for a written list of questions; the questions would be sent back to the scientist, who would be asked to provide a written list of responses. The scientist's answers would spin their way through Ottawa media relations staff as they decided what the official Government of Canada position would be. As indicated in the PowerPoint presentation circulated to Environment Canada staff, this could include:

Asking the programme expert to respond with approved lines

Having media relations respond

Referring the call to the Minister's Office

Referring the call to another department

Motivating this Orwellian control of science was a desire to ensure that Environment Canada had "one department, one voice" since "interviews sometimes result in surprises to Minister and Senior Management." Ottawa's manufacturing the message of science had two effects. The first was that Environment Canada scientists stopped doing interviews. It was simply too much of a hassle and a headache. The second was that the media stopped going to Environment Canada scientists for assistance with their science stories. The reporters could not afford to wait for days while Ottawa bureaucrats decided the politically appropriate scientific explanation. As a taxpayer, I am incensed that publicly funded scientists are no longer able to convey their expertise to the public via the media.

The editorial writers of *Nature*, the world's most prestigious scientific journal, obviously thought so too. In a scathing piece entitled

"Science in retreat: Canada has been scientifically healthy. Not so its government" published February 21, 2008, they criticized the Harper government for its "manifest disregard for science," citing evidence of the government's skepticism of the climate change science as one of many examples. As noted by Margaret Munro in her February 21 Canwest News Service story:

> … a chorus of leading and increasingly frustrated Canadian scientists say the editorial is pretty much bang-on

And this included the president of the prestigious Royal Society of Canada's Academy of Sciences.

Nature is not to be taken lightly. The journal is read by scientists of all disciplines in countries around the world. In fact, the article was brought to my attention by a former student living in New Zealand. What message are we as a nation sending to the world?

We Can't Wait for Federal Leadership

"Alberta to cut projected emissions by 50 per cent under new climate change plan," read the headline of the January 24, 2008, news release from the Alberta government. At first glance, this sounds very impressive. But closer inspection reveals that this 50% reduction is measured relative to emissions that would occur in the absence of policy (i.e., business as usual). In actual fact, the Alberta plan, which is heavily dependent on the capturing of emissions associated with oil sands production and storing these emissions in underground reservoirs, would lead to a 14% reduction from 2005 levels by 2050.

Alberta currently produces about 31% of all Canada's emissions. The Harper government has further pledged an *aspirational* greenhouse gas reduction target of 60% to 70% by 2050. So if Alberta only cuts its emissions by 14%, everyone else in Canada must cut their emissions by 81% if Canada is to reduce its emissions nationally by 60%. That's more than the 80% reduction legislated in British Columbia. If Canada aspires to reduce its emissions 70% by 2050, then everyone apart from Albertans would have to cut their emissions by 96%! The disconnect between Alberta and federal initiatives is staggering.

On June 4, 2007, Stephen Harper told European leaders in Berlin, Germany, that climate change was "perhaps the biggest threat to confront the future of humanity today." Yet the February 26, 2008, federal budget, advertised under the title "Responsible Leadership," gave no indication that the government took these words seriously. Rather than sending a price signal to the market and allowing its efficiency to come up with the technological solutions to global warming, the government decided it knew best. Funding was doled out to the energy and automobile sectors to facilitate their investment in new technologies. While British Columbia is introducing incentives to promote the purchase of eco-friendly automobiles, the federal government cancels their programs to do the same. In essence, the government was promoting the status quo.

The visionary leadership of British Columbia continues to fill me with optimism. I look forward to other provinces following its lead (and other states following California's lead) in the move toward carbon neutrality. Waiting for federal leadership is no longer an option. The time to deal with global warming is now.

Acknowledgments

OVER THE YEARS I have been fortunate to have worked with some truly outstanding graduate students and post-doctoral fellows, most of whom have taught me much more than I have ever taught them. Their enthusiasm for learning and their dedication to understanding their fields of research continues to inspire me.

My writing benefited from discussions with far too many individuals to list here. I am particularly grateful to Julie Arblaster, Seth Borenstein, Max Boykoff, Matthew Bramley, Ken Caldeira, Michael Eby, Greg Flato, John Fyfe, Nathan Gillett, Kevin Grandia, Jonathan Gregory, Slava Kharin, Alvaro Montenegro, Margaret Munro, Val Shore, Dáithí Stone, Stephen Toleikis, Kevin Trenberth, and Diana Varela for their advice, comments, discussions, or other input. Thanks also to Tom Richardson of AtmosClear Water Company for his endless supply of five-gallon water containers that continually replenished my home office water cooler as I wrote this book.

I am especially grateful to my colleagues Stephen Johnston and Edward Wiebe, as well as my father, John Weaver, for reading and providing extensive comments on each chapter as it was written. I thank Chris Avis, Jeremy Fyke, Theodore Raptis, and Ralph Shaw for their comments on the first draft of the whole book and Tom Pedersen, Ken Denman, Kirsten Zickfeld, and Katrin Meissner for their detailed review of individual chapters. Heather Sangster at Strong Finish did a marvellous job with the copy-editing. I sincerely appreciate the care with which she examined early drafts. Her perceptive editorial eye certainly improved the presentation enormously.

Some of the analysis in this book relies on simulations obtained from the University of Victoria (UVic) Earth System Climate Model. I am indebted to Michael Eby, who conducted most of the simulations and is responsible for building and maintaining the UVic model. I am further indebted to Edward Wiebe, who has put together our computing network and climate model visualization tools, and Wanda Lewis, who ensures that my research laboratory operates smoothly. And of course, without the financial and infrastructure support from the Canada Research Chairs Program, the Canadian Foundation for Climate and Atmospheric Sciences, the Natural Sciences and Engineering Research Council, the Canadian Foundation for Innovation, the Killam Research Fellowship Program, and the University of Victoria, none of my research over the years would have been possible.

Finally, without the continued support of my wonderful family I would never have been able to complete this book. I dedicate this book to them.

Sources

Introduction: A Change in the Wind

Folland, C.K., T. Karl, J.R. Christy, R.A. Clarke, G.V. Gruza, J. Jouzel, M.E. Mann, J. Oerlemans, M.J. Salinger, and S.-W. Wang. 2001. Observed climate variability and change. In *Climate Change 2001: The Scientific Basis. Contribution of Working Group I to the Third Assessment Report of the Intergovernmental Panel on Climate Change*, eds. J.T. Houghton, Y. Ding, D.J. Griggs, M. Noguer, P.J. van der Linden, X. Dai, K. Maskell, and C.A. Johnson, 99–181. Cambridge, U.K.: Cambridge University Press.

Gillett, N.P., A.J. Weaver, F.W. Zwiers, and M.D. Flannigan. 2004. Detecting the effect of human induced climate change on Canadian forest fires. *Geophysical Research Letters* 31, L18211, doi:10.1029/2004GL020876.

Groisman, P.Y., B.G. Sherstyukov, V.N. Razuvaev, R.W. Knight, J.G. Enloec, N.S. Stroumentova, P.H. Whitfield, E. Førland, I. Hannsen-Bauer, H. Tuomenvirta, H. Aleksandersson, A.V. Mescherskaya, and T.R. Karl. 2007. Potential forest fire danger over Northern Eurasia: changes during the 20th century. *Global and Planetary Change* 56:371–386.

Le Page, M. 2007. Climate change: A guide for the perplexed. *New Scientist Online*, May 16. Available at http://environment.newscientist.com/channel/earth/dn11462.

Stocks, B.J., J.A. Mason, J.B. Todd, E.M. Bosch, B.M. Wotton, B.D. Amiro, M.D. Flannigan, K.G. Hirsch, K.A. Logan, D.L. Martell, and W.R. Skinner. 2003. Large forest fires in Canada, 1959–1997. *Journal of Geophysical Research* 108(D1), 8149, doi:10.1029/2001JD000484.

Westerling, A.L., H.G. Hidalgo, D.R. Cayan, and T.W. Swetnam. 2006. Warming and earlier spring increase Western U.S. forest wildfire activity. *Science* 313:940–843.

Zhang, X., F.W. Zwiers, G.C. Hegerl, F.H. Lambert, N.P. Gillett, S. Solomon, P.A. Stott, and T. Nozawa. 2007. Detection of human influence on twentieth-century precipitation trends. *Nature* 448:461–465.

Chapter 1: Global Warming in the News

Azenabor, A.A., P. Kennedy, and S. Balistreri. 2007. Chlamydia trachomatis infection of human trophoblast alters estrogen and progesterone biosynthesis: an insight into role of infection in pregnancy sequelae. *International Journal of Medical Sciences* 4:223–231.

Begley, S. 2007. The truth about denial. *Newsweek*, August 13. Available at www.newsweek.com/id/32482.

Boykoff, M.T. 2007. Flogging a dead norm? Newspaper coverage of anthropogenic climate change in the United States and United Kingdom from 2003–2006. *Area* 39:470–481.

———. 2008. Lost in translation? United States television news coverage of anthropogenic climate change, 1995–2004. *Climatic Change* 86:1–11.

——— and J.M. Boykoff. 2004. Balance as bias: global warming and the U.S. prestige press. *Global Environmental Change* 14:125–136.

Bramley, M. 2007. Analysis of the Government of Canada's April 2007 greenhouse gas policy announcement. Pembina Institute Report. Available at http://pubs.pembina.org/reports/Reg_framework_comments.pdf.

CBC-TV's *the fifth estate*. 2006. *The Denial Machine*, first aired November 15. Available at www.cbc.ca/fifth/denialmachine/.

Christy, J.R., D.E. Parker, S.J. Brown, I. Macadam, M. Stendel, and W.B. Norris. 2001. Differential trends in tropical sea surface and atmospheric temperatures since 1979. *Geophysical Research Letters* 28(1):183–186.

Folland, C.K., T. Karl, J.R. Christy, R.A. Clarke, G.V. Gruza, J. Jouzel, M.E Mann, J. Oerlemans, M.J. Salinger, and S.-W. Wang. 2001. Observed climate variability and change. In *Climate Change 2001: The Scientific Basis. Contribution of Working Group I to the Third Assessment Report of the Intergovernmental Panel on Climate Change*, eds. J.T. Houghton, Y. Ding, D.J. Griggs, M. Noguer, P.J. van der Linden, X. Dai, K. Maskell, and C.A. Johnson, 99–181. Cambridge, U.K.: Cambridge University Press.

Gelbspan, R. 1998. *The heat is on: The high stakes battle over Earth's threatened climate.* New York: Addison-Wesley.

———. 2004. *Boiling point: How politicians, big oil and coal, journalists, and activists have fueled the climate crisis—and what we can do to avert disaster.* New York: Basic Books.

Holland, M.M., C.M. Bitz, and B. Tremblay. 2006. Future abrupt reductions in the summer arctic sea ice. *Geophysical Research Letters* 33:L23503, doi:10.1029/2006GL028024.

Jaccard, M. and N. Rivers. 2007. Estimating the effect of the Canadian government's 2006–2007 greenhouse gas policies. C.D. Howe Institute, Working Paper, June.

Leggett, J., W.J. Pepper, and R.J. Swart. 1992. Emissions scenarios for the IPCC: an update. In *Climate Change 1992: The Supplementary Report to the IPCC Scientific Assessment*, eds. J.T. Houghton, B.A. Callander, and S.K. Varney, 69–95. Cambridge, U.K.: Cambridge University Press.

Lemke, P., J. Ren, R.B. Alley, I. Allison, J. Carrasco, G. Flato, Y. Fujii, G. Kaser, P. Mote, R.H. Thomas, and T. Zhang. 2007. Observations: changes in snow, ice and frozen ground. In *Climate Change 2007: The Physical Science Basis. Contribution of Working Group I to the Fourth Assessment Report of the Intergovernmental Panel on Climate Change*, eds. S. Solomon, D. Qin, M. Manning, Z. Chen, M. Marquis, K.B. Averyt, M. Tignor, and H.L. Miller, 337–383. Cambridge, U.K.: Cambridge University Press.

Montgomery, C. 2006. Mr. Cool: Nurturing doubt about climate change is big business. *Globe and Mail*, August 12. Available at www.charlesmontgomery.ca/mrcool.html.

Nakicenovic, N., J. Alcamo, G. Davis, B. de Vries, J. Fenhann, S. Gaffin, K. Gregory, A. Grübler, T.Y. Jung, T. Kram, E.L. La Rovere, L. Michaelis, S. Mori, T. Morita, W. Pepper, H. Pitcher, L. Price, K. Riahi, A. Roehrl, H.-H. Rogner, A. Sankovski, M. Schlesinger, P. Shukla, S. Smith, R. Swart, S. van Rooijen, N. Victor, and Z. Dadi. 2000. *IPCC Special Report on Emissions Scenarios*. Cambridge, U.K.: Cambridge University Press.

Stroeve, J., M.M. Holland, W. Meier, T. Scambos, and M. Serreze. 2007. Arctic sea ice decline: faster than forecast. *Geophysical Research Letters* 34:L09501, doi:10.1029/2007GL029703.

Trenberth, K.E., P.D. Jones, P. Ambenje, R. Bojariu, D. Easterling, A. Klein Tank, D. Parker, F. Rahimzadeh, J.A. Renwick, M. Rusticucci, B. Soden, and P. Zhai. 2007. Observations: surface and atmospheric climate change. In *Climate Change 2001: The Scientific Basis. Contribution of Working Group I to the Third Assessment Report of the Intergovernmental Panel on Climate Change*, eds. J.T. Houghton, Y. Ding, D.J. Griggs, M. Noguer, P.J. van der Linden, X. Dai, K. Maskell, and C.A. Johnson, 235–336. Cambridge, U.K.: Cambridge University Press.

Chapter 2: A Passage Through Time

Arrhenius, S. 1896. On the influence of carbonic acid in the air upon the temperature of the ground. *Philosophical Magazine and Journal of Science* 41:237–276.

Broecker, W.S. 1975. Climatic change: Are we on the brink of a pronounced global warming? *Science* 189:460–463.

Callendar, G.S. 1938. The artificial production of carbon dioxide and its influence on climate. *Quarterly Journal of the Royal Meteorological Society* 64:223–240.

CBC News. 2007. Harper's letter dismisses Kyoto as 'socialist scheme,' January 30. Available at http://www.cbc.ca/canada/story/2007/01/30/harper-kyoto.html.

Christianson, G.E. 1999. *Greenhouse: the 200-year history of global warming.* New York: Walker Publishing Company.

Fleming, J.R. 1998. *Historical perspectives on climate change.* New York, U.S.A.: Oxford University Press.

———. 1999. Joseph Fourier, the 'greenhouse effect,' and the quest for a universal theory of terrestrial temperatures. *Endeavour* 23(2):72–75.

———. 2007. *The life and work of Guy Stewart Callendar (1898–1964), the scientist who established the carbon dioxide theory of climate change.* Boston: American Meteorological Society.

———. and J. Fleming. 2007. *The papers of Guy Stewart Callendar, digital edition.* Boston: American Meteorological Society.

Fourier, J.B.J. 1824. Remarques générales sur les températures du globe terrestre et des espaces planétaires. *Annales de chimie et de physique* 27:136–167.

IPCC. 2004. Who is who in the IPCC, IPCC secretariat, Geneva, Switzerland. Now available at www.ersilia.org/canvi_climatic/documents/IPPC/IPCC_Whoiswho.pdf.

———. 2006. Principles governing IPCC work. Available at www.ipcc.ch/pdf/ipcc-principles/ipcc-principles.

Keeling, C.D. 1970. Is carbon dioxide from fossil fuel changing man's environment? *Proceedings of the American Philosophical Society* 114(1):10–17.

Le Treut, H., R. Somerville, U. Cubasch, Y. Ding, C. Mauritzen, A. Mokssit, T. Peterson, and M. Prather. 2007. Historical overview of climate change. In *Climate Change 2007: The Physical Science Basis. Contribution of Working Group I to the Fourth Assessment Report of the Intergovernmental Panel on Climate Change*, eds. S. Solomon, D. Qin, M. Manning, Z. Chen, M. Marquis, K.B. Averyt, M. Tignor, and H.L. Miller, 94–127. Cambridge, U.K.: Cambridge University Press.

Manabe, S. and R.T. Wetherald. 1975. The effects of doubling the CO_2 concentration on the climate of a general circulation model. *Journal of the Atmospheric Sciences* 32 (1):3–15.

Marland, G., T.A. Boden, and R.J. Andres. 2007. Global, regional, and national fossil fuel CO_2 emissions. In *Trends: A Compendium of Data on Global Change.* Carbon Dioxide Information Analysis Center. Oak Ridge, Tenn.: Oak Ridge National Laboratory, U.S. Department of Energy.

McCormick, R.A. and J.H. Ludwig. 1967. Climate modification by atmospheric aerosols. *Science* 156:1358–1359.

Meehl, G.A., T.F. Stocker, W.D. Collins, P. Friedlingstein, A.T. Gaye, J.M. Gregory, A. Kitoh, R. Knutti, J.M. Murphy, A. Noda, S.C.B Raper, I.G. Watterson, A.J. Weaver, and Z.-C. Zhao. 2007. Global climate projections. In *Climate Change 2007: The Physical Science Basis. Contribution of Working Group I to the*

Fourth Assessment Report of the Intergovernmental Panel on Climate Change, eds. S. Solomon, D. Qin, M. Manning, Z. Chen, M. Marquis, K.B. Averyt, M. Tignor, and H.L. Miller, 747–845. Cambridge, U.K.: Cambridge University Press.

Molina, M.J. and F.S. Rowland. 1974. Stratospheric sink for chlorofluoromethanes: chlorine atom-catalysed destruction of ozone. *Nature* 249:810–812.

Montenegro, A., V. Brovkin, M. Eby, D.E. Archer, and A.J. Weaver. 2007. Long term fate of anthropogenic carbon. *Geophysical Research Letters* 34: L19707, doi:10.1029/2007GL030905.

National Research Council. 1979. *Carbon dioxide and climate: A scientific assessment.* National Academy of Sciences. Washington, D.C.: National Research Council.

————. 1983. *Changing Climate.* National Academy of Sciences. Washington, D.C.: National Research Council.

Nobel Foundation. 1903. Nobel Prize in Chemistry. Available at nobelprize.org/nobel_prizes/chemistry/laureates/1903.

————. 2007. Nobel Peace Prize. Available at nobelprize.org/nobel_prizes/peace/laureates/2007.

Rasool, S.I. and S.H. Schneider. 1971. Atmospheric carbon dioxide and aerosols: effects of large increase on global climate. *Science* 173:138–141.

Revelle, R. and H. Suess. 1957. Carbon dioxide exchange between atmosphere and ocean and the question of an increase of atmospheric CO_2 during the past decades. *Tellus* 9:18–27.

————., W. Broecker, H. Craig, C.D. Keeling, and J. Smagorinsky. 1965. Restoring the quality of our environment. Report of the Environmental Pollution Panel, President's Science Advisory Committee, 111–133. Washington, D.C.: The White House.

Seidel, S. and D. Keyes. 1983. *Can we delay a greenhouse warming?* Washington, D.C.: U.S. Environmental Protection Agency.

Tyndall, J. 1859. Note on the transmission of radiant heat through gaseous bodies. *Proceedings of the Royal Society of London* 10:37–39.

————. 1861. The Bakerian lecture: On the absorption and radiation of heat by gases and vapours, and on the physical connexion of radiation, absorption, and conduction. *Philosophical Transactions of the Royal Society of London* 151:1–36.

Weart, S.R. 2007. *The discovery of global warming.* Cambridge, MA: Harvard University Press.

WMO. 1986. Report of the international conference on the assessment of the role of carbon dioxide and of other greenhouse gases in climate variations and associated impacts, Villach, Austria, October 9–15, 1985. WMO Report No. 661.

————. 1988. Proceedings of *The changing atmosphere: implications for global security,* Geneva, Switzerland. WMO Report No. 710.

Chapter 3: The Nature of Things

Alley, R.B. 1998. Icing the North Atlantic. *Nature* 392:335-337.

Berger, A. and M.F. Loutre. 2002. An exceptionally long interglacial ahead? *Science* 297:1287–1288.

Bindoff, N.L., J. Willebrand, V. Artale, A. Cazenave, J. Gregory, S. Gulev, K. Hanawa, C. Le Quéré, S. Levitus, Y. Nojiri, C.K. Shum, L.D. Talley, and A. Unnikrishnan. 2007. Observations: oceanic climate change and sea level. In *Climate Change 2007: The Physical Science Basis. Contribution of Working Group I to the Fourth Assessment Report of the Intergovernmental Panel on Climate Change*, eds. S. Solomon, D. Qin, M. Manning, Z. Chen, M. Marquis, K.B. Averyt, M. Tignor, and H.L. Miller, 385–432. Cambridge, U.K.: Cambridge University Press.

Caldeira, K. 2007. What corals are dying to tell us about CO_2 and ocean acidification. *Oceanography* 20(2):188-195.

———., M. Akai, P. Brewer, B. Chen, P. Haugan, T. Iwama, P. Johnston, H. Kheshgi, Q. Li, T. Ohsumi, H. Poertner, C. Sabine, Y. Shirayama, and J. Thomson. 2005. Ocean storage. In *IPCC Special Report on Carbon Dioxide Capture and Storage. Prepared by Working Group III of the Intergovernmental Panel on Climate Change*, eds. B. Metz, O. Davidson, H.C. de Coninck, M. Loos, and L.A. Meyer, 277–317. Cambridge, U.K.: Cambridge University Press.

Calvin, W.H. 1998. The great climate flip-flop. *The Atlantic Monthly* 281(1):47-64.

Etheridge, D.M., L.P. Steele, R.L. Langenfelds, R.J. Francey, J.-M. Barnola, and V.I. Morgan. 1996. Natural and anthropogenic changes in atmospheric CO_2 over the last 1000 years from air in Antarctic ice and firn. *Journal of Geophysical Research* 101:4115–4128.

Gagosian, R.B. 2003. Abrupt climate change: should we be worried? Prepared for a panel on abrupt climate change at the World Economic Forum, Davos, Switzerland, January 27, 2003. Available at www.whoi.edu/page.do?cid=9986&pid=12455&tid=282.

IPCC. 2001. *Climate Change 2001: Synthesis Report. A Contribution of Working Groups I, II, and III to the Third Assessment Report of the Intergovernmental Panel on Climate Change*, eds. R.T. Watson and the Core Writing Team. Cambridge, U.K.: Cambridge University Press.

Jansen, E., J. Overpeck, K.R. Briffa, J.-C. Duplessy, F. Joos, V. Masson-Delmotte, D. Olago, B. Otto-Bliesner, W.R. Peltier, S. Rahmstorf, R. Ramesh, D. Raynaud, D. Rind, O. Solomina, R. Villalba, and D. Zhang. 2007. Palaeoclimate. In *Climate Change 2007: The Physical Science Basis. Contribution of Working Group I to the Fourth Assessment Report of the Intergovernmental Panel on Climate Change*, eds. S. Solomon, D. Qin, M. Manning, Z. Chen, M. Marquis, K.B. Averyt, M. Tignor, and H.L. Miller, 433–497. Cambridge, U.K.: Cambridge University Press.

Joyce, T. 2002. The heat before the cold. *The New York Times*, April 18, A27.

Lemley, B. 2002. The new ice age. *Discover* 23(9), September, 35–40.

Meehl, G.A., T.F. Stocker, W.D. Collins, P. Friedlingstein, A.T. Gaye, J.M. Gregory, A. Kitoh, R. Knutti, J.M. Murphy, A. Noda, S.C.B. Raper, I.G. Watterson, A.J. Weaver, and Z.-C. Zhao. 2007. Global climate projections. In *Climate Change 2007: The Physical Science Basis. Contribution of Working Group I to the Fourth Assessment Report of the Intergovernmental Panel on Climate Change*, eds. S. Solomon, D. Qin, M. Manning, Z. Chen, M. Marquis, K.B. Averyt, M. Tignor, and H.L. Miller, 747–845. Cambridge, U.K.: Cambridge University Press.

Monnin, E., E.J. Steig, U. Siegenthaler, K. Kawamura, J. Schwander, B. Stauffer, T.F. Stocker, D.L. Morse, J.-M. Barnola, B. Bellier, D. Raynaud, and H. Fischer. 2004. Evidence for substantial accumulation rate variability in Antarctica during the Holocene, through synchronization of CO_2 in the Taylor Dome, Dome C and DML ice cores. *Earth and Planetary Science Letters* 224:45-54.

Montenegro, A. V. Brovkin, M. Eby, D.E. Archer, and A.J. Weaver. 2007: Long term fate of anthropogenic carbon. *Geophysical Research Letters* 34:L19707, doi:10.1029/2007GL030905.

Petit, J.R., J. Jouzel, D. Raynaud, N.I. Barkov, J.-M. Barnola, I. Basile, M. Benders, J. Chappellaz, M. Davis, G. Delayque, M. Delmotte, V.M. Kotlyakov, M. Legrand, V.Y. Lipenkov, C. Lorius, L. Pépin, C. Ritz, E. Saltzman, and M. Stievenard. 1999. Climate and atmospheric history of the past 420,000 years from the Vostok ice core, Antarctica. *Nature* 399:429-436.

Rahmstorf, S. 1997. Ice-cold in Paris. *New Scientist* 153:26-30.

Royal Society. 2005. Ocean acidification due to increasing atmospheric carbon dioxide. Policy document 12/05, Royal Society, London, U.K. Available at www.royalsoc.ac.uk/document.asp?id=3249.

Schwartz, P. and D. Randall. October 2003. An abrupt climate change scenario and its implications for United States National Security. Emeryville, CA: Global Business Network.

Self, S., M. Widdowson, T. Thordarson, and A.E. Jay. 2006. Volatile fluxes during flood basalt eruptions and potential effects on the global environment: A Deccan perspective. *Earth and Planetary Science Letters* 248:518–532.

Weaver, A.J. and C. Hillaire-Marcel. 2004a. Ice growth in the greenhouse: a seductive paradox but unrealistic scenario. *Geoscience Canada* 31, 77–85.

———. 2004b. Global warming and the next ice age. *Science* 304:400–402.

Chapter 4: The Human Footprint

Bindoff, N.L., J. Willebrand, V. Artale, A. Cazenave, J. Gregory, S. Gulev, K. Hanawa, C. Le Quéré, S. Levitus, Y. Nojiri, C.K. Shum, L.D. Talley, and A. Unnikrishnan. 2007. Observations: oceanic climate change and sea level. In *Climate Change 2007: The Physical Science Basis. Contribution of Working Group I to the Fourth*

Assessment Report of the Intergovernmental Panel on Climate Change, eds. S. Solomon, D. Qin, M. Manning, Z. Chen, M. Marquis, K.B. Averyt, M. Tignor, and H.L. Miller, 385–432. Cambridge, U.K.: Cambridge University Press.

CFCAS. 2001. Canadian Foundation for Climate and Atmospheric Sciences Mandate. Available at www.cfcas.org/overview_e.html.

Damon, P.E. and P. Laut. 2004. Pattern of strange errors plagues solar activity and terrestrial climate data. *EOS Transactions of the American Geophysical Union* 85(39):370, 374.

De Souza, M. 2007a. Tories' reason for ending fund irks researchers; 'I truly think they don't understand what research means.' *Ottawa Citizen*, November 9, A5.

———. 2007b. Nobel scientists blast government on environment; Atmosphere is changing faster than expected, wise policies require more research, they say. *Times Colonist* (Victoria, B.C.), November 5, A3.

Friis-Christensen, E. and K. Lassen. 1991. Length of the solar cycle: an indicator of solar activity closely associated with climate. *Science* 254:698–700.

Gelbspan, R. 1997. *The heat is on: the high stakes battle over Earth's threatened climate.* New York: Addison-Wesley.

Hegerl, G.C., F.W. Zwiers, P. Braconnot, N.P. Gillett, Y. Luo, J.A. Marengo Orsini, N. Nicholls, J.E. Penner, P.A. Stott. 2007. Understanding and attributing climate change. In *Climate Change 2007: The Physical Science Basis. Contribution of Working Group I to the Fourth Assessment Report of the Intergovernmental Panel on Climate Change*, eds. S. Solomon, D. Qin, M. Manning, Z. Chen, M. Marquis, K.B. Averyt, M. Tignor, and H.L. Miller, 663–745. Cambridge, U.K.: Cambridge University Press.

IPCC. 1996. *Climate Change 1995. The Science of Climate Change. Contribution of Working Group I to the Second Assessment Report of the Intergovernmental Panel on Climate Change*, eds. J.T. Houghton, L.G. Meira Filho, B.A. Callander, N. Harris, A. Kattenberg, and K. Maskell. Cambridge, U.K.: Cambridge University Press.

———. 2001. *Climate Change 2001: The Scientific Basis. Contribution of Working Group I to the Third Assessment Report of the Intergovernmental Panel on Climate Change*, eds. J.T. Houghton, Y. Ding, D.J. Griggs, M. Noguer, P.J. van der Linden, X. Dai, K. Maskell, and C.A. Johnson. Cambridge, U.K.: Cambridge University Press.

———. 2007. *Climate Change 2007: The Physical Science Basis. Contribution of Working Group I to the Fourth Assessment Report of the Intergovernmental Panel on Climate Change*, eds. S. Solomon, D. Qin, M. Manning, Z. Chen, M. Marquis, K.B. Averyt, M. Tignor, and H.L. Miller. Cambridge, U.K.: Cambridge University Press.

Jones, P.D. and A. Moberg. 2003. Hemispheric and large-scale surface air temperature variations: an extensive revision and an update to 2001. *Journal of Climate* 16:206-223.

Lemke, P., J. Ren, R.B. Alley, I. Allison, J. Carrasco, G. Flato, Y. Fujii, G. Kaser, P. Mote, R.H. Thomas, and T. Zhang. 2007. Observations: changes in snow, ice and frozen ground. In: *Climate Change 2007: The Physical Science Basis. Contribution of Working Group I to the Fourth Assessment Report of the Intergovernmental Panel on Climate Change,* eds. S. Solomon, D. Qin, M. Manning, Z. Chen, M. Marquis, K.B. Averyt, M. Tignor, and H.L. Miller, 337–383. Cambridge, U.K.: Cambridge University Press.

Le Treut, H., R. Somerville, U. Cubasch, Y. Ding, C. Mauritzen, A. Mokssit, T. Peterson, and M. Prather. 2007. Historical overview of climate change. In *Climate Change 2007: The Physical Science Basis. Contribution of Working Group I to the Fourth Assessment Report of the Intergovernmental Panel on Climate Change,* eds. S. Solomon, D. Qin, M. Manning, Z. Chen, M. Marquis, K.B. Averyt, M. Tignor, and H.L. Miller, 94–127. Cambridge, U.K.: Cambridge University Press.

Lockwood, M. and C. Fröhlich. 2007. Recent oppositely directed trends in solar climate forcings and the global mean surface air temperature. *Proceedings of the Royal Society, Series A* 463:2447–2460.

Mann, M.E., R.S. Bradley, and M.K. Hughes. 1998. Global-scale temperature patterns and climate forcing over the past six centuries. *Nature* 392:779-787.

Natural Resources Canada. 2001. Canadian Climate Impacts and Adaptation Research Network (C-CIARN) Objective. Available at www.c-ciarn.ca/index_e.html.

Stott, P.A., D.A. Stone, and M.R. Allen. 2004. Human contributions to the European heatwave of 2003. *Nature* 432:610-614.

Trenberth, K.E., P.D. Jones, P. Ambenje, R. Bojariu, D. Easterling, A. Klein Tank, D. Parker, F. Rahimzadeh, J.A. Renwick, M. Rusticucci, B. Soden, and P. Zhai. 2007. Observations: surface and atmospheric climate change. In *Climate Change 2001: The Scientific Basis. Contribution of Working Group I to the Third Assessment Report of the Intergovernmental Panel on Climate Change,* eds. J.T. Houghton, Y. Ding, D.J. Griggs, M. Noguer, P.J. van der Linden, X. Dai, K. Maskell, and C.A. Johnson, 235–336. Cambridge, U.K.: Cambridge University Press.

Vincent, L.A. and E. Mekis. 2006. Changes in daily and extreme temperature and precipitation. Indices for Canada over the twentieth century. *Atmosphere-Ocean* 44:177–193.

Chapter 5: Turbulent Times

ACIA. 2005. *Arctic climate impacts assessment.* Cambridge, U.K.: Cambridge University Press.

CEC. 2007. *Limiting global climate change to 2 degrees Celsius: The way ahead for 2020 and beyond*. Communication from the Commission to the Council of the European Parliament, The European Economic and Social Committee, and the Committee of the Regions, Commission of European Communities. Brussels, Belgium, January 10.

den Elzen, M. and M. Meinshausen. 2006. Multi-gas emission pathways for meeting the EU 2°C climate target. In *Avoiding Dangerous Climate Change*, eds. H.J. Schnellnhuber, W. Cramer, N. Nakicenovic, T. Wigley, and G. Yohe, 299–309. Cambridge, U.K.: Cambridge University Press.

EU Council. 1996. Community strategy on climate change—council conclusions. CFSP Presidency Statement, Presse 188, Number 8518/96, Luxembourg, June 25.

Fischlin, A., G.F. Midgley, J.T. Price, R. Leemans, B. Gopal, C. Turley, M.D.A. Rounsevell, O.P. Dube, J. Tarazona, and A.A. Velichko. 2007. Ecosystems, their properties, goods, and services. In *Climate Change 2007: Impacts, Adaptation and Vulnerability. Contribution of Working Group II to the Fourth Assessment Report of the Intergovernmental Panel on Climate Change*, eds. M.L. Parry, O.F. Canziani, J.P. Palutikof, P.J. van der Linden, and C.E. Hanson, 211–272. Cambridge, U.K.: Cambridge University Press.

Forest, C.E., P.H. Stone, and A.P. Sokolov. 2006. Estimated PDFs of climate system properties including natural and anthropogenic forcings. *Geophysical Research Letters* 33:L01705, doi:10.1029/2005G:023977.

Government of Canada. 2007. Greenhouse gas emissions reductions. Available at www.budget.gc.ca/2007/bp/bpc3e.html and www.pm.gc.ca/eng/media.asp?id =1683.

Gregory, J.M. and P. Huybrechts. 2006. Ice-sheet contributions to future sea-level change. *Philosophical Transactions of the Royal Society, Series A* 364:1709–1731.

IPCC. 2007. *Climate Change 2007: The Physical Science Basis. Contribution of Working Group I to the Fourth Assessment Report of the Intergovernmental Panel on Climate Change*, eds. S. Solomon, D. Qin, M. Manning, Z. Chen, M. Marquis, K.B. Averyt, M. Tignor, and H.L. Miller. Cambridge, U.K.: Cambridge University Press.

————. 2007. *Climate Change 2007: Synthesis Report. Contribution of Working Groups I, II and III to the Fourth Assessment Report of the Intergovernmental Panel on Climate Change*, eds. Core Writing Team, R.K. Pachauri, and A. Reisinger. Geneva, Switzerland: IPCC.

Liberal Party of Canada. 2007. Balancing our carbon budget. White Paper, March. Available at www.liberal.ca/pdf/docs/whitepaper_EN.pdf.

McGranahan, G., D. Balk, and B. Anderson. 2007. The rising tide: assessing the risks of climate change and human settlements in low elevation coastal zones. *Environment and Urbanization* 19:17–37.

Meehl, G.A., T.F. Stocker, W.D. Collins, P. Friedlingstein, A.T. Gaye, J.M. Gregory, A. Kitoh, R. Knutti, J.M. Murphy, A. Noda, S.C.B. Raper, I.G. Watterson, A.J. Weaver, and Z.-C. Zhao. 2007. Global climate projections. In *Climate Change 2007: The Physical Science Basis. Contribution of Working Group I to the Fourth Assessment Report of the Intergovernmental Panel on Climate Change*, eds. S. Solomon, D. Qin, M. Manning, Z. Chen, M. Marquis, K.B. Averyt, M. Tignor, and H.L. Miller, 747–845. Cambridge, U.K.: Cambridge University Press.

Meinshausen, M. 2006. What does a 2°C target mean for greenhouse gas concentrations? A brief analysis based on multi-gas emission pathways and several climate sensitivity uncertainty estimates. In *Avoiding Dangerous Climate Change*, eds. H.J. Schnellnhuber, W. Cramer, N. Nakicenovic, T. Wigley, and G. Yohe, 265–279. Cambridge, U.K.: Cambridge University Press.

Nakicenovic, N., J. Alcamo, G. Davis, B. de Vries, J. Fenhann, S. Gaffin, K. Gregory, A Grübler, T.Y. Jung, T. Kram, E.L. La Rovere, L. Michaelis, S. Mori, T. Morita, W. Pepper, H. Pitcher, L. Price, K. Riahi, A. Roehrl, H.-H. Rogner, A. Sankovski, M. Schlesinger, P. Shukla, S. Smith, R. Swart, S. van Rooijen, N. Victor, and Z. Dadi. 2000. *IPCC Special Report on Emissions Scenarios*. Cambridge, U.K. and New York: Cambridge University Press.

Theil, H. and R. Finke. 1983. The distance from the equator as an instrumental variable. *Economics Letters* 13:357–360.

———. and J. Galvez. 1995. On latitude and affluence: the equatorial grand canyon. *Empirical Economics* 20:163–166.

UNFCCC. 1994. United Nations Framework Convention on Climate Change Objective. March 21. Available at http://unfccc.int/essential_background/ convention/background/items/1353.ph.

Wigley, T.M.L. 1998. The Kyoto Protocol: CO_2, CH_4 and climate implications. *Geophysical Research Letters* 25:2285–2288.

Chapter 6: Investing in the Future

BCLA 2007. *Report on the budget 2008 consultations*. British Columbia Legislative Assembly, Select Standing Committee on Finance and Government Services. 1st Report, 3rd Session, 38th Parliament, November 2007. Available at www.leg.bc.ca/cmt.

Burrows, M. 2007. Petro-giants will accept a carbon tax. *The Georgia Straight*, December 6. Available at www.straight.com/article-123594/petro-giants-will-accept-a-carbon-tax.

CCCE 2007. Canada's business leaders call for aggressive action to tackle climate change, drive energy innovation and strengthen economic performance. Available at www.ceocouncil.ca/en/media.php.

Gurney, N. and E. Gurney. 1965. *The king, the mice and the cheese*. New York: Beginner Books, A division of Random House.

Lake Victoria Commonwealth Climate Change Action Plan. [2007]. Commonwealth Heads of Government Meeting. Uganda, November 24, 2007. Available at www.thecommonwealth.org/document/34293/35144/173014/climateaction-plan.htm.

Monbiot, G. 2006. *Heat: how to stop the planet from burning.* Toronto: Doubleday Canada.

Rudd, J. 2007. Try environmental carrot first, B.C. legislature report says. *Times Colonist,* November 16, A4.

Simpson, J., M. Jaccard, and N. Rivers. 2007. *Hot air: meeting Canada's climate change challenge.* Toronto: McClelland & Stewart Ltd.

Epilogue

Babbage, Maria. 2008. McGuinty says one of Canada's largest polluters won't be looking at carbon tax. Canadian Press. 21 February. Available at http://cnews.canoe.ca/CNEWS/Canada/2008/02/21/4866016-cp.html.

Environment Canada. 2007. Media relations protocol. PowerPoint Presentation, Executive Management Committee, Communications Branch. 14 November. Ottawa: Environment Canada.

Government of Alberta. 2008. Alberta to cut projected emissions by 50 per cent under new climate change plan. News Release, 24 January.

Harper, Stephen. 2007. Prime Minister Stephen Harper calls for international consensus on climate change. European Union-Canada Summit, Berlin, Germany, 4 June. Available at www.ecoaction.gc.ca/speeches-discours/20070604-eng.cfm.

Munro, Margaret. 2008. British journal blasts Tory government for 'dismal' track record on science. Canwest News Service. 21 February. Available at www.canada.com/ottawacitizen/news/story.html?id=3ae6976c-887b-4d14-8eef-76db706ffe1d.

Prince of Wales's Corporate Leaders Group on Climate Change. 2007. The Bali Communiqué. Available at www.balicommunique.com/communique.html.

Rynor, Becky. 2008. Federal environment minister OK with B.C. carbon tax. Canwest News Service. 20 February. Available at www.nationalpost.com/news/canada/story.html?id=322378.

Taylor, C. 2008. B.C. minister of finance 2008 budget. 19 February. Available at www.bcbudget.gov.bc.ca/2008/default.htm.

Wong, Craig. 2008. Canada needs common carbon tax regs: Flaherty. Canadian Press. 14 January. Available at http://cnews.canoe.ca/CNEWS/Science/2008/01/14/4772287-cp.html.

Credits

Grateful acknowledgment is made to the following for permission to reproduce material:

Illustrations

"Temperature Distribution." Reproduced from Folland et al. (2001) with permission from the IPCC.

"Forest Fire Area Burnt." Reproduced with permission from Gillett et al. (2004).

"Arctic Sea Ice in 2007." Reprinted with permission from the National Snow and Ice Data Center in Boulder, Colorado.

"Will Your City Survive?" Used with permission of American Media Inc.

"Joseph Fourier and Svante Arrhenius." Used with permission of The Granger Collection, New York.

"Joseph Tyndall and His Experimental Apparatus." (Joseph Tyndall) Used with permission of The Granger Collection, New York. (Apparatus) Used with permission of the Royal Society of London.

"Guy Callander." Used with permission of James R. Fleming.

"Frost Fair on the Thames River, January 31–February 5, 1814." Reproduced with permission from the UK Secretary of State for Culture, Media and Sport. © Crown copyright: UK Government Art Collection.

"The Earth's Energy Balance." Reproduced with permission from FAQ 1.1, Figure 1, of Le Treut (2007).

"Four Hundred Million Years of Atmospheric CO_2 Levels." Redrawn from the top panel of Figure 6.1 in Jansen et al. (2007).

"Antarctic Ice Core Record." Reproduced from Figure 6.3 of Jansen et al. (2007).

"Great Ocean Conveyor Belt." Reproduced with permission from Figure 4-2 of IPCC (2001).

"D-O Oscillations, Heinrich Events, and Bond Cycles." Adapted and redrawn from a figure originally published in Alley (1998).

"Northern Hemisphere Temperature Reconstructions." Reproduced with permission from Figure 6.10 of Jansen et al. (2007).

"Upper Ocean Heat Content." Reproduced from Figure 5.1 of Bindoff et al. (2007).

"Solar Cycle Lengths." Taken from Damon and Laut (2004) and reproduced with permission of American Geophysical Union.

"Annual Mean Warming Trends." Redrawn from Figure 3.9 of Trenberth et al. (2007).

"Seasonal Mean Temperature Trends, 1979 to 2005." Redrawn from Figure 3.10 of Trenberth et al. (2007).

"Mean Sea Level Changes, 1870 to 2006." Reproduced with permission from Figure 5.13 of Bindoff et al. (2007).

"Changes in the Cryosphere Since 1960." Reproduced with permission from FAQ 4.1, Figure 1 of Lemke et al. (2007).

"Interactive Components of the Earth System." Reproduced with permission from FAQ 1.2, Figure 1 of Le Treut et al. (2007).

"Observed and Simulated Temperature Trends." Reproduced with permission from Figure 9.6 of from Hegerl et al. (2007).

"Regional Climate Changee Detection." Reproduced with the permission of Dr. Dáithí Stone.

"Projected Global Mean Surface Temperature Change, 2090 to 2099." Redrawn from Figure 10.29 of Meehl et al. (2007).

"Projections of Surface Temperatures." Reproduced with permission from Figure TS.28, page 72 of IPCC 2007.

"Projected Global Mean Sea Level Rise, 2090 to 2099." Redrawn from Figure 10.33 of Meehl et al. (2007).

"Projected Annual Mean Change in Precipitation, 2080 to 2099." Produced by and reproduced with permission from Julie Arblaster at the Australian Bureau of Meteorology Research Centre.

"Fossil of the Day Awards." www.avaaz.org/fossils.

Text

"How Dangerous Is Global Warming?" Reproduced with permission from the *Los Angeles Times* and Richard Lindzen.

"Projected Regional Impact Examples." Reproduced with permission from Table SPM.2 on pages 11–12 of the "Summary for Policymakers" of the IPCC AR4 Synthesis Report available at www.ipcc.ch/ipccreports/ar4-syr.htm.

Index

Page numbers in italic represent graphs, charts, etc.

acid rain, 25, 76, 101, 117, 119, 197
acidity, 120–21, *121* (*See also* pH balance)
Ad Hoc Working Group on Long-term Cooperative Action under the Convention, 275
adaptation, 23, 139, 187, 188, 203, 222, 225–26, 230, 257
advertising, 42, 276
aerosols, 48, 76, 80, 83, 87–89, *91*, 93–94, 117, 118, 190, 197, 232
afforestation, 17, 226, 257
Africa, 132, 137–38, 218, 219, 222, *261, 262*
Africa Group of Nations, 264
agriculture, 71, 92, 96, *97*, 151, 219, 221, 222, 223, 224 (*See also* food production; growing seasons)
air conditioners, 92
air pollution, 35, 266
air travel, 20, 21, 266
airports, 8, 9, 10, 215
Akkadian Empire, 155
alarmism, 19–20, 27, 40–43, *41*, 45, 47, 53, 70, 89, 139–44
Alaska, 181, 228
albedo, 80–81, 83, 93–94, 130, 150, 173, 209
Alberta, 4, 5, 23, 27, 33, 35–36, 96–97, *96*, 219–20, 268, 291–92
aleatoric uncertainty, 63–64
alkalinity, 20, 264 (*See also* pH balance)
Allen, Myles, 174
alternative energy technologies, 20–21, 266–70
Ambrose, Rona, 107
American Meteorological Society, 11, 27
American Philosophical Society, 98
amphibians, 116
An Inconvenient Truth (film), 2, 33, 67
ancient atmosphere, 111–13 (*See also* climates, past)
Anderson, David, 185–86
anomalies, 3, *180, 204*, 212, 268

Antarctic
    ice cap. *See* ice sheets
    ice core records, *127*, 149–50
    and ozone depletion, 92
Antarctica, 125–27, *126*, 132, *133*, 141, 147, 177, 179, 202, 212
anthropogenic aerosols, 48
anthropogenic forcing (ANT), 190, 197, 198, 199, 203, *204*
aphelion, 128, *129*, 130
Archer, David, 85–86
Arctic
    impact of global warming on, 224–25
    research, 187
    sea ice. *See* sea ice
    sovereignty, 40
Arctic Climate Impact Assessment (2005), 225, 237
Arctic Council, 225
Arctic Ocean, 179, 181, 220, 278–79
Area (journal), 67
Arrhenius, Svante August, 72, 73–74, *73*, 77, 78–79, 87, 102, *103*, 110, 115
Aruba, *95*
Asia, 214, 222–23, 260, *261, 262*, 272
Assessment Reports (IPCC), 21–22, 27, 51, 57, 67, 104, 105–9, 110, 273 (*See also* First Assessment Report; Fourth Assessment Report; Second Assessment Report; Third Assessment Report)
asteroids, 116, 117, 119
AT & T, 274
Athabasca (glacier), 179
Athabasca (river), 179
Atlantic meridional overturning circulation (MOC), 135, *136*, 137, 138, 146–47
Atlantic Monthly, 140
Atlantic Ocean, 134–37, *136*, 176 (*See also* North Atlantic conveyor)
atmospheric window, *80*, 82, 92
atoms, 113–14
attribution studies, 181–82
audio conferences, 21, 22
Australia, 34, *95*, 132, 218, 223, *242*